D0388861

HOW *to* BE
a HAPPIER
PARENT

AVERY

an imprint of Penguin Random House

New York

HOW *to* BE *a* HAPPIER PARENT

RAISING A FAMILY,
HAVING A LIFE,
AND LOVING (ALMOST)
EVERY MINUTE

KJ Dell'Antonia

AVERY

an imprint of Penguin Random House LLC
375 Hudson Street
New York, New York 10014

Most Avery books are available at special quantity discounts for bulk purchase for
sales promotions, premiums, fund-raising, and educational needs. Special books
or book excerpts also can be created to fit specific needs. For details, write
SpecialMarkets@penguinrandomhouse.com.

ISBN 9780735210479

Printed in the United States of America
1   3   5   7   9   10   8   6   4   2

BOOK DESIGN BY MEIGHAN CAVANAUGH

To my parents, Jon and Jo Dell'Antonia,

who gave me my first happy family,

and to Sam, Lily, Rory, and Wyatt, who became my second.

Most of all, to my husband, Rob. With you beside me

I am fearless—and so, so much happier.

CONTENTS

introduction

THIS COULD BE FUN

I'd been a parent for close to twelve years by the time it occurred to me to ask myself if the whole thing had to suck quite as much as it seemed to most days.

I have four children. Four amazing, glorious, delightful, stubborn, challenging, bickering other human beings live in my house, plus one equally wonderful, but mostly not all the other things, husband. I expect to spend twenty-some years in the thick of family life, driving, hugging, negotiating, laughing, cooking, playing, cleaning, reading, and all the rest of it. That's a big piece of my expected life-span. What's more, it's a piece I looked forward to. We planned this, my partner and I. We chose this life. This is what we wanted.

I don't want to spend that time in a haze of resigned exhaustion, longing to be or do something else. I want to raise my family, have my life, and love almost every minute of it. I am lucky to have all this, the house and the SUV and the washer-dryer and the healthy, loving kids. I want to like it.

But up until recently, it wasn't working out that way. The workload was overwhelming, from the laundry to the dishes to the cooking. The children were sometimes cute, but too often actively unpleasant: they fought with one another and with me; they refused to do the simplest of chores; they started from a baseline of entitlement and seemed to go downhill from there. Far too many days were what I called "get your skates on" days, when my husband and I both got up at dawn, drove children all over creation in the name of education or sports, worked a full day, drove more children to still more places, fed them, tended them, cleaned up after them, devoted an hour to inking in the next day's continuing insanity, and then collapsed into bed after bickering weakly with each other about whose day blew more chunks. We were always running, often late, and rarely without a child making us all suffer in the name of hating "transitions."

There was nothing really wrong—far from it. On the surface, we had everything we ever wanted, and below that surface, we had even more. We had good health, loving children, and enough money to do and have the things we really needed and many things we only wanted. We had had a stillborn child, a tragedy, but that was years ago. We'd come through it. There was nothing to complain about, but complain we did. It was just not as great I thought it would be.

I could say that about a lot of things—zip lines, for example, or sitting in the copilot seat of a commuter jet, or nearly every flume ride I've ever been on—but in this case, I'm talking about a whole lot more than a ride. This was a lifetime commitment. If it wasn't turning out like I'd hoped, I needed to find a way to turn it around.

The one thing I knew, as I began to contemplate the question of why I wasn't more satisfied with my life as a parent, was that I wasn't alone. During the course of those early years I began to write about family, first for a variety of print magazines, later for *Slate*, and then for the *New York Times*, where I ran the *Motherlode* blog and later became part of its Well Family page. I interviewed hundreds of parents over the course of that decade. Most found happiness more elusive than they'd hoped.

At the same time, research was revealing a dismaying level of stress and dissatisfaction among my parenting peers, even those who are secure in the basics (food, shelter, health) and without any immediately obvious bonus challenges at any given moment. We tell researchers we'd rather do laundry than spend time with our children. We give up our own hobbies and pleasures in pursuit of our children's betterment. We answer surveys about our satisfaction with our lives and families in ways that lead to headlines like "How Having Children Robs Parents of Their Happiness" and books like *All Joy and No Fun: The Paradox of Modern Parenthood*, and then we devour the results as vindication of our overwhelming sense of being caught up in a race we can't win. Parenting, writes Judith Warner in her book *Perfect Madness: Motherhood in the Age of Anxiety*, has become "poisoned" through a "cocktail of guilt and anxiety and resentment and regret."

What's up with that, and how can we make it stop? Sure, some moments, and even some days or weeks, are truly terrible. Death, illness, job loss, accidents—those things stalk us all, but most days feature only the ordinary ups and downs of mornings, homework struggles, stuffed in-boxes, and dirty dishes. Why do we have such a collective sense of distress around these fates that we have chosen?

When things are steady, we could be finding satisfaction in our lovely modern lives, so filled with convenience and possibility and abundance. And when the worst happens, those ordinary moments with the families we've built should be a comfort and a refuge, not an additional source of anxiety. But I didn't feel like that was the life I was creating, and I saw the parents around me struggling in the same ways.

So I set out to discover how parents could find the way to our own personal version of happily ever after. How could we bring more joy, pleasure, and even fun to those ordinary days that make up the measure of our lives? What was contributing to our individual and collective unhappiness, and more importantly, what could we do about it?

I turned first to the community of parents and educators I've built up over the years. *What makes you unhappy?* I asked. *When do you feel like you're not where you want to be, or doing what you want to be doing?* I read everything I could find on happiness in general. Books piled up next to my bed: *Hardwiring Happiness*; *Stumbling on Happiness*; *If You're So Smart, Why Aren't You Happy?*; Gretchen Rubin's Happiness trilogy: *The Happiness Project*, *Happier at Home*, and *Better Than Before*; and more. I read books and research studies on parent and family happiness in particular: *All Joy and No Fun* and *Perfect Madness*, of course; plus *Overwhelmed: Work, Love, and Play When No One Has the Time*; *Maxed Out: American Moms on the Brink*; *Unfinished Business: Women Men Work Family*; and *The Way We Never Were: American Families and the Nostalgia Trap*.

I read research studies on happiness and life satisfaction, on time use and leisure, on community and dinner and wealth and volunteering and sleep, and then I read some more. (I knew it was time to stop when I found one study linking happiness to nudism.) And then, because I still had questions, I worked with Fordham University professor Matthew Weinshenker to create our own research into how choices around common parenting activities like helping with homework and driving to after-school activities affected our overall life satisfaction. We surveyed just over a thousand parents nationwide, and we asked them to tell us how being a parent had changed their approach to things like vacations and eating, and to take a deep dive into what made them happy and what didn't.

What I found convinced me that we can be happier. It doesn't even have to be that difficult. We can start by changing the stories we tell ourselves about our lives as individuals and as parents, and reveling in the meaning and excitement that comes from the adventure of raising a family instead of trying to measure our success. Wanting to be happier has its own happiness-increasing effect. The way we interpret our own lives and the way we talk to ourselves about our experiences has an enormous impact on how we perceive them. We can choose to feel satisfied with the (imperfect) lives we have, and comfortable and confident in how we're raising our kids. When we make that choice, or even when we decide to strive for it, something shifts in our mind-set, and we're more able to see and appreciate what's already there.

As I've changed how I think about my own parenting, I've found that I come back to ten mantras that invite me to see things differently or approach them with more confidence. I've listed those at the end of this introduction. But as useful as it is to change how we think about our family lives, it's not enough. Positive thought is powerful, but you cannot bring about more joyful mornings or less stressful evenings just by wishing it so (sadly, that is not "the secret" to happier parenting).

As we change how we think, we must also change what we do. In our day-to-day lives, we can build stronger partnerships and friendships, share leisure activities with our families, and spend time with our children doing things that are pleasant for all parties. We can increase the things in our lives that correlate with happiness and what researchers like to call "a sense of parental efficacy" (feeling like we're pretty good at this thing, which is a common measure of parent satisfaction).

Happier parents in general do four things well. They shift from heavier involvement to fostering independence as their children become more capable. They don't put their children's everyday needs above their own. They look for the good in day-to-day experiences, and they know what's really important and what's just noise and fury.

But those are big, amorphous goals, and here's something else you find out when you research happiness: most of us are better at making specific changes than we are at fulfilling vague, unwieldy intentions. So how should I divide those big goals into manageable bits we can tackle a bite at a time to create a blueprint for happier family lives?

I considered the chronological—how to be happier when life includes a baby, a toddler, a tween, or a teen. But what if you've got all four? Maybe, I suggested to some friends on Facebook, I should structure the book around some of the larger things that parents who are satisfied with their lives often do. I could research and describe the ways people become part of a community of faith or intention, restructure their careers in creative ways, or build a life around a passion, and find lessons we could apply to ourselves in large and small ways.

"I do absolutely none of those things," responded one friend. "I can think of no better way for you to make me feel like crap." Scratch that, then.

Ultimately, I kept coming back to what felt like the most obvious plan—taking it one trouble spot at a time. Those big questions of how to foster independence, keep your sense of self, make room for happiness, and see the forest for the trees don't come up all by themselves. They come up again and again, all day, every day, within the seemingly smaller challenges. How can I get these children to go to bed? How can I get them to stop fighting? Should I let my ten-year-old use Instagram? What's for dinner?

So each of the chapters of *How to Be a Happier Parent* focuses on a single challenge spot for parents. To find those challenges, I started by doing exactly what any of you would do—I listed the things that were the most difficult for me and my family. (Mornings. Homework. Sibling relationships.) Then I turned to my research and found a surprising consensus—just under a third of the parents who responded to an open-ended question about what they liked least about parenting offered up some variation on "discipline": "Enforcing rules, taking away privileges." "I don't like having to punish my children." "Discipline. I know it's important to have consequences, but it is still hard to discipline." We know we need to teach our children to behave and meet the expectations of the family and community they're a part of, but it seems we really don't enjoy it.

I'd start with discipline, then, but where to go from there? "You cannot write this book without talking about screen time," said Bruce Feiler, author of *The Secrets of Happy Families*. "Everyone is trying to figure that out."

"What about chores?" said one of my editors at the *Times*. "I can't believe your kids do chores every morning before school. We can barely get out the door." After I corrected her vision of my children skipping off to work in our barn every morning with a merry whistle like so many of Snow White's dwarfs, I promised to cover chores.

To their ideas and to that formal survey, I added the results of a more informal version, in which I asked a few thousand parents to name their top three challenges. Two of mine (homework and sibling bickering) also appeared at the top of many lists, followed by screen time ("SnapFREAKINGchat"), meals, driving, "so many negotiations," mornings and bedtimes, activities, "dressing the toddler," manners, chores, getting no respect, and lack of sleep. I turned those two lists into chapter headings and went from there.

For every topic, from discipline through mornings, siblings and vacations and leisure time, I start by describing what commonly goes wrong, for me and for other parents. The first thing I do is to consider what lies underneath the seemingly straightforward challenge of things like getting children up, fed, dressed, and out of the house by 7:37 every weekday morning. Yes, there are things we can do to make it better. But it's important to look around us and see what's holding us down. In so many ways, from school hours and vacations to typical activity schedules to the challenges of finding good, flexible childcare, our society makes it difficult to manage both caregiving and breadwinning, whether two parents have largely divided those roles, one parent is riding them solo, or your family has two adults working on all fronts. It's hard to find happiness when every day is a race against a clock we don't set, but knowing what we're up against can help us change what we can, and accept what we can't. *How to Be a Happier Parent* is focused on creating the best possible family life we can with the hand we've been dealt.

Then I get at the larger question: what can we do about it? I've taken each of those tough spots and I've tackled them with fellow parents and experts to look at what works. How can we make things like dealing with homework or grocery store temper tantrums better? Over and over again, as I considered topics from discipline to vacations, I found the same pattern. First, we need to change how we think about it. Then, we need to change what we do about it. The bulk of every chapter gets into the nitty-gritty of that last part. Mornings (or sibling battles, or screen time arguments, or mealtimes) suck. *So what do we do to make it feel better?*

How to Be a Happier Parent isn't a memoir. Far from it. I'm still right with you, learning how this is done every day. But let's own this much: it is a "self-help" book. I didn't set out to research what makes for happier families without hoping that the results of my work would actually help some parents—that would be you and me both—find a way to a life that's regularly, consistently satisfying, that includes ample joy and fun, one that allows you to look around and sigh and let your shoulders drop down out of your ears and say, yes, this is what I wanted. Maybe not every single minute of it. Maybe not the dog barf I just cleaned up or the mid-vacation who-will-sleep-in-which-bed squabble or the dirty dishes in the sink, but the children and the dog and the vacation and the dishes and the sink, yes, this is the journey I want to be on.

So while *How to Be a Happier Parent* contains my story of finding a place of joy and satisfaction with my life and my family life, it's more often a guide to how you can find your own way to that place of your own, and the answer certainly isn't "by doing everything just exactly like KJ does, because KJ's life is perfect, rah-rah!" If I feel like I've got a handle on something, you'll hear about it. But more often, you'll join me in working through advice and ideas from other parents and families, in the hope of finally finding a better approach to the things that challenge you most. It worked for me—I am now living proof that it is possible to be happy and satisfied with your life as a parent even while there is a child on the floor of your kitchen, screaming and writhing because dividing with fractions is *just too hard*.

It's also possible to be happy, or at least happier, when your life includes real challenges. In interviews for this book, I've spoken with parents with physical disabilities, with histories of abuse or addiction, or who have lost partners or children. I've talked to parents whose children deal with mental illness, learning disabilities, or other issues, or who have lost jobs or struggle financially. Those parents were still looking for, and finding, ways to be happier. Sometimes things are hard. We're sandwiched between a rock and a hard place, and it's rainy and cold and the forecast is for snow, and no one is suggesting you be happy about that. But you're still getting up in the morning, and the kids still need school lunches—and they'll still surprise you with a hug, delight you by learning something new, or move you to tears by helping you out when you need it most.

We can find happiness even when things aren't great, and it's okay to want to be happier, no matter what else is going on in your life or in the world. If you need an excuse, happier people make better employees. They volunteer more. They're more creative, healthier, more productive. They spread their happiness to the people around them, and they have stronger relationships—and children who have better relationships with their parents are happier, too.

Which brings me to another important point. This whole happier thing isn't a destination. You don't become a happier parent and then put a finish coat on it and call it done. The goals I set for myself, and the ideas you'll find for setting your own goals and making your own changes, aren't goals of achievement. They're goals of motion. If, on any given day, things feel better, go more smoothly, leave us putting our heads on our pillows with a sense of pleasant expectation for tomorrow, then we lick the back of a gold star and keep going. Because while there is an end goal of parenting (raising functional adults), this book isn't about getting there. Just the opposite. It's about not wanting to rush to the end, because you're right in the middle of everything you love.

When I did that survey asking people to describe their trouble spots as parents, mixed in with all the terrible mornings and chore battles and one awesome picture of an infant peering up from between his mother's legs in front of the toilet upon which she was seated, I found these complaints:

They grow up.

Long-distance calls (not enough of them).

They're far away.

This period—this time we have with everyone packed into the house and living life so fully intertwined—it ends. And yes, we know that. We've all been stopped by someone as we slog through the grocery store with three children under five and reminded to "enjoy it, because it goes so fast." We know the truth of Gretchen Rubin's saying: "The days are long, but the years are short." As I write this book, my oldest child is fifteen; by the time you read it, it's likely we'll know where he's going to college.

Our family lives will change. That's all the more reason to do everything we can to make these years as good while they're happening as they'll be in hindsight. A satisfying family life is attainable, and it isn't about raising great kids and churning them out at destination: success. It's about finding happiness—real happiness, the kind you look back on, look forward to, and live for—along the way.

interlude

TEN MANTRAS
FOR HAPPIER PARENTS

Before we go any further, I'll go ahead and reveal the book's ending, at least for me: I'm happier. When I started to apply what I've learned, things changed. My children get along better, and I handle it better when they don't. Mornings aren't ultra-stress sprints anymore, and while homework is scarcely making anyone in the house happy, it's not a big drain on my personal resources at the end of a long day. That leaves me with more to give at bedtime, and more ability to do things for myself as the evening winds down.

Some of what got better came from doing things differently, and the details—the ideas and tips and hacks—are coming, topic by topic. But so much of what shifted for me wasn't in what I did, but in how I thought about it. I was like Dorothy with her sparkly red shoes: I had what I needed to get where I wanted to go all along, but I still needed to travel my own road.

As I did, I found that I kept coming back to a few fundamentals. There were basic rules that applied again and again, and those came to form the guiding principles of my own life as a happier parent. When I'm uncertain, reaching for my next move, or about to lose my mind over a seeming "crisis," these are words I come back to. I hope they'll work that way for you, too.

What you want now isn't always what you want later. So many times, I would rather just take the easy way out. I can clear a child's dishes off the table. I can tell her the answer to that math problem. I can email his teacher to get him out of a jam. But me doing those things now doesn't teach my kids to do them later. In the short run, it means I'll spend a lot of time doing their work, and in the long run, it will mean I haven't given them what they need to grow up. In parenting, you mostly have to go the long way.

There is nothing wrong. This came from a book I read years ago with a very Buddhist slant (Sarah Susanka's *The Not So Big Life*). In her usage, there never was anything wrong, and there never could be anything wrong, because whatever had happened had already happened and was therefore the way it was, and not wrong.

I can't take it that far (which is why I am not a Buddhist), but I find this a comforting place to return to when things are *going* wrong. Child tantrum, job troubles, teenager in crisis, sickness, broken bones . . . fundamentally, nearly always, things are still okay. As philosopher Michel de Montaigne put it, "My life has been full of misfortunes, most of which never happened." I often say this one as *there is nothing really wrong*, but editors famously dislike the word "really." So I try to go all in, and most of the time, it's exactly true: *There is nothing wrong.*

People, including children—especially children—change. I'm a first-class catastrophizer. If something isn't going well, I tend to think it never will. He will *never* like school. She will *never* eat yo-gurt. Those two will *never* get along. I'm almost always wrong. Picky eaters evolve. Lazy students get motivated. Kids learn. That's kind of the point. But it's very important that we let them, instead of getting in their way by assuming they'll stay where they are.

You don't have to go in there. This is my shorthand for reminding myself not to be infected by my family's moods, from my daughters' dramas to my husband's occasional grumps. It comes from the ten-dency of one child to go into her closet and slam the door when she's upset. While it's true that sometimes I need to literally "go in there" to be with her, I don't need to go into her mood, and it won't help ei-ther of us if I do.

If you see something, don't always say something. I don't have to leap into every sibling battle or correct every minor infraction, espe-cially if a child is having a bad day. Many things go better if I don't intervene, and it's possible to learn even the lessons that need the most repetition while occasionally getting a pass.

You do you. I have friends who do a lot of great things with their children. They take them on hundred-mile-long cross-country-ski camping trips. They spend a year in Madrid. They build a treehouse, volunteer at a soup kitchen, jam on their guitars, build a stone wall, rescue endangered turtles, have board game tournaments, show cows, take their crepe cart to farmers' markets.

We do not do any of those things. Importantly, I do not *want* to do any of those things. We do our things, some of which sound just as fantastic and some of which don't, and that's okay. I can't raise my kids as traveling circus acrobats because I am not a traveling circus acrobat, even if that would make a fantastic college application essay. A corollary to this is *you can't do everything*. You can't. The end—or at least, it should be.

You can be happy when your children aren't. It isn't my missing Thomas the Tank Engine. It isn't my homework. It isn't my sports team. It isn't my college admission. Our kids will have disappointments. They will make terrible decisions. Other people will screw them over. Luck won't always fall their way. Sometimes we will ache for them. Sometimes we will be struggling not to say "I told you so."

Either way, we can keep our own inner equilibrium. Sympathy and empathy don't have to mean that our worlds come crashing down around us when that's how it feels to our kids. Usually, we have something our children don't: perspective. We know that Thomas will turn up or be forgotten, that the homework will get done, and that there are other teams and colleges. We know what's big and what isn't. In her book *Rising Strong*, Brené Brown says that we need permission to feel our emotions. This phrase is permission to understand your child's feelings from the security of your own, and to give your child the distance she needs to experience her own emotions without a sense of being responsible for yours.

Decide what to do, then do it. Being a parent can mean doing a lot of waffling. TV or no? Candy? Snack? Rabbit? Sleepover? Hoverboard? Scary movie? Concert? We weigh alternatives. We reconsider. We think, sometimes too much. *Decide what to do, then do it* reminds me that most of these choices aren't life-altering. It also reminds me to actively decide and then stick with it, instead of answering thoughtlessly and then giving in to begging later.

You don't have to get it right every time. Actually, you're not going to get it right every time. You're not even supposed to. No one does. Sometimes, you will yell when you wish you'd been calm. You will accuse an innocent child, and let a guilty one off the hook. You will help too much, or too little. You will bring the wrong child to the dentist, you will buy dinner from a vending machine, and you will realize that there isn't always a "right" choice anyway. And then you'll get another chance tomorrow.

Soak up the good. Unlike the rest of the mantras, *soak up the good* reminds me to do something I want to do instead of avoiding the things I don't. In his book *Hardwiring Happiness*, Rick Hanson (you'll hear more from him later) describes the way humans are wired to put more weight on negative experiences than on positive ones, in part because it's more important to remember to avoid a tiger than that the berries on this bush are sweeter than the ones from the tree over there.

We can be happier, he says, if we train our brain to revel in the positive. Hanson is a neuropsychologist, and according to his research, noticing when things are good and making an effort to soak that in feeds dopamine (a positive, calming neurotransmitter) to our amygdala, helping it to want and seek out more dopamine. I'm paraphrasing here, but essentially, the more you *soak up the good*, the more good you see to soak up, and the more your brain is able to stay in that calm, more positive place.

Thanks to Hanson, I've been pausing to absorb even the simplest of good moments. We're all in the car talking and no one is squabbling. The sun is shining and my kid is excitedly sharing plans for the afternoon. It even works when things aren't obviously going

well—when one of my kids comes to me with a problem or a disappointment, even while I sit with that child, holding and talking, a
part of me takes in the pleasure of being there. *Soak up the good* builds
a reservoir of happiness for when things feel bad. Fill that reservoir,
and you have happiness that stays with you.

one

MORNINGS ARE THE WORST

For us, a family headed by two night owls and populated by children who are slow to move at the best of times and can easily lose twenty minutes to the discovery of a yo-yo on the floor of a closet, mornings are the worst. They start so early. They go so quickly. They involve so very many have-tos and where-is-mys and snooze buttons and tardy bells.

I should find some more positive way to put it. Mornings are *challenging*, I should say. It takes a lot of effort for me to get up and get going at all, let alone to help others get up and get going. And it generally feels impossible to get up and get going in a manner that does not spread misery and gloom among all those around me. "Challenging" is a lovely word, suggesting as it does a spirit of enthusiasm, of embracing the day. It's so much more in keeping with the spirit of bringing happiness back into our family lives.

But really, mornings are the worst.

It all starts with mornings, too. A good morning sets the tone for your whole day; a bad morning either does the same or sets us all up with something to overcome first thing. Becoming a parent changes most things, but it really does a number on your morning routine. Gone are the days of staying up until two and sleeping until ten, or leaping out of bed at the last possible moment to allow for an almost on-time arrival at work or in class.

Now, not only do we have to get up early, but we have to get up early enough to get others up, to do the things for them that they can't do for themselves, and to help them learn to get up and get going. Worse, we have to do that with good grace, both to give everyone a pleasant start to their day and to teach by example: when something has to be done, stomping around and screaming at everyone while you do it only makes it worse. (I haven't done that for months. Well, weeks.)

What Goes Wrong (Besides Everything) in the Morning

The process of getting yourself and your entire family moving in the morning is hard. It's hard for nearly everyone. Aside from a few exceptional parents who are making quinoa crepes for breakfast (or are willing to lie about it for articles with headlines like "The Morning Routines of People Who Are More Awesome Than You"), mornings are the great equalizer. It's not that you're overscheduled. It's not that you're insufficiently present, or that your children have too much screen time or are hovered over, or any of the other guilt inducers of the modern parent. The problem is straightforward: it's hard to feel happy when everyone has to be somewhere earlier than almost anyone wants to be anywhere, and some of the people in this equation are too young to take responsibility for getting themselves out the door.

Parents are up against a lot in the mornings. What goes wrong? Some answers: "They start too early." "It's dark and cold." "I have to make coffee before I've had coffee." "Having to rush everyone." "High school starts at 7." "Elementary school starts at 7:45." "Whining." "My child who gets up at five a.m. no matter what." Everything from the weather to our children seems to conspire against us, and the boulders of morning doom start to pile up before we even go to sleep the night before, invariably too late to get enough sleep to face another dawn.

Lack of sleep is a big problem, but it's far from the only problem. Mornings are packed chock-full of other parent challenges. Transitions. Multi-tasking. Things to remember. Deadlines, time limits, and cutoffs enforced by people and places outside of our control. Mornings are unforgiving and for most of us they come with a built-in performance evaluator ticking away on the wall of the kitchen and the car dashboard. How are we doing? We can see the answer right there on the face of the clock.

Then there are the children. The younger ones scoff at your foolish demand for punctuality. Time is meaningless to the baby who has a set-in-stone routine of blowing out his diaper the moment he's placed in his car seat. The toddler with separation issues cares nothing about your need to punch in at work. A slightly older child may seem as if she can understand the kindergarten teacher marking her tardy and even dislike the feeling of running in to join morning circle after the bell, but that possible future pales in comparison to the allure of the plastic sheep she just found on the kitchen floor, which needs to join its flock, which she is pretty sure she put under her bed somewhere, or maybe in the laundry room.

Middle graders and teenagers have some of the same organizational problems parents have in the morning, but without even our dubious ability to get it all done in time. One forgot to print out his homework; another forgot an assignment entirely. Your daughter didn't pack her hockey bag; your son really believes he can make a complex sandwich for his lunch in the thirty seconds he has before he leaves to catch the bus. You've coached them through the process a hundred times, and you'll do it a hundred more before they're capable of the kind of planning it takes to make a morning run smoothly, but meanwhile, your nine o'clock call doesn't want to hear it.

Mornings can be better. There exist parents, not all naturally early risers, and not even equipped with superpowers, who have figured out ways to feel happier amid the morning madness along with getting the whole thing to run more smoothly. There are researchers and experts with data that might finally convince us to make some changes that can benefit our own health and happiness and that of our kids. One big hint: it starts the night before.

The Single Biggest Thing We Can Change About Mornings

Bed. It's the most inviting place in the world early in the morning for older kids, teenagers, and adults—and the last place some of us can make ourselves go at night. Meanwhile, those younger kids, the ones that pop up at five a.m. and appear in our rooms, all sunshine, and then pinch our cheeks and shout, "GET UP, MOMMY! DADDY, GET UP!"? They don't want to go to bed, either. Going to bed, and getting others to go to bed, is hard. But the later we go to bed, the more painful it is when morning comes.

Everything eats away at bedtime, from the jobs we've put off until the last minute to our desire to extend the part of day when we get to do what we want to do instead of what we have to do. The minute we go to bed, it's practically tomorrow (an effect that's worsened when tomorrow is Monday). When our children are young, the time after we tuck them in is our grown-up time. It's time with your partner, if you have one. It's time for yourself, to get things done or just enjoy the opportunity to read a book without interruption. As our kids get older, they start to feel the same frustrations. Especially if they're loaded up with homework, or even if they're busy after school with things they enjoy, they share that sense that the minute their time becomes their own, it's time to go to bed, or they won't get enough sleep.

What's "enough"? The number of hours needed does vary, but not nearly as much as we think. Most people who say they do fine on five or six hours are kidding themselves. Seven is the happy medium for adults and the sweet spot where many can function at their best, which includes being a successful part of your family. I need eight at a minimum, and I guarantee you'll like me better if I'm getting that eight hours consistently, not just on the occasional lucky weekend.

Children and teenagers need even more sleep than we do: eleven to thirteen hours for toddlers and preschoolers; ten hours for younger school-age children; nine to ten for teenagers. Those hours make a difference in grades, health, behavior, and general quality of life. More sleep means happier parents, children, and teens, and happier people work better together to have happier, and thus more manageable, mornings.

Even with all of that research pointing us toward counting

backward from the number on our alarm clock and turning off the lights on time, most of us have trouble doing it. Relatively few adults, teenagers, or children get the sleep they need. How can we make that change?

Sell Your Kids on More Sleep

If bedtimes for your children have slipped, take a hard look at how much sleep they're able to get after lights out. Upping that number probably means you're going to have to put in some tougher bedtimes for a few weeks while you establish or reestablish an earlier routine. It's hard to start dinner earlier, run the tub earlier, or cut short your family evening (especially if you or your partner often work late), but the morning benefits will quickly convince you that it's worth it, and the long-term benefits are even greater.

You can help make the shift by changing the way you talk to your children about sleep and bedtime. Researchers have worked with preschoolers and seventh graders and found that, in both groups, learning the value of sleep led to children getting more. Both groups were given positive sleep education about the benefits of sleep in age-appropriate ways. Parents often get caught up in describing bedtime as a "have to," as in "You have to go to bed now." For little kids, sleep demands that they trade in a bright world of fun and company for a dark and lonely room (or at least, that's how many see it) while older kids share the problems we adults have. At night, finally done with their homework, they're doing their own thing. Bedtime just means morning and the school routine come sooner.

Researchers created a program for preschoolers that included teaching children how to put a teddy bear to sleep using a routine, followed by simple lessons on the importance of sleep and routine for people, too. They were taught that more sleep helped them be cheerful and get along with others, and given a bedtime chart and stickers to use to follow their own routine. The program, designed for low-income families, also included parent and teacher education on sleep. A month later, the children were averaging half an hour more sleep a night, even though their parents appeared to retain very little of their own sleep education.

For seventh graders, the same researchers designed a program that taught children about the ways sleep, or a lack thereof, could affect their grades, mood, health, and relationships. They offered lessons on basic sleep hygiene, including a bedtime ritual, consistency in waking and sleeping times, a dark room, and avoiding caffeine late in the day. Those students maintained better sleep times and sleep quality for nearly a year before reverting to earlier habits.

What these studies show us, as parents, is that how we talk about sleep and how much our kids understand the need for it is important. We can establish and maintain our own sleep routines and talk about how we give up evening hours in exchange for better mornings. And when we observe the impact of a lack of sleep in ourselves or our kids, we can note it, along with a plan to do better. Kids can see how differently they feel after a full night's sleep, and although it's not likely to make them hop into bed without the usual foot-dragging, it does make a difference.

With teenagers especially, parents tend to be too tolerant of activities that interfere with sleep but seem to help children reach other goals, like studying or sports practices. That's shortsighted. Instead of looking the other way when our kids stay up late cramming for a test or a play rehearsal runs late into a school night, we should remind children that more sleep means better academic performance and help them spread out their studying over a longer stretch of time—even if it means we're paying attention to details we'd usually leave to them. When it comes to other activities that bleed into sleep time, take action. If your child is young enough, step in and don't send her to an activity that will go too late, and remind a coach or instructor that nine hours of sleep at night plus a seven a.m. bus equals a nine p.m. bedtime. Even if you end up compromising once in a while, teaching your child that you take sleep seriously sets them up to better manage their own sleep.

Get More Sleep Yourself

To really feel happier in the mornings, parents need to get more sleep, too. We're better at everything when we've had more sleep, and most importantly for better mornings, we've got more patience and more ability to give our children the help and support they need to get going. Too little sleep, and we're jumpy and reactive. Our brains are more likely to flood us with adrenaline in a stress response to what really isn't a life-or-death situation, and that makes it really difficult not to blow up at the kid who got the waffle stuck in the toaster. (There's more on this in Chapter 7, "Discipline: This Hurts Me More Than It Hurts You.") But we're parents, and that means we can't always sleep when we want to, even if it would be better for everyone.

There's no denying that infants make getting enough sleep impossible. Not nearly impossible, or practically impossible, but actually impossible. A survey of one thousand new parents by a British bed manufacturer found that two-thirds were sleeping only four contiguous hours or less. Five hours of sleep at night (still not nearly enough) during the first two years of parenting would be 3,650 hours; four hours a night is 2,920. That leaves new parents with a sleep deficit of 730 hours—or the amount of sleep you'd need, at five hours a night, for about five months. Looking to get a healthy seven hours? As a new parent, after two years, you're more than a year behind.

You can do three things during this phase of life. You can allow enough time for sleep, putting yourself to bed early enough that if the baby was to sleep, you'd get what you needed. You almost certainly won't, but many of us shoot ourselves in the foot by not even setting up the opportunity to accumulate those hours. Work with your partner, if you have one, to create trade-offs. Even if one of you is working and the other isn't, you both need an equal shot at sleep. Next, create the best possible opportunity for sleeping when the baby allows. Shawn Stevenson, author of *Sleep Smarter*, says that when you can't get quantity sleep, the sleep you get should be as high-quality as possible. His suggestions include giving yourself a caffeine curfew, timing your exercise for morning hours, and avoiding the second-wind syndrome at bedtime. Let yourself go to sleep when you need to.

Finally, go easier on yourself (and on your partner) when it's impossible to get the sleep you need, whether it's baby or kid sleep troubles or your own insomnia that's keeping you up. Let some things go, in your mood, in your home, and in what you expect of yourself. You're running uphill and that makes a difference in everything you do.

Once you're out of the baby years, set an example for your children by making sleep a priority for yourself. Create a bedtime, stick with it, and talk about it. Set a curfew for digital devices, even those in nighttime mode. It's not just the light that's stimulating, it's the constant input from tech and television that keeps our brains firing long after we've shut our eyes. If you're in the habit of staying up late for pleasure or productivity, it will probably feel difficult to shut down sooner. *What you want now isn't always what you want later.* Your to-morrow morning self will thank you for the gift of more sleep.

Changing My Morning Story

Even beyond working toward better sleep, there's a lot left to improve about the average morning. Setting out to make mornings happier at our house was daunting and packed with failure. Take, for example, my attempt to adopt Gretchen Rubin's "sing in the mornings" resolution from her book *The Happiness Project*. Rubin's daughter Eliza was asked at school to describe how her parents woke her up in the morning. "With a good-morning song," she said.

Now, lest you misjudge Rubin, this was apparently not at all accurate. "I'd only done that a few times in her whole life," she said. But after Eliza described it in school, Rubin thought it must have made a real impression on her daughter. She vowed to make a habit of it, and succeeded. In her world, "singing in the morning really had a cheering effect."

It didn't in mine. Singing seemed like going too far, so I thought a morning mix of get-moving tunes might be the way to go. I created a Happy Morning playlist for the kitchen and tried, for weeks, to let those cheerful songs set our morning mood.

I hated it. I do not want to be nudged out of my morning fog by ABBA; I am not a morning dancing queen. But the real problem with my attempt to drown out my morning grumpies with a rousing version of "Everything Is Awesome" wasn't that I didn't like the music. It was that I was still fundamentally misunderstanding mornings. I thought I hated them, and I do. But I kind of love them, too. And it took a bigger failure to figure that out.

Paying someone else to do the things you hate to do to free yourself up for what's important is a classic strategy, beloved by the "highly successful" and the "get it done" crowd. About the same time as I attempted to institute musical mornings, our sister-team of house cleaners moved, leaving us bereft. And since I'd long admired the household of friends, both doctors and the parents of five children ranging in age from two to twelve, I asked them how they did it. They had a housekeeper, an "Alice," and she did mornings.

So instead of replacing the cleaning team, I hired one person, Betty, for the same amount of money. Betty, a naturally early riser, was not just willing but enthusiastic about arriving at our house at six a.m. and helping us get our day started, three days a week, before putting in a few hours of cleaning and heading home to her husband and hobbies. Even as I write about it, it sounds brilliant. Not a morning person? Hire a morning person! I could have an extra hour of sleep under my belt right now.

It was not brilliant. Not for me. To this day, hiring Betty stands out as the moment when I realized that what I thought I wanted was not what I wanted at all. I thought I wanted easier mornings for me. What I really wanted were happier—and easier—mornings for all of us.

A lot happens in the morning. Plans and lunches are made and discussed. Homework is gathered. Tests quickly reviewed for. Clothing is found to be too short or too full of holes. There were many pies being made in the morning, and before Betty's arrival, my husband and I had our fingers in all of them. The advent of Betty meant losing a connection to our children's day that I hadn't realized how much I relied on. Instead of outsourcing so I could focus on the important things, I'd outsourced something that was itself important. Pretty soon we started joining back in, and there were too many cooks in the breakfast kitchen. In a matter of months, Betty moved on.

What was true for us in the mornings turned out to be true about a lot of things to do with the daily work of raising our family. I didn't want to not do it. I just wanted it to be more fun, or at the very least less miserable. We regrouped after Betty. I knew what I didn't want in the morning. I didn't want to be late. Didn't want to feel rushed. Didn't want to spend it yelling. But when I focused on the didn'ts, things didn't get much better. I quickly found myself once again sending a child off to school with a parting shout of "See, I told you you'd be late," a slammed door, and a screech of angry tires. *Wow*, I thought, as I churned off, fuming. *This is a really lousy way to start the day.*

That was when I finally figured out what I did want. I wanted to give the kids—and myself—a good start. I *wanted* to be there in the morning. I *wanted* to be a part of that part of their day. And if I wanted to be there, then it had to be possible to turn mornings around.

Fortunately, a good start, in my mind, doesn't require quinoa crepes or the family sitting down around the table together. If you can do that, you can probably move on to another chapter, because you've got mornings licked. A good start looked simple to me: it looked like a morning where children knew what they needed to do, had enough time to do it, and weren't being yelled at every step of the way, even if things were going wrong. Even if they were going to be late. A good start looked like a morning where everyone worked together toward a common goal: getting the car out of the garage early enough to get to school not smack on at the starting bell, early enough that they could settle into their day. Once I knew what I wanted, it was easier to start figuring out how to get there. Here's some of what I did, and what other families suggest, for turning your mornings around.

Making Mornings Better

GET UP EARLIER

Many, many ideas for improving the morning involve rising earlier. In her book *I Know How She Does It*, Laura Vanderkam analyzed 1,001 days in the lives of working mothers earning at least $100,000 a year. Many found more time to spend with young children, who naturally get up early, by embracing that early morning time instead of trying to keep the children up after dinner to play with parents who didn't make it home until seven or eight. Other parents swear by getting up early enough to have a cup of coffee before the rest of the household appears, or to work on a personal project, read, or exercise. They have sex or balance their checkbooks. Like the White Queen in Lewis Carroll's *Through the Looking-Glass*, they believe six impossible things before breakfast.

Although I've finally managed to do this (I get up half an hour earlier to run a mile on a treadmill five days a week), I still resent the people to whom this comes easily. If you're one of them, and if you can help your children to get up early enough not to feel rushed in the morning, you can probably change the tenor of your mornings more easily than those of us who wake up grumpy and never, no matter how much sleep we've had, want to get out of bed. Mornings at your house will probably be more pleasant than many. But even for families of early risers, it's still hard to get out the door.

GET UP DIFFERENTLY

Until very recently, I never thought I was capable of getting up a minute before I had to. Instead, I focused my attention on getting up differently, and helping the children get up differently as well. For many years, my husband started the morning at our house, and going up the stairs to shake the children out of their sleep was his least favorite moment of the morning (and theirs). Our heaviest sleepers were, at the time, in the two top bunks, meaning that on many mornings, he was making his way up to the top to shake a child awake. That made him irritated, and it irritated the sleeper as well, setting off a chain reaction that more than once ended in a morning temper tantrum.

That is definitively not a good start to the day. The solution seems obvious—alarm clocks—and after some trial and error, and one child who kept setting her alarm for the wee hours by mistake, this helped a lot. The natural anger anyone feels at an alarm clock was directed at the clock, not Dad. There's still a fair amount of checking to be done that they actually get up, but the onus is on them, not on us.

You can also wake the kids up differently by staggering their schedules. Naomi Hattaway, a mother of three in Virginia, found that when her kids woke up at the same time, everyone was stumbling over each other and getting in each other's way. So instead, she encourages her youngest (her "morning child") to get up first. "She gets time to adjust, wake up, greet the day, have one-on-one time with parents before her older siblings get up." As children get older, the same system minimizes the rush on the bathroom.

ENLIST KIDS TO HELP

Because there's so much at stake in the mornings—and yet, on a global scale, so little—mornings are the perfect time to let your children take responsibility for themselves. Depending on their age, they can, and should, be the ones charged with remembering their hats and mittens, sneakers, backpacks. They can make their own breakfasts, set their own alarms, help with siblings.

But what if they fail? Hit snooze and roll over, arrive at school without a coat in a New England January, leave the homework they worked so hard on in the middle of the kitchen table? Within the constraints of what works for you and your family, making those little failures their problem and not yours will go a long way to making your mornings happier in the long run. Parents who say they're happier in the mornings put kids in charge of the things the kids can handle, and let their children's responsibilities grow with the kids.

"One day our youngest (a first grader at the time) told us he knew it was time to get up for school because he could hear us screaming at his older brother," says Angela Crawford, a mother of three in New Jersey. "That was our aha moment—something had to change. Every morning we were constantly battling to get him to do what he needed to do: print out his homework, pack his backpack."

So, she says, they set rules for who did what and when. "Children pack their own backpacks, and we won't bring them forgotten homework. I pack lunches in elementary school; once you hit middle school, you do your own. I once received an email from a teacher that my child had forgotten their homework and they asked if I would drop it off and I told them no and explained why. For two of my children getting a zero was punishment enough, for my oldest not so much, so if he missed a homework he would not be able to play with friends after school that day. We ask them (and remind them) to plan ahead and be considerate of us as well, and to ask for things like permissions slips or a ride home from sports practices before they're walking out the door, but we don't look for those things. If they don't ask, it doesn't happen."

Other parents set a departure time and hold firm to that. Leon Scott Baxter, father of two and author of *Secrets of Safety-Net Parenting*, says his daughters lagged and dragged and lingered every morning amid his constant harrying: "Let's go! Get your shoes on! I'm going to be late!" Eventually he told the girls he'd be leaving at 7:25, with or without them. "My oldest must have been in third or fourth grade and she was lagging. At 7:25, I told her I was leaving, and I walked out the door. I got in my car. She looked out the window. I backed the vehicle out of the driveway. She scrambled out the door with backpack and papers in hand. She tumbled into the van. A minute later she realized she was wearing her bedroom slippers. She begged me to go back. I didn't. She wore her slippers at school the entire day." The same child, he said, started college this year and is "incredibly responsible." That's not something he credits to the slippers incident, but to many years of expecting her, and her younger sister, to take charge of themselves when it was appropriate, even if they didn't always get things right. "I think allowing her to feel some discomfort as a result of her own choices and mistakes when she was younger has helped her turn into someone who can rise to the occasion as a young adult," he says.

A key to making this work successfully for your family is deciding what you'll do when your kids blow it (and they will). I've read stories of parents who stepped over a forgotten lunch in the mudroom, just to make the point that it's the child's job to remember, and your parents won't be there to save you every time. That's not our style, if for

no other reason than I have proven many times that if you are counting on me to remember your things, you have backed the wrong
horse. I will put the wrong skates in your hockey bag and am just as
likely to forget that lunch as you are, and maybe more.

But if I do see the lunch, I'll grab it—because, as my friend Catherine Newman, author of *Waiting for Birdy*, puts it, independence is
not always the goal, and never the only goal. (Imagine, for a minute,
what you'd say if your thirteen-year-old stepped over your eight-year-
old's forgotten lunch without comment.) Encouraging children to
take responsibility for some elements of their mornings makes mornings go more smoothly. Letting them feel the consequences of a failure will make everyone happier in the long run, as they learn to take
care of their needs, but that doesn't mean you have to force those
consequences on them. In most families, those things will happen
often enough without your "help." Working together for a successful
morning makes everyone happier, too.

DO MORE THE NIGHT BEFORE

I do better in the mornings if I prepare. Most mornings, my husband
is the preferred parent to get breakfast going for everyone. (He says,
"I'm grumpy, but at least I don't bite.") If he's out of town, I get ready
for morning in a way he doesn't feel the need to, setting out everything I need for any breakfast plans, leaving notes for any kids who
might need instructions before I get up at the last possible minute,
and structuring things so that I don't need to make any decisions. I'm
not at my best in the morning, and I know it.

I stole this idea from a friend, a fellow mother of four, who set a
breakfast table nightly right down to the bowls of cereal, filled and
covered in plastic wrap. The same friend, when all of those children

were very young, put them to sleep in their school clothes, a strategy I would totally have emulated if I'd known about it before my kids got attached to their pajamas. Similarly, another friend bought only fleece-lined shoes and slippers for her children when they were in preschool and did away with socks altogether. "I hate socks," she said. "They're nothing but trouble."

Make or help with lunches the night before. Help with the packing of backpacks, then remind regularly about the packing of backpacks. Lay out clothes, especially if one of your children is indecisive in the morning. When my kids were small, I bought four sets of hanging shelves for their closet and put one day's school clothes on each shelf straight from the laundry basket, underwear and socks and all.

Fill the coffeemaker. Lay out your own clothes. Hang your keys in their spot. Do everything you can for morning you, and do it right after dinner, not last thing before bed.

TURN OFF THE TECH

There are typically two stages of family morning life: the one where the kids naturally get up earlier than most people can function, and the one where it feels impossible to get them up at all. When you're in the first stage, television and other gadgetry can be a lifesaver. They let you shower, make breakfast, or go back to sleep for a little while (more on that in Chapter 6, "Screens Are Fun, Limiting Them Is Not").

But once you get past the TV-as-babysitter stage, you quickly enter the TV-as-distraction stage, along with a multitude of other gadgets. For many families with older children, early-morning tech is a shortcut to a tardy slip. "No screens in the morning," says Jen Mann, a mother of two in Kansas City. "It makes a huge difference. Everyone can focus on what needs to be done and not get distracted so easily. I'm embarrassed to admit how long it took us to realize that was our issue." If your children are heading straight for phones or screens when they wake up, they're probably not getting their lunches or homework together, and they might not even be eating that breakfast sitting in front of them. Instituting a no-screens rule will help them get moving—and if you're checking emails and skimming Facebook yourself, try setting those things aside until you can give them your full focus. You might find you move a little faster, too.

MASTER GOOD TIMING

The other day in the car, I asked my kids, "How long do you think it takes you to brush your teeth and get your coats and things after breakfast?" "Nine minutes." "I don't know." "Fifteen minutes." "Five minutes. It should take five minutes."

Nope, I said. Twenty. Twenty, almost without fail, maybe fifteen if there are extenuating circumstances, like a school day everyone is looking forward to. And then I proved it, setting a timer when I first told them to go brush their teeth, and turning it off only when they were all in the car.

If they knew I was timing them, they could go faster, but the real goal of the timer wasn't speed. It was more practical. I know that to get places on time, I need to count backward from when we're supposed to be there, and to do that I need to know how long things take. Twenty minutes is fine—if you allot twenty minutes. But humans are notoriously poor estimators of time, and young human beings doubly so. Sometimes it just seems like it ought to be faster. Sometimes we just so badly want it to be faster.

Since magical thinking is as little help here as it is in other areas of parenthood, time yourselves, and don't fall for the old "that was not a typical morning" routine. There is no typical morning. Someone will always be able to find only one shoe, and someone will always drop her entire binder on the floor, the one with the easy-open rings. Given that, how long does it take your family to get from "brush your teeth and get your backpacks" to completely out the door? Count backward from that, and that's when the whistle blows. Any later and you're fooling yourself. You may get lucky once in a while, but it's the lucky morning that's not "typical."

Timing ourselves is itself fun. We can try to break our record, or simply marvel when each and every person in the car had to stop and go back in for, in descending age order, coffee, sneakers, recorder, homework, and jacket, with the result that eleven minutes passed from the moment the first person got in the car to the moment we left the garage—and then another three when someone else turned out to have forgotten her gym shoes.

SET IT TO MUSIC

"We literally have a soundtrack," says Whit Honea, a father of two in Los Angeles. "It plays from rise to door and all their cues are marked accordingly." If a full, timed playlist seems like too much, try a song that's the "get ready to get out the door" cue, whether it comes on automatically (if your household is equipped to make that happen) or whether it's just something you play manually at the same time every morning. *You do you.* For some families, a little music makes everything better. I didn't like the morning playlist when we tried it the first time, but I'm going to give it another shot.

CHANGE SOMETHING BIG

If your mornings are particularly painful because of some external problem—school start times, long commutes, one parent's daily eight a.m. class overlapping with the other parent's daily 7:30 staff meeting—it's worth thinking about changing something big. Friends of ours who were extreme night owls, and who kept their daughters on a schedule that allowed for a lot of evening family time after relatively late work nights, chose their daughters' elementary school based on the late start time. We don't have that kind of school choice where I live, but if you do, and if it's an affordable choice that better suits your life, why not?

Ponn Sabra, a Connecticut mother of three, says she has to laugh when she considers what her family did to make their morning routine easier: they quit. After too many hectic mornings (and with a life that includes a lot of international travel), she chose to homeschool her daughters. Mornings, she says, became "a fun, lively time to enjoy being all together." That's an extreme solution to mornings that most of us can only dream about (and many of us, myself included, would consider a nightmare—I can't imagine a parent less suited to homeschooling her children than I am), but sometimes imagining the extreme can open you up to ideas that, while "out there," might be achievable, like petitioning the high school to change its start time or moving to a home where your children could walk to school.

If something about your job makes your mornings miserable, like a regularly scheduled staff meeting that requires you to catch a train that leaves before your children are even awake or a commute that's beginning to feel unsustainable, try to change that one thing, at least part of the time. Ask to move the meeting. Explore working part-time from home. Look ahead, because even a change that makes things better next year can make this year easier. Changing jobs to increase your happiness is the subject of many a book beyond this one. But you do mornings, well, every weekday morning. If your job is making your mornings miserable, that's a lot of miserable.

If a small change isn't enough change, think big. Or maybe make mornings a little more fun just by imagining a big change. The school is unlikely to install a gondola ski lift between our second floor and theirs, but we can hope.

GET UP FOR SOMETHING YOU WANT TO DO

After all of that (and I've just described more than a decade of evolving mornings), the very weirdest thing we did at our house to improve mornings, the single one thing that meant the children would be on time nearly every day for school and that everyone had time to take a breath and get over whatever morning madness had set in and wake up all the way and head into the day, was the one thing I thought would make us permanently late for everything, forever.

We bought a house with a big barn. And then we put a few horses in that barn, and then we let the apartment above the barn to a wonderful young couple, Kristyn and Greg, and they put even more horses in the barn, and Kristyn and I rescued some horses and put them in a new shed because they didn't even fit in the barn, and then we added some chickens and then Kristyn and Greg added a baby and then we added some chicks and all of those things had to be taken care of, every morning, by all of us, and so we got up even earlier.

I still don't like getting up in the morning. It doesn't matter how much sleep I've had, or what kind of alarm I use. I just don't spring out of bed with a joyful step, and it seems likely that I never will. But when I threw myself headlong into a project I love, helping to run a horse barn, I put myself in a position where, most mornings, I *have* to get up earlier.

We leave the house at seven-ish for the barn. We leave the barn at 7:40, no -ish, for school, after we do whatever needs to be done. On a really busy morning, we feed the horses (there have been up to nineteen), blanket them, put them out, muck the stalls, put hay in the fields for them, fill the water troughs, feed the chickens, and sweep the aisle. On an easy morning, when the weather is glorious and all the horses slept outside and the fields are conveniently growing grass for them to eat, we bring in a few horses who need grain in the morning, put them back out and clean up after them, then feed the chickens.

Going to the barn is not always a "fun" proposition. There is always one kid who doesn't want to drag the hose out over the ice and snow to fill the tub in the back field and another who thinks she's doing more work than anyone else. But even then, when it's done, everyone has stretched out, everyone has accomplished something, everyone has had some fresh air and done some work that had to be done for some other creature that can't do it for him- or herself. The work itself may not be fun, but the satisfaction that comes with it is, as is the part where we are always among the earliest cars in the drop-off line.

I'm not suggesting that you run out and buy a farm to make your mornings happier. But maybe making mornings more fun for you means doing something totally unexpected that takes longer, something that isn't just "get up earlier" but "get up earlier *for this*." A weekly diner breakfast. Morning family runs. A stop at an elderly neighbor's to see if he needs anything, twenty minutes dedicated to getting dinner prepped together, taking time with one child to make a proper breakfast for the rest of the family. I don't know. I hate getting up in the morning, but I get up earlier for the horse barn, and I'm happier for it.

LET HAPPINESS IN

There is nothing wrong. As I discovered after I tried to outsource my morning madness, when you're in the middle of that getting-out-of-the-house swirl, you're probably exactly where you want to be, doing exactly what you want to do—under the circumstances. Second only to the dinner hour, mornings are when families spend the most time all together, all in the same place. You're all there. You're all engaged, interacting, moving around one another in that complicated family kitchen dance. This is your time to be the people you are together, and that matters more than the clock or the forgotten algebra assignment. That doesn't mean you don't keep making things happen or you aren't still going to hold the child assigned to empty the dishwasher to her job. It just means there really is something to enjoy in the mornings, although I struggled to find it until I pulled off the whole "get more sleep" thing.

When something big really does happen, a catastrophe, or even just unexpected news, many of us find ourselves longing for the ordinary life we lived before everything suddenly changed. This is it. If we can shift our attitudes just a little, we can find a way to appreciate this time in all its abundance while it's here, instead of when it's gone. You can even put a little reminder in a good place, like a note on a mirror or your phone or computer home screen. I have a bracelet inscribed with the words "an ordinary day," and when I look at it, I take my shoulders out of my ears and *soak up the good*. Even if it doesn't feel that great.

Mornings are still the worst. But they're also part of the best. We get one a day, every day, until they're gone.

two

CHORES: MORE FUN IF SOMEONE ELSE DOES THEM, AND YOUR CHILD SHOULD

Children should do chores. That's a controversial premise, although not everyone will admit it. A few parents will declare outright that their children are "too busy for chores" or that "their job is school." Many, many more of us assign chores, or believe in them, but the chores just don't get done.

If this is true in your house, it's a big part of the reason you're not getting as much joy as you could be out of your family life. There aren't that many issues upon which I'll plant the parenting expert flag, but I'm a firm believer in chores. If you're clearing your eleven-year-old's dishes after every meal, then unless your child has physical or mental special needs that require this service, you are doing it wrong—as are most of our fellow parents. In a survey of 1,001 US adults, 82 percent reported having had regular chores growing up, but only 28 percent said that they require their own children to do them.

Our children are capable of helping us look after our homes and do the work it takes to keep everything clean, pleasant, and running smoothly, and in some families, they do. In pediatrician Deborah Gilboa's family, children take on a big responsibility every year, depending on age, and keep that chore until the next child is ready to step up. At seven, they become responsible for the family laundry. At nine, they become the lunch maker for the family; at eleven, they become the designated dishwasher emptier; and at thirteen, they become responsible for making dinner once a week. Because her kids do those things, Dr. Gilboa and her partner are freed up to do, as she puts it, "the things the kids can't. They can't pay the bills. They can't mediate sibling disputes. The only way we have the time and energy to do those things is if we delegate some of the rest." Jennifer Flanders, a mother of twelve children (the oldest is twenty-nine; the youngest, seven), says something similar. "It quickly became clear that they could make messes much faster than I could clean them up." For her children, the expectation that they will do chores is a given, and by the time they're in college, each child is capable of the cleaning, cooking, lawn mowing, and general tending it takes to make a household work. For more on how that works, keep reading.

What Goes Wrong

Chores themselves mostly aren't fun (although they can be). But when children don't help out with household tasks, their absence, and our resentment, gets in the way of families having fun together and detracts from our children's sense of being part of a larger whole. Children who don't do chores also miss out on the chance to make their own fun that much sweeter by adding in the satisfaction that comes from having had a job to do and seeing it through. When we don't give our children age-appropriate responsibilities (and expect them to fulfill them), we're not respecting who they are now or the adults they will later become, and we're leaving them with a sense of being adrift in a world where everyone wants to feel needed.

We can blame culture, a little bit. If your child is coming home with five hours of homework every night and is in even one sport, that doesn't leave much time for anything else. If every other child in the community plays three sports a year on top of Kumon and robotics club, you can get sucked into a schedule that makes chores hard to establish without even realizing you've been had. And although you should put absolutely no faith at all whatsoever in your child's declaration that "no one else has to do the dishes," he may be right—and being part of a community where most kids aren't expected to contribute around the house does rub off.

That works the other way around, too. If you're surrounded by families who respond to your invitations for their child to join yours for a day of sledding with "as soon as he's done with his chores," and if your child is seeing friends being told to "clean up your room" and helping with the dinner dishes, your job will be (a little) easier, and when you're the family that expects children to do their share, you help spread that expectation.

The sheer effort of getting the children to do the chores is also a big factor in why it just doesn't happen. Studies show that it takes, on average, five years of nightly nagging before a child will, without a reminder, clear her own plate from the dinner table. The fact that those studies were entirely unscientific and done in my kitchen on a sample set of four should not make you believe in them any less. The struggle is real. It's easier to do it yourself until, suddenly, it's not—but if you wait until then to start nagging, you have a rough five years ahead. If you can pay someone to clean your house for you (we do), the load on the parents is lighter, making it even more tempting to skip the nagging and just do it yourself.

That's the choice many of us make. Of parents who said they had chores themselves but didn't expect their kids to do them, 75 percent said they believed regular chores made kids "more responsible" and 63 percent said chores teach kids "important life lessons." We believe in chores. We talk a good game. But when we look honestly at who's doing what in our kitchens, laundry rooms, and bathrooms, many of us (including me) struggle to do what it takes to get kids to help at home.

Research not performed in my kitchen also backs up our instinct that we're not asking enough of our children. Between 2001 and 2005 a team of researchers from UCLA's Center on the Everyday Lives of Families (CELF) recorded 1,540 hours of footage of thirty-two middle-class, dual-earner families with at least two children, all of them going about their regular business in their Los Angeles homes. They found that the Los Angeles parents did most of the housework and intervened quickly when the kids had trouble completing a task. Children in twenty-two families made it a practice to ignore or resist their parents' requests for help. In eight families, the parents didn't actually ask the children to do much of anything. (This research was described by one of the younger social scientists as "the very best birth control ever.")

Unfortunately, if you wish your children did more around the house (as I do), the brutal truth is that it's on us if they don't. Children whose families have established an expectation that they will contribute to the workings of the household, do—whether it's a five-year-old in Peru's Amazon region climbing trees to harvest papayas and "helping haul logs thicker than her leg to stoke a fire" or a seven-year-old doing the household laundry every weekend. They may not whistle while they work; they may require near-constant reminders; they will almost certainly not do the job to your standards without years of training, but children (including mine and yours) can and will do the work if you require it of them.

There are two ways to make this happen. The first is to make it a priority—to say what you mean and mean what you say around chores, to enforce consequences, to nag, to ground, to request and request and request and never let up—or just do it yourself or conclude that you can live with unmade beds or un-put-away laundry.

This first course takes serious dedication. You're swimming against the tide—most parents, as I've said, don't pull this off (and as you'll see as you read further, I'm still working on it). I suspect it's worth it, and the parents I've talked to whose children (after years of training) genuinely do regular chores with efficiency, if not grace, assure me that it is so.

The second way to get your children to do chores is to need the help—and this is why middle- and upper-class families with two healthy parents are at a rare disadvantage, and one few would want to change. If you can't manage without help because one parent is chronically ill, because you're a single parent, or because you're working two jobs just to keep the basics covered, your children are more likely to step up. They will learn to prepare food, produce clean laundry, and take care of younger children. This can be a bad thing (see Jeannette Walls's memoir, *The Glass Castle*), or it can be a good thing (think Mary and Laura in *Little House on the Prairie*). It can also be a bad thing that leads to good things.

You can't, and wouldn't want to, artificially create a situation in which your life demanded that your three-year-old boil her own hot dogs, as Jeannette Walls describes (she was badly burned as a result).

But watch. There will come a time when you are faced with an injured family member or animal, or your car goes off the driveway into a snowdrift, or you are traveling alone with four young children and one toddler is barfing and the baby is crying and the preschooler needs to go poop. At that moment, you will look at whatever child is even close to physically capable of whatever you need and you will say, "I cannot do this without you." And that child will perform miracles.

You can be very, very glad that you're not in that place very often— but recognize that the capable child who comes through in a pinch is the same child sitting at the dinner table reading a comic book while you clear and wash the dishes generated by the meal you cooked half an hour ago. He is not physically different from the children born to less who do more, or the kids from that big family down the street who are always so polite and helpful when they come over.

All of which means that, as much as we don't want to, we really need to nudge that child up and teach him to properly load the dishwasher—which also means we must find a way to get over our own distaste for the task. In my research, I asked 1,050 parents an open-ended question: *what do you least like about parenting?* The most popular answer, without contest, was "discipline" in various forms, and that included enforcing chores and other responsibilities. Among the things we don't like? "Enforcing the rules, especially about house-hold chores," the challenges of "chores and disciplining a child," and having to nag kids to do simple chores. Many parents wish they had begun enforcing the rules and started a routine of chores earlier when their kids were younger instead of "fighting teeth and nails to get something done" when they are older. We may think our children should do chores, but we really don't want to have to make them— but it's worth noting that we don't like "doing all the chores myself" either.

We will all, parents and children alike, be happier if we parents overcome our reluctance to be the chore enforcer. "It's not good for kids to be outside playing and Mom to be inside doing all the work," said Jennifer Flanders. "They benefit more from helping and from working side by side with us, and then we can all play together." Children who help more at home feel a larger sense of obligation and connectedness to their parents, and that connection helps them connect to others and weather life's more stressful moments—in other words, it helps them be happier. Their help, even when it's less than gracious, helps us be happier, too. We know we shouldn't shoulder all the work of the household alone, and we know, too, that children raised to get up and help when there is work to be done become a more productive part of any group they join.

"We want to raise our children with joy," said Flanders, and that means building a family that works together to sustain and support one another. "I don't want to be a martyr, always complaining about all the work the kids create. Why would you raise kids you're not happy to live with?"

When Should Chores Start for Kids?

The short answer to that question is now. Although it's never too late to start, the younger kids are when we create an expectation that they'll help around the house, the better. If you're doing work that's necessary to the running of the house and your children are sitting and watching (or more likely, sitting nearby and watching something else), get them up and get them involved.

Wondering what kids can do? Probably more than you think. Look back in time a little, or even just to your own childhood, and ask yourself—when did kids start milking cows and churning butter? Mowing the lawn? Washing the dishes? Usually, the answer is something like "As soon as they could do so safely," an assessment parents once made by working alongside their kids until they felt the kids were ready to take over, allowing the parent to move on to other work.

"What chores should children do at what ages?" is a common question, and there are plenty of answers (just search "age-appropriate chores" online). But before you do a Web search for a chore list, ask yourself a more localized question. What are you doing when you do the things that make your house run? Are you vacuuming and sweeping? Gathering or folding laundry? Feeding chickens? The question isn't really what kids can do, it's what needs to be done at your house. The jobs that absolutely need to be done for your family are the jobs you want to be teaching and eventually delegating, whether they're as generic as washing dishes or as specific as piloting the houseboat through the lock. This is not about, as one popular chore chart suggested, training a four-year-old to sanitize doorknobs—unless, of course, sanitizing doorknobs takes up a lot of your time. It's about learning to work together to all make the house run, so that you can all enjoy everything else life has to offer.

But What About All That Homework?

Here's the most common question, or maybe excuse, brought up by parents of older kids who aren't doing nearly what they could to help the house run smoothly: how can we ask the high schooler who barely got to dinner after sports practice to put in fifteen minutes of kitchen time before setting off for his three hours of homework, especially if, as discussed in Chapter 1, we're trying to put a family priority on getting enough sleep?

We can—once we understand that this is truly important. Who do you want this child of yours to grow up to be? Almost all parents respond to surveys and questionnaires by saying they are deeply invested in raising caring, ethical children, and most parents tell researchers that they see these moral qualities as more important than achievement. Other research suggests that many of our children aren't getting that message. In a survey of more than ten thousand students from thirty-three schools in various regions of this country, Harvard psychologist Richard Weissbourd found that almost 80 percent valued achievement of their own happiness over caring for others—and what's more, most thought their parents agreed.

Although household chores are a small thing, the subtle but pervasive message of requiring them isn't small at all. Requiring that high schooler to contribute to the family well-being and the smooth running of the household before turning his attention to his books conveys the value you place on that contribution. Schoolwork is important, but so is your place in this family community. You're not saying "you must do dishes instead of homework" (although it's likely your high schooler will claim to see it that way). You're saying "you must find a way to balance these competing responsibilities that does not shirk your role as part of this family."

It's so, so tempting to give the kid a pass, and so hard to see how often we hand over that get-out-of-chores-free card. But *what you want now isn't always what you want later*. "Our interviews and observations over the last several years also suggest that the power and frequency of parents' messages about achievement and happiness often drown out their messages about concern for others," says Dr.

Weissbourd. Your "message" about helping to care for one's family needs to be repeated often, especially if it involves doing the dishes.

But what if that fifteen minutes a night leads to a B in Spanish, which is ultimately the reason the Harvard admissions office—home of the noted researcher Richard Weissbourd, quoted earlier—puts your snowflake in the "no" drift?

You can't look at it that way. (Note that if I didn't sometimes lean toward looking at it that way myself, it probably wouldn't occur to me.) You do not just want to raise the child you can hothouse and coddle into the Ivy League. You want to raise the adult who can balance a caring role in the family and community with whatever lifetime achievement goals he chooses. Teaching that balance has value. Asking—and expecting—children to contribute is important. One small longitudinal study, done over a period of twenty-five years, found that the best predictor for young adults' success in their midtwenties was whether they participated in household tasks at age three or four. That researcher, Marty Rossmann, used data from a longterm study that her own family had participated in, which included questions about children's participation in family work at ages three to four, nine to ten, and fifteen to sixteen, along with a brief phone interview when child participants were in their twenties. She found that earlier work meant more, helping children to internalize the idea that household responsibilities are shared responsibilities—which extended, then, to a sense of responsibility and empathy in other areas of their lives.

I don't want to make too much of a small study, and there's really no need. All the research in this area does is confirm what we already know. The new boyfriend who rises to help his hosts clear the table when meeting his partner's family, the young employee who steps up to help employees in other jobs, the student who doesn't just finish her lab work but makes sure her work area is ready for the next class—those kids are more self-sufficient, better prepared for adulthood, and more successful in relationships with family and friends. Success is not all about gold stars and letter grades.

So How Do We Make Chores Happen?

Our family history of chores is mixed. Our kids do farm work that most others don't, which they would argue should count when I'm considering how much they help around the house (I disagree). For household chores, though, I'd rate my performance at about a C. I suspect we're average, my husband and I. We have tried every single available system for assigning and enforcing chores, and after more than fifteen years as parents, we achieved children who mostly clear their own dishes, including one who does it every time and one who has to be reminded almost every time. That was it. They knew how to do a variety of other things, particularly cooking things, which might go on the credit side of our ledger, but they do not actually do them unless we demand it, or at least not in a useful way. (Okay, brownies are useful. But it's just not what I mean.)

They fed the dogs and cats and chickens, albeit with much stomping and dish slamming and grumping about siblings who didn't have to do the job when it was their week and the general unfairness of a life that includes opening a can of cat food once daily. I'd estimate that I chose to feed the animals myself rather than endure the fuss about half of the time. Maybe more often. There was a child assigned to empty the dishwasher daily, to set the table, to clear the table, to do the dishes, and to take out the trash—but if we didn't demand that those things happen, they didn't.

What had we tried? Star charts. Reward chips that could be cashed in at the Mom Store. Fines for failure to perform. Bonuses for stellar performance. Offering their allowance in the form of single dollars in a cup and taking a dollar out every time a chore wasn't done. Docking allowances for complaining about chores. Countless other strategies that I have forgotten.

Here's what I've learned, through my own experience and interviews with other parents: any of those things can work. So why didn't they work for us? Because we didn't stick with them. We got tired of the effort of implementing the charts. We foolishly promised rewards that involved things like trips to the ice-cream store that we did not want to do. We got angry and punished inconsistently. And, again and again, we gave up, and no one was happy—because as much as they fussed about chores, the kids didn't want to have to watch us griping about doing them, either. It started to seem as though "happy" was unobtainable.

Have we found a way to make it better? Yes. And we certainly got happier—kids and parents alike. Some families really have got it figured out—they've established routines that have been working decently for years; they're comfortable with the amount of reminding required, and their family is in a good place with this one.

Here's what those parents had to say about making chores a happier part of family life, and how we used their advice to change.

THEY'RE NOT CHORES, THEY'RE LIFE SKILLS

Laundry, loading a dishwasher, cooking a meal, keeping a living space orderly—when you do them, they're chores. But when you teach your children to do them, they're life skills. Cleaning a shower is not rocket science, but it does require some coaching, starting with the fact that a shower—which is just filled with soap and water, right?—has to be cleaned at all. You don't want to raise that roommate you once had who put greasy dishes in the cabinet because he didn't know how to wash them, or the babysitter who made boxed macaroni and cheese for my children by opening the box and the cheese packet, pouring both into the pan, adding water and then turning on the heat.

Looked at that way, it's easier to see the persistence it's going to take to persuade your child to do a job correctly, without you standing over her, in a different light. Restoring a kitchen to order after a meal is a skill adults need—as is the acceptance that sometimes you do that even though you do not want to. Even though you are tired, or would rather watch TV, or still have work to do, you still get the taco stains and shredded cheese off the counter.

In her book *How to Raise an Adult*, Julie Lythcott-Haims, a former dean of freshmen at Stanford University, described the life-skill-building strategy a friend developed for building skills in children:

- First we do it for you.
- Then we do it with you.
- Then we watch you do it.
- Then you do it yourself.

It's easier to get our kids through those first four steps when we remind ourselves that if we don't, they'll start off at step five in a dorm room or an apartment filled with empty food containers and unwashed dishes: you deal with the cockroaches.

STICK WITH IT AND THEN STICK
WITH IT SOME MORE

I was joking earlier in the chapter when I said it took five years for a child to learn to clear a plate from the table without being asked—but I might not be far off. Most parents whose kids do specific chores regularly describe a process that takes not days or weeks, but months, and probably years, no matter when you start.

"My son has to clean his room, water the plants, and clean the toilets before he is allowed screen time on weekends," Sarah Maxell Crosby, a mother in White River Junction, Vermont, said. "We've been doing this for about two years; he'll be seven this month. For several months, he would drag it out, not getting screen time until Sunday afternoon, or at all, if he was really resistant, but we stuck to our guns, and the time to completion became shorter. Now, most Saturdays, he has finished his chores before I even wake up."

She's describing a process that took months to implement and more than a year to feel confident in. Other parents say much the same. "It took time and persistence." "Reiteration and patience." "Training and follow-up." "Tolerating the complaints and resistance." "I did have to hang in there for a lot of whining and incompetence for a while." "My kids are now ten and fifteen—they've been assigned simple chores forever, but it's taken this long to have some peace with some of them!!" Parents who stop and start, change chores and strategies, and give up and do it all themselves for months on end—like me—will find themselves, as I have, back at square one again and again.

Deborah Gilboa, the pediatrician whose youngest child, at seven, is responsible for the family laundry (and whose three older children manage other tasks that help the whole household), says sticking to the plan (without making it bigger than it has to be) has been a key to her family's success. "I don't expect them to enjoy it," she says. She just expects them to do their part. Over the years, the family has learned that while some flexibility is required, adjusting to changing schedules doesn't mean everyone doesn't contribute. If a child who is expected to empty the dishwasher will be gone all day and the dishwasher has run, "I'll throw them some compassion," she says, but that favor—emptying the dishwasher so that others can fill it—comes with a text offering a choice of other things that need to be done.

Julie Lythcott-Haims says she didn't really begin to require chores with any consistency until her children were ten and twelve (not so coincidentally, about when she began writing her book). "They were all, 'WHAT?!'" she says. Now fifteen and seventeen, they need little reminding to do their own chores (laundry, taking the trash bins to the curb, setting and clearing the table, unloading the dishwasher, and dealing with trash and recycling). "It's fun to hear them negotiating over whose turn it is to do what. And my elder is great at doing things 'for' the younger to be nice."

Which sounds fantastic—but don't focus on whether your kids would ever reach the point of helping one another out with chores. Focus on the fact that even someone who literally wrote the book on raising independent kids didn't start her kids off as young as she wished she had, and had to go through the same long days, weeks, months, and years of prodding that we all do before it got better. *You don't have to get it right every time.* When it comes to getting kids to do chores, you just have to keep trying.

MAKE CHORES A HABIT, AND GIVE
THE HABIT TIME TO STICK

When I first set up our chores, they were a timing mishmash. The child assigned to "laundry" could arguably do it any time, while the child feeding the dog needed to perform precisely at six (our dogs can tell time better than I can in that respect). Then I read Gretchen Rubin's book on forming habits, *Better Than Before*, along with Charles Duhigg's *The Power of Habit*, and realized that I was inadvertently making it harder to turn chores into any kind of a routine. The regular chores now come paired with a repeated activity, one to be done as soon as you get downstairs in the morning, one right before dinner, and one after dinner. It's easier to do something every day than once in a while. Tying a chore to something that happens daily makes it much easier to remember.

But for a habit to stick, it has to be practiced regularly. The parents I spoke to who were happiest about the ways their children contributed to the running of the house didn't assign daily chores, or weekly chores, or even monthly chores.

They assigned a chore for a year. A year.

A year of laundry. A year of lunch-making. A year of loading the dishwasher after dinner. That's true in pediatrician Deborah Gilboa's family, and in Jennifer Flanders's large family as well (Flanders runs the Flanders Family Homelife website, a resource with a Christian message for homeschoolers and large families). More than two decades ago, when her children's ability to make messes outpaced her ability and willingness to clean them up, Flanders decided to abandon her mother's approach ("to let them help when they wanted to help") in favor of a system she hoped would teach all of her kids, regardless of gender, to do everything that has to be done to run a household. Every child is expected to keep a tidy room and to make the bed daily; beyond that, each has a responsibility for the year: set the table, load the dishwasher, sort the laundry, etc.

"By the time the year is over, they're efficient and they've stopped complaining," she says. "Sometimes they've come up with a way to do it that's better than mine."

Giving a child a chore for the year means that chore can really become an established part of the routine, for both parent and child. It also puts a little more slack in the system—feeding the dogs Friday night because a child is at a soccer game isn't as big a deal if that child still has 364 days of dog-feeding ahead. "I'll sometimes just help out, and sometimes I'll tell them that because they weren't there to do it, they've got something else to do," says Flanders. A full year of a chore gives a child the opportunity to really master both the chore itself and the will it takes to get up and do it over and over and over again.

Flanders gives easier jobs to younger children (sometimes manufacturing a job for a child that's too young for most things) and graduates them to more difficult chores as they age. At the end of the year, "they do get a little bit of say in what they get next, but not much," she says. Eventually everyone gets every job and learns to do it right.

In the Flanders family, most chores are done at the same time, usually daily, and the family works together to get all the jobs done, a routine that keeps the kids on track. Deborah Gilboa ties the timing of weekly chores to privileges. In her son's case, it's "no screens on Sunday until the laundry is done"—a particular challenge, she says, if there's a football game on. On weekdays, chores must be done before anyone can play or have screen time.

"I think one important thing, though, is that I don't get offended when they don't remember," she says. "But I don't ever let them off the hook."

That's a message echoed by many parents, and a reassuring one. When it comes to chores, it's important to separate two goals—that our children do the work, and that they remember to do the work without prompting. Both are great, but it's getting the job done consistently that really matters.

"As long as they do it, I wouldn't feel bad about having to ask every single time," Susan D'Entremont, a mother in Albany, told me. "My oldest is eighteen and she's finally started doing things without being asked." Doing it without being reminded can wait until the next battle.

EXPECT HELP

One friend wrote this on Facebook:

> My kids have been doing chores since they were tiny. They all unload the dishwasher if it is full of clean dishes, do their own laundry, make their beds, clean communal areas, and take out recycling and garbage without being reminded. My youngest daughter loves to sweep the foyer and my older daughter cooks if I am not feeling well. The boys are college age but still mow the yard in the summer and spring. I don't know why they are like this. They have never been paid to do chores or rewarded for it. I have always told them we are a team and that every team member plays an important role in making the family run smoothly. I also have always done chores with them. So . . . yeah. I don't know, but I am

grateful. Also, my kids are typical teens and young adults. We butt heads and argue. We are far from perfect . . . but they do chores and four of five have jobs outside the home. Personality maybe. Other responders have mentioned consistency. That is also a huge part of it.

She doesn't know why her kids are the way they are—but I do. I don't think it ever occurred to her that they wouldn't help, and so they do. Hers is a large family, with a strong tradition of service based on their religious faith, and they are surrounded by a community with similar values. Hard work is part of the package.

For some families, the expectation that everyone will contribute seems to be baked in. It can come with religious practice, yes, as it does with my friend and with the Flanders family, but it can also come with a sustainable living ethos, or farm work, or a home or family business. There's something about an accepted need to all pull together that turns kids into part of the team. I've singled out this friend, but I've seen it again and again, and I imagine you have, too— the children in the family that runs the local restaurant, or the CSA, or whose single mother runs a sales business out of their home—those children know how to work, and they do. But if that's not your family, you can still use the mind-set. Farms, family businesses, family service work—those take a lot of effort, but so does running any household. It takes everyone.

You can declare it a need, and even tie it to a change in your life, if there's a reason you're looking to your kids for more help. Or you can just own your previous failures. Jessica Lahey, my friend and neighbor and author of *The Gift of Failure: How the Best Parents Let Go So Children Can Succeed*, told her two sons that she'd been doing too much for them, and it was time for that to change (proving, as with Julie

Lythcott-Haims, that there is nothing like writing a book about raising children with life skills to light a fire under a parent). Expect help. Demand it, insist on it, stand over your children until they give it. You deserve their support—and they deserve to be allowed to contribute, even if they don't think they want to.

DON'T PAY KIDS FOR CHORES UNLESS
YOU'D PAY SOMEONE ELSE

Parents who give their children an allowance tend to fall into two camps—those who consider the allowance an exchange for chores, and those who do not. My *New York Times* colleague Ron Lieber, the author of *The Opposite of Spoiled*, has convinced me to remain firmly in the non-payment camp. In his view, an allowance is a tool to teach children to value and manage money, while chores are an expectation for anyone who is a part of the family.

Why? In part, because if you're "paying" your kids to do chores, there will likely come a point when they'll just shrug. Fine. Take it away, I have the money Grandma sent me for my birthday, or I don't want to buy anything anyway. More importantly, although getting paid for work is a part of adult life, most chores fall into the category of things we do without pay, like brushing our teeth and feeding our pets (or, for that matter, our children). "I don't even get out of bed unless I get paid" may make a funny T-shirt, but it's a terrible approach to life.

That said, there are times when you will pay a child to do a chore. At our house, I'll pay a kid for some things I'd pay an adult to do, like lawn work, although I don't pay older children for babysitting younger ones. I might pay a child to do a sibling's chore, if the task was large enough and the sibling unavailable (usually those chores involve chickens and a driving snowstorm). Once I paid a kid five bucks to make me a batch of Rice Krispies treats. (What can I say? I had a craving. *You do you*.) Lieber agrees that some things are worth paying for. He had a great suggestion for "big, nasty, one-off chores" that I'll be trying: "Post the chore with green cash money pinned to a bulletin board—first kid to complete the task gets the money."

He also endorses paying for excellent work—a performance bonus, if you will, for, say, a week of doing a chore without being reminded, or picking up the slack for an injured sibling.

It's tempting to take allowance away for excessive complaining or for not getting the work done, although I haven't found that to be a successful tactic (maybe because I'm usually doing it in anger). "We also dock allowance if chores are not done competently or for too much complaining. But this doesn't work as well as the more positive strategies," says Patty Chang Anker, a mother of two from Westchester County, New York. Taking away allowance after the fact doesn't really help you achieve the goal of a child who gets the chores done, and it lets a parent off the hook for the hard work of enforcing the requirement that a child contribute at the moment when the contribution is necessary. It's a cop-out, and that (along with our inconsistent application) is probably why it doesn't work.

WORK TOGETHER, OR ALL AT THE SAME TIME

"We have Power Hour on the weekend for chores," says Shannan Ball Younger, a mother in Naperville, Illinois. "It's scheduled, not every single weekend but at least twice a month, and everyone participates." That rhyme is popular. "We do an 'hour of power' on Friday nights where everybody spends one hour diligently cleaning/decluttering and then we all watch a movie afterward," says Liz Whalley, a mother of two from Seattle.

Also popular is the idea of all doing the chores together, at a set time, for a set time, often with music or a fun reward to follow. "We didn't hire a cleaning person when we moved to a new city," says Abby Klemmer, a mother in Birmingham, Michigan. "Now, every two weeks we do a family cleanup day. My kids clean their bedrooms and bathrooms, change their bed linens, vacuum. We do pay them a few dollars for this, but it's not optional."

"It's amazing how much can get done in a relatively brief amount of time and it helps with the idea of 'we all live here so we all pitch in,'" says Younger. In Berryville, Arkansas, Laura Hudgens's three kids work in rotating zones—the kitchen, the living spaces, and the entrance to their home. When they were younger, every day at four o'clock they did a "twenty-minute tidy" in their zones, but as they got older and busier, the time became hard to stick to and the plan slipped. This year, Hudgens reinstated it, but she now allows the kids to choose when they work. "One of the best things about zones is how it frees me from having to worry about assigning chores," she says. "I don't have to think about whose turn it is to vacuum or clean out the lint trap. And the kids have already stopped arguing about that kind of thing."

As Laura discovered, keeping to a set time weekly gets more difficult with older, more active children, but if you can find a time that works for almost everyone almost every week, that will do, and work much better than rescheduling chore time every week. Consistency is your friend, and a moving target will probably never be hit in this instance. It will involve complaining, almost every week, almost certainly, about whatever child "never has to do their share," but it's not as if there would be no complaining if everyone were present. They'd just be complaining about something else.

CONSEQUENCES

In our house, if you fail to do your own personal "chores" well, or at all (like putting your own hockey gear in the bag that needs to be brought to your practice after school, or putting last night's homework in your backpack), it comes with natural consequences. I have accidentally put many an assignment in the recycling—easily fished out, yes, but since it's not sitting on the counter to remind you, it probably doesn't get turned in on time. And it's unlikely that I, who played hockey only briefly, will manage to take every single piece of gear off the drying rack (there are *so many*), and that I'll be able to pick out your shin guards from your sister's (gross!). And I certainly won't check to see if you got it all in your bag. Both that job, and the consequences, are on you.

One of our kids arrived at hockey missing a key piece of equipment so many times that he had to sit and watch practice three times in a row—and the fourth time, I got an email from the coach. "Where," he asked, "is [child]?" "Well," I replied, "I dropped him off . . ." After a few minutes of mild worry (we live in a small town, and that child knows everyone at the rink), the coach emailed again. The child had been found hiding in the bathroom, too embarrassed to admit to having to sit out practice once again. Consequences provided, with no help from me.

But with most household chores, the "natural consequences" bother us more than they do our children. They're blind to overflowing trash and dishes in the sink. If they cared about a clean room, they'd have cleaned it. Which means that if we want to use consequences as motivation, we have to come up with something they care about—and we have to ensure that it's not an empty threat.

What might that consequence be? The loss of screen time is the most popular (with children who have their own devices, suggests

Ron Lieber, the Wi-Fi password might change). Maybe you won't drive a child to practice until the chickens are in or the dog is fed. Suddenly, the coach who requires laps if anyone is late is in charge of your consequences, which is a beautiful thing. Choose something that matters to your child, and take it away.

LET KIDS PICK THEIR CHORES

When our kids were younger, we rotated chores, because even if you'd actually prefer to feed the chickens, it is *not fair* if you're the only one who does it. But especially with older kids, it's possible that they'll just agree—one would rather wash the dishes, the other would rather clear the table and wipe the counters. "We sat down with a huge list of things that get done around the house and I let them pick things they disliked the least, explaining that this is how my husband and I originally divvied up the work—I do the cooking because I don't really mind it. He does the dishes because I really hate that," says Karen Smith from Glen Ellyn, Illinois, of her two kids.

"Speaking as someone who did a lot of chores as a kid," says Melody Schreiber, a mother in Washington, DC, "I would listen to the kids about which chores they despise and which ones they enjoy. I hate dishes but love vacuuming and laundry, so my mom played that up. And if I wanted to complain, she reminded me that I chose them."

The most popular area of choice is dinner—kids who cook (and even a nine- or ten-year-old should be able to cook a simple meal—watch *MasterChef Junior* if you don't believe me) can also choose. "I recently started asking my kids to each make dinner one night a week," says New Jersey mother Aileen Carroll. Her seventeen-year-old and two sixteen-year-olds each sign up for a night weekly, and she makes sure that they have a plan so that items are defrosted or ingredients are on hand. "It works surprisingly well and no more complaints about the menu!"

IT'S NEVER TOO LATE TO START

Maybe you just never established a chore routine at your house—first the kids were too young, then you were too busy—and now they're however old (five, eight, fifteen) and you're wishing you'd made this happen. As with anything, you can't start any younger. But it's really not too late. One strategy, suggested by Dr. Gilboa, is to address the entire question of whether you treat your children with the respect due to their age and ability together. Most kids, she points out, "are so annoyed with you that you don't understand how grown-up they are, and you treat them like a baby."

So talk to them, she said. Tell them—and I mean this sincerely, not with a trace of irony—that you haven't done right by them. There are privileges they feel old enough for, and there are responsibilities they are old enough for, and they can earn the privileges by stepping up to the responsibilities. Say, "I'm going to teach you to do the laundry, and once you can do it, we'll start the clock, and after you've shown me that you can handle that for a month, you can take the bus to the mall alone," or whatever you're willing to let them do.

"Grown-up privileges are tied to grown-up responsibilities," she says. "That's the way life works, and it's the way you should work."

START WHEN LIFE CHANGES

Many parents who have been at-home caregivers go back to work when their children reach a certain age. Make that a moment to bring about the chore transition. You're going to need more help, and that's not an occasion for guilt, but rather an opportunity. Other life changes can present the same need, whether it's long term and ongoing like a partner who deploys for the military or a decision to bring another child into the family, or it's a temporary measure because of family need, a death or divorce, a job loss, a move, or the purchase of a family business.

Some of those circumstances are obviously not things you'd choose (to say the least), but addressing the physical challenges they're going to present for your family as well as the emotional ones directly can give everyone something different to hold on to (and even something different to be upset about). Change can be very hard, but change can also allow children and families to grow.

LET THEM WHINE

Once they're past that "helpful" stage, most children really don't want to do anything that could be described as a chore. (Sadly, this usually coincides with their becoming able to actually help.) Or maybe they do like some chores, but they don't want to do them when you need them done. And any child with siblings is going to know, for certain-sure and with all her heart and soul, that she does more than they do, and she's going to say so.

That's okay. In this case *if you see something, don't always say something* becomes *if you hear something, pretend you didn't.* It's so easy to let the griping get to you. *Really?* Really they're complaining about feeding the dog when you just worked a full day and made dinner and you've got laundry to do and a full list of other stuff before bed? Worse, whining over chores can really hit us where we live. Who but a totally entitled, spoiled child would put on this kind of production over clearing the table?

More than anything else, the complaining over simple chores can make us doubt our entire parenting strategy. We hate "making them do chores" as a piece of discipline in part because their reaction makes us feel terrible on so many levels. We hate that they're unhappy, we hate that our asking them to help us out would make them unhappy, and we hate the whole process of feeling our own emotions while dragging them through their resistance.

But it's deeply ironic that we often choose to skip the whole thing (thus increasing the odds that we really are raising a spoiled and entitled child who can't do anything for herself) instead of just skipping something simpler: our reaction.

So what if they complain? So what if they don't want to do it? You probably don't want to do it, either; you've just learned that complaining only makes it worse. They'll learn that, too, eventually. Meanwhile, let it go when you can, for the sake of your own happiness.

A few other simple pieces of advice:

Lower your standards. Not, perhaps, with respect to clean dishes—but there really are multiple ways to successfully load a dishwasher.

Simplify the chore. "I gave my three daughters their own laundry duty as early as possible," says Dana Laquidara, a mother of three now-adult children in Upton, Massachusetts. "I taught them to wash the whole load in cold when their hamper (which doubled as a laundry basket) was full. No sorting required."

Keep a few good lines in your pocket. It helps to have a few go-to things to say when you'd rather shout, "Just shut up and do it!" Here are some ideas: "We do chores 'CQC'—cheerfully, quickly, and completely," says Laura Hudgens. "When they're whining, I ask them if they really think they have that horrible of a situation or if they thought that maybe it wasn't that bad, and then get back to me," says Judi Fusco Kledzik, who lives with her husband and three kids in California. "I try to take the path of commiseration," says Rebecca Wadsworth Blythe, also from California, adding, "' I know! I hate laundry, too! Just imagine how horrible it would be if *one* person had to [gasp] fold and put away laundry for the *whole* family!'" Just imagine.

Teach them how to remember. Kledzik teaches her three daughters to use the same tools she uses: notes, phone reminders, setting something right by the door the night before so it won't be forgotten in the morning.

Have someone else teach them. "As a young widow trying to run a business and raise two kids, I quickly discovered I lacked the attention, patience, and perseverance to get them to do their chores. My solution was to hire an after-school nanny. He was that impartial third party who could teach them how to do laundry, wash dishes, vacuum, and apply the implacable follow-through they needed. He saved my sanity and allowed me to enjoy the kids when we were together," says Joy Imboden Overstreet. Now a grandmother who lives in Oregon, she says, "when I visit my busy daughter, I am the one who rides herd on her kids."

Settle in for the Long Haul
(Or, What Happened at Our House)

It's still a struggle to get the chores done at our house—but it's a struggle that we're happier about. As I interviewed parents for this chapter, I realized more and more that children who just do this stuff every time without a reminder, whether it's clearing a plate or doing the laundry, are few and far between, and that it takes a long time—longer than I ever would have imagined—for most of us to get there. And children that do their chores without complaining are even more rare. The children who happily get up and clear the table at your house? I talked to their parents. They're not like that at home.

Really establishing a chore routine requires a consistency that we can rarely achieve at our house. The one area where we achieve that is the horse barn. Every morning, before school, we go to the barn to help with whatever feeding and mucking is required (it varies by season and weather). Three things make this work: it happens every weekday at the same time; I'm working, too; and the job has to be done. It's the essence of routine, and it gets more difficult (and the complaining increases) in the summer or any time the routine is interrupted.

When it comes to household chores, though, the routine is always changing, which meant we needed to find consistency in something else. After interviewing parents for this chapter, I made changes to my expectations for my kids, and for myself and my spouse. First, my husband and I agreed: chores matter, and we're going to expect that they're done, even when there is homework, even when there are sports, even when it would be far easier to just do it ourselves. Then, we changed our approach. Each child has one significant chore for the year (making lunches, feeding household animals, emptying the dishwasher, or taking out the trash nightly). The remaining chores—the before- and after-dinner ones—rotate monthly instead of weekly, and the children sat down and agreed on how the after-dinner cleanup, in particular, could be fairly divided. It's early days yet, but the shift seems to be working. There's somehow more gravitas to "this is your September chore" than there is to "it's your turn to clear the table." Still, there is complaining, and there is forgetting, and there is always some degree of resentment that someone else's load is somehow lighter.

Accepting those things—that this takes time, that it's important enough to make the time, and that no matter what we say or do, our children are going to complain—made us a lot happier. We expect to remind our children about their chores, and we don't feel like failed parents every time we do it, which helps us to skip the yelling and just say it again. We expect to need to give direction and to periodically require that a chore done poorly be done over. It's our job to teach them to do theirs.

What's consistent isn't the chores, or their timing, or what it takes to get the children to get the work done. It's something we control: our expectation that our children will help us daily as well as when we ask and that they'll do their jobs right. When we make that the focus, as opposed to their memory or their attitude, we can feel good about what we're doing even when things don't seem to be going so well.

three

SIBLINGS: THEY CAN BRING THE FUN, AND THEY CAN TAKE IT AWAY

"Get out!"

"It's my room, too! I don't have to!"

"But I came up here with my homework to get away from you. I'm working!"

"I'm doing my homework, too! I have to memorize this! 'Sing to me of the man, Muse, the man of twists and turns, driven time and again off course . . .'"

"Stop it!"

"'Once he has plundered the—the heights—the hallowed—'"

"STOP IT!"

"But I have to learn this! I have to!"

"MOOOOOMMMMMM!"

Wouldn't it be fun to have siblings who loved each other, played together, stood up for each other, and took care of each other? If only. Instead, those of us with big families too often find ourselves in the Mafia don role of overseeing ever-shifting rivalries and loyalties, while parents of two children watch one-on-one versions of the same games of envy, competition, love, and hatred. And of course, if you're the parent of an only child, the complaints often come from the outside. Will he be selfish, spoiled, self-centered, unsocialized? (Research says no.) I just heard a story of someone changing pediatricians because one doc kept offering what was apparently a saying in her family: "Only children are lonely children."

If you're the parent of a single child, you can skip over this chapter, enjoy the schadenfreude, or read it for ideas that might work when friends are around or extended family is in town. Sibling battles aren't sucking away any of your happiness. (Although if the general tenor of the societal reaction to your family choice is, you should read Lauren Sandler's *One and Only: The Freedom of Having an Only Child, and the Joy of Being One*.)

If you do have multiple kids, then read on. Sibling battles are without a doubt in my top three when it comes to the question, "What sucks for you about parenting?" (Mornings and homework are my other two.) In fact, over the period of writing this book, sibling battles edged out the other two for the top spot. My two daughters, then eleven and twelve, were at a low point in their relationship.

The opening lines of the battle described above (accompanied by the opening lines of *The Odyssey*) were launched in some form many, many times a day, along with such classics as "That's my charger!," "Stop singing!," and "I was sitting there!" Their fights became the center of all of our family interactions, the first thing I brought up with other parents, the thing that kept me awake at night, and, at one point, the talk of their entire hockey team. They were, I told my husband, ruining our lives.

Here's the good news: as I researched and wrote this chapter, two things happened, in this order:

I figured out how to get a grip on my own reaction to their end-less, escalating bickering.

And things got better.

What Goes Wrong

Of course I'm going to tell you what changed. But first, let's look, as in every other chapter, at "what goes wrong" here—and, for a change, at what goes right, which we may be losing sight of amid all the chaos. Becoming a happier parent of multiple children isn't just about how we approach the conflict. It's also about appreciating all the other moments. Brothers and sisters fight, yes. Parent-reported and obser-vational studies put the number of conflicts between young siblings (seven and under) at between three and seven an hour, and the amount of time spent on those conflicts at about ten minutes of every hour.

Ten minutes. I don't know about you, but I would have guessed way higher. And my overemphasis on those conflicts may be part of the problem. It's easier to see what's wrong than what's right. Re-search suggests brothers and sisters have good and natural reasons for conflict. In children of all ages, but especially younger children, the urge to compete for parental attention is innate, and not all bad. Among teens specifically, sibling conflict helps them work out their need to differentiate from family and one another, and to set their own bound-aries. Some jostling, at a minimum, is probably inevitable, and pitched verbal and physical battles are normal and even expected.

That doesn't mean parents, with help from our usual accomplice society, can't still make things worse. Focusing on the bad times rather than the good is only one of our many well-intentioned mistakes. We compare our children, stick ourselves in the middle of their battles, favor one over the other, or get drawn into their need that everything be "fair." We expect too much in the way of love and affection between them or demand too little in the way of tolerating differences and playing safe. We put all our effort and attention onto the fighting and conflict, and leave the good times to happenstance. We stick a different label on our children collectively, one that says, "They don't get along."

The world around us contributes by offering up a view of siblings in media that emphasizes the fighting far more than the family. When one researcher created a program exposing children to books and cartoons that included sibling conflict resolution on the theory that they might help aid children in learning to solve their own problems, she found that the children learned something else. As described in Po Bronson and Ashley Merryman's *NurtureShock*, "After six weeks, the sibling relationship quality had plummeted." Why? Because the media taught the kids "novel ways to be mean to younger siblings they'd never considered." Siblings, the children in the study learned, were supposed to fight and tease. In her later study of 261 books that portrayed sibling relationships, the same researcher found that the average book "demonstrated virtually as many negative behaviors as positive ones." Those unintentional demonstrations, it seems, are just as effectively conveyed as the everyone-gets-along-again endings, and maybe more so.

Along with portraying their relationships in a negative light, much of the way society encourages us to structure our children's lives today pushes them apart. In a world of fewer activities and smaller houses, siblings might have spent more free time together, and more time in unscheduled free play, still together, with neighbors and other families. Now, many children spend large chunks of time in age-segregated activities. Although about two-thirds of children still share a room (as mine do), in middle- and upper-middle-class suburbs, increasing numbers of children sleep on their own. That decrease in time spent together lessens the need to resolve conflict and condenses the time available in which to do it.

The research does offer some good news. The constant give-and-take of a sibling relationship can help children learn to handle conflict, negotiate, hone their verbal skills, regulate their emotions, and gauge the emotions of others. And while our children may spend less time with their siblings than did earlier generations, they're still clocking plenty of hours together: at age eleven, children spend about 33 percent of their time with their siblings (more than with friends, teachers, parents, or even alone). Even teenagers spend about ten hours a week with their brothers and sisters.

Sibling relationships are formative. As parents, we can see that the way our children treat one another helps to shape who they are at home and out in the world. We want them to be loving, and it's hard for us to be happy when it feels as if they're not, and even harder when every night includes a battle that draws the whole family in and leaves everyone emotionally drained. So how can we as parents reduce the level of conflict we live with, remain calm when children bicker, and—better yet—strengthen sibling bonds to make for a happier family overall?

Managing the Conflict, and Making It Better

Conflict between siblings may not actually be inevitable, but if you're experiencing it, it's almost inevitably making you and your family life less happy overall. It's also hard to strengthen bonds and increase the joy in the time your whole family spends together when two or more of its members are locked in what feels like mortal combat. So let's start there: what can you do when the battles rage and the cease-fires are temporary?

One of the most important ways to maintain your own happiness even when the squabbling begins is to know your own strategy and to have confidence in it. *Decide what to do, then do it.* Research shows that parents with some training in managing sibling conflict also feel better able to manage their own emotional response to the fighting. Parents of children between five and ten years old were taught to help children by interrupting the conflict to describe each child's perspective, and then invite them to suggest solutions. Those strategies might work for you (and there's more detail in the next section), but even if other responses work better in your situation, you can reduce your own emotional involvement by making active choices around how you'll handle whatever is happening at your house instead of reacting minute by minute. Here are some ideas to get you started.

INTERVENE OR IGNORE?

When it comes to what to do when they start fighting, the first question is the obvious one. Do you intervene, or do you ignore? It's both a philosophical debate—what, as a general rule, will you do?—and a situation-specific one—what will you do right now?

Considered as a bedrock of parenting strategy, "intervene or ignore" is often presented as a black-and-white question. Either "good parents know that children need to be taught to manage their emotions and resolve conflict" (intervene) or "good parents know that conflict is really about parental attention, and so they let children figure it out for themselves" (ignore). In theory, all you have to do is decide which kind of a "good parent" you are, and then carry on with either giving each child equal time to air their side of the story before engaging them in conflict resolution or shouting "you kids work it out" from the couch.

Is anything ever that simple? Rather than being a single debate, the "intervene or ignore" question turns out to be a continuum. To answer it, you need to assess your larger situation—what do your children need from you now—and know that it's an evolving process. Broadly speaking, younger siblings need more help. Three- to five-year-olds tend to behave even more antagonistically when parents don't intervene, while even slightly older children (five to nine) are better able to resolve a situation on their own. That generalization, though, serves as little more than a starting place. In your family, what do your children typically fight about, and have you given them tools they can use to either solve a dispute or recognize an impasse (or bait) and walk away? If you don't feel that they have those abilities, you can expect to invest time in helping them now before you let yourself leave them to it later.

When younger children are at odds, don't minimize their problem, says Joanna Faber, coauthor (with Julie King) of *How to Talk So Little Kids Will Listen*. "Don't tell them that 'blocks aren't worth fighting over.'" To them, there's nothing more important at that moment. Instead, agree. "Say, 'Boy, this is a tough problem,' then narrate what you're hearing," she suggests. *Cleo wants to build with blocks, but Colin needs all of them for his tower.* "If you come up with solutions with them, they'll quickly start to do that with each other," she says.

"By offering a sort of color commentary on their problem, you're doing two things," agrees her coauthor, Julie King. "You're showing them that you hear them and that you understand. And you're slowing things down so that they can hear each other as well. Taking another's perspective is one of the most important skills we can teach our kids."

Older children should be more able to see the situation from their sibling's point of view, but that doesn't mean they'll do so without coaching (or prodding). If you're hearing a dispute between kids who can't move on from argument to problem-solving, your next move should be based on the situation and where you think they are in terms of knowing what to do next (as well as what will preserve your sanity). They may each be well aware of the other's perspective and be choosing to ignore it, or the battle may be so heated that their normal problem-solving skills are obscured by emotion.

Those are challenges that children have to deal with eventually, but now may not be the time. If you do need to step in, the goal is the same as with younger children—showing them that you hear them and understand, and helping them to do the same for one another—but the strategy may be different. You may need to wait and talk to them when they've cooled down, or use humor to take the edge off. (Approaching them with the singsongy voice of a preschool teacher can be pretty effective.)

You may also just want to let them work it out on their own, even if you can tell it's not going well, or you may decide to stomp in yourself and remove whatever's at the center of the argument. You don't have to get it right every time. Sometimes you'll intervene and wish you'd ignored; sometimes it will go the other way around. Chances are, you'll have another opportunity to make that call sooner than you'd like.

The Conflicts

Typically, sibling battles fall into one of four categories: jealousy, property rights, space occupation, and pure deviltry. Any one of those can fit in anywhere on yet another continuum—that of minor, everyday bickering up to emergency room visits or words that truly wound.

The first is tolerable, or can be; the progression obviously moves toward unhappiness for all. The more you can teach your children to handle at least some conflict on their own, the more likely things are to stay on the bickering side of the curve, whether you choose to intervene or not—and particularly as children get older, "not" is the goal.

"All I do is get stressed when I become a referee," said Lori Zimmerman, a mother of two teenage girls in Delaware. It doesn't matter what she actually says or does, but how the girls hear it. "It always appears to one that I'm taking the other one's side."

Backing yourself out of that referee role will make you a happier parent, but it involves setting expectations—for yourself and your kids—on the front end. Establish a family philosophy in the problem spots: this is how property/space/emotions/annoyances are handled at our house. Help your kids learn to apply it, starting with lots of involvement, listening, and repeating of feelings. Teach them to see what's really wrong (siblings are a safe space to take out a lot of frustrations) and learn to empathize at least a little with one another. Finally, step back to let them work it out. (That last, incidentally, is very much where I fell down, but more on that later.) That's a good overarching strategy—here's how to approach it on each of the most common battlegrounds.

JEALOUSY

"Hey! She got a bigger piece!" So much of sibling rivalry boils down to just that—she got a bigger piece of cake. Of the backseat. Of the pretend pork chop cooked in the toy kitchen. Of *you.*

This is one that starts early. There you are, holding that baby, all the time. Baby, baby, baby. And suddenly, there's your big kid, the one who really wanted a baby sister, administering secret pinches, slamming doors when you're trying to get that baby down for a nap, and taking the baby's squeaky giraffe toy at every opportunity.

Here's my favorite strategy for jealousy, and it comes pretty much straight from the pages of *Siblings Without Rivalry* by Adele Faber and Elaine Mazlish: do you need some more?

> *I see you have the baby's giraffe. Do you want me to help you find your baby toys?*

> *I see you're having a hard time staying quiet while I try to get the baby to nap. Do you need more hugs and snuggles for yourself when she's asleep?*

> *Oh, you think she got a lot of spaghetti. There's plenty—do you want more?*

Now, I hear you. This is not a cure-all. You've got "buts": But I still have to get the baby to nap. But she doesn't want her old baby toys, she wants the baby's toys. But there isn't always more spaghetti. Or if there is, it's a waste to give it to her because she won't eat it. But that kid is always going to want what her sister has.

All arguably true. But instead of looking at this as a single strategy, try considering it a philosophy. In our family, there is enough for everyone. You will never do without the love or spaghetti you need. That doesn't mean everyone always gets everything they want. Sometimes, it's "I see you're upset that she got new sneakers. When you need them, we will get you new sneakers, too," or "Oh, you wish you could go to Joey's birthday party. Wouldn't it be fun if your friend had a birthday party at the same time as Joey?" Approach the jealousy as about the envious child, not about the envied. What do you need? Is there something you can do to get there?

By consistently saying, "Let's think about you and what you're feeling, wanting, and wishing instead of what someone else has," you're shifting the focus to a better place. Your child will never be able to control what happens with her sibling—or, for that matter, with anyone else. There will always be times when he wants something someone else has. What he can control is how he reacts to those feelings.

BUT THAT'S NOT FAIR

You'll be a happier parent if you can tattoo the following somewhere within your brain: *fair doesn't always mean equal.* The teenaged hockey player does get more spaghetti than his six-year-old sister, even though she plays hockey, too. They don't always have to all get new winter coats. Just because you had time to drive one to a friend's house yesterday does not mean you're obligated to drive another to the playground today.

Fair doesn't even have to mean you're trying to be "equal," especially when questions of responsibility and privilege are afoot. "If your children don't think you're unfair sometimes, you're not doing your job," said Dr. Kenneth Ginsburg, a pediatrician at the Children's Hospital of Philadelphia, a professor of pediatrics at the University of Pennsylvania School of Medicine, and the author of *Raising Kids to Thrive: Balancing Love with Expectations and Protection with Trust.* "You're supposed to change the boundaries according to what they can handle."

Again, what you're hoping to do for your child is to defuse the comparison mechanism as best you can. This is about your plate, your coat, today as opposed to yesterday. It's a good idea to have some sort of plan for recurring debates, like who pushes the button in the elevator or who rides in the front seat. My favorite idea there comes from Sharon Van Epps, a mother of three in Seattle. "Each child has a day, and if it's your day, you do all the things. You get the one leftover cookie, you get to go first, you get to sit next to Mommy." Every week, each child has two "days," and the seventh day is Mommy's. Her children are teenagers now, and they've been successfully doing this since they were toddlers.

You can also give your children tools for deciding these things themselves. There's the classic "you cut, I choose" option for splitting things like cookies and cake, or "tit for tat" for a shared job (you pick up one, I pick up one). You want them to seek "fairness" when they're resolving things together, so especially when they're younger, you will be teaching them to seek out compromises and solutions. But you don't want to become the court of final appeal on all such questions. Leave them totally without resources, and although research does support the idea that they'll start leaving you out of the equation, it also suggests that the younger or weaker child will constantly wind up on the losing side, and that both children might believe you tacitly endorse that result. That's why, in this case, you intervene to teach the skills you expect them to learn to use themselves.

"It's not parental intervention that's the problem," says Laura Markham, a clinical psychologist, mother of two, and the author of *Peaceful Parent, Happy Siblings*. "It's taking sides." So, especially with younger children, if you sit down and facilitate a happier ending when you're able, they'll be more likely to try to achieve the same thing when you're not around. What does each child think is "fair"? Can she put herself in her brother's shoes and ask what might be "fair" to him, too?

Maybe she can, maybe she can't. Maybe, in the end, you're going to stop the dispute by removing its cause, whatever it is. "No television for anyone if you can't agree on what to watch"; "The Thomas tracks are going to be put away for now if you can't play together." That's okay. The evolution of your children's relationship to one another will be gradual and packed with what look like setbacks—but if you feel like you're on the right track, it's much easier to roll with that. Your goal is to teach them to tell each other what they want (not what they don't want the other to have), to consider the other perspective, and to find their own "fair" resolution—or cope with your solution, which will nearly always be neutral but negative. The dispute is resolved, but now nobody's happy. Except you, because *you can be happy when your children aren't.*

Of course you treat them fairly. Don't you? There's a larger issue at hand, one that's far more important than just who has more chips in her bowl. Are you basically "fair"? Parents and children are people. Some pairs click more easily than others, some stages of childhood are easier to relate to or more intensely demanding. Some years may find you coaching your daughter's hockey team, or feeling constantly at odds with a child who tends to argue. Some of us find younger children easier, others deal better with teenagers.

"Parents need to focus on whether we're meeting individual needs instead of worrying whether each one is getting the exact same thing at the exact same time," says Dr. Markham. "We get really annoyed when we hear 'that's not fair,' because it feels like an attack on us." Instead, she suggests, come back to what we know to be true—we basically put all our kids on an equal footing. Worry about it only if you have a sense that, lately, that hasn't been the case, because the baby is taking up all of your time, or you've been really giving your attention to your middle schooler's class play.

If that's where you are, adjudicating a momentary cake dispute is not the time to put things right. Instead, choose another time to talk to your child ("Hey, I feel like I haven't seen enough of you lately—what can we do together this afternoon?") or just make a plan and put it into action. Some parents keep specific "date nights" with their children while others (like me) track these things more loosely, but you should feel a strong separate connection with each of your kids. That's how you keep things "fair." The child whose bucket of good times with a parent is full is more capable of watching the baby be rocked to sleep than the one whose bucket is empty (and some children have bigger buckets than others). The best way to stop "that's not fair" before it even starts is to try to keep things as balanced as you can among your children's differing needs and to make sure every child feels seen, treasured, loved, and important within the family fold.

PROPERTY RIGHTS: DO YOU HAVE TO SHARE?

"That's mine!"

"But you're not using it!"

"But that's mine! Give it back!"

"I found it in the garage. You haven't even touched it in months!"

"I don't care. I was looking for it. Give it!"

"You only want it because I have it!"

(In unison) "DAAAAAAD!"

And you're off on one of the most common sibling debates of this or any century. What is "it"? It doesn't matter. It could be a Rubik's cube, a gold coin, or a paper insert from the *American Girl* magazine.

The only way to maintain your own sanity here (which is to say, your only chance at preserving a little happiness under the assault) is to know, at root, what your family policy is in this or any of the other similar disputes—the one about the toy in the toddler's hands, the one about the shirt from a sister's closet, and worst of all, the one about the only findable hat of the four identical hats from the Capitals game that a well-meaning relative bought for each of your children. Whose is it? You have no idea. Neither do they, really. Except that they do. It's "MINE!"

Before you can resolve property disputes like this, you need to answer one basic question: do your kids have to share?

Unless you're already familiar with Heather Shumaker's book *It's OK Not to Share*, that might sound like a crazy question. But Heather's mother teaches at a preschool in Columbus, Ohio (where Heather herself went as a child), where she applies what she calls "renegade" ideas. One of those ideas is that the children don't have to share. If they're playing with a toy, they, and they alone, decide when it's time to give another child a chance.

"Young children aren't ready to share," Shumaker writes. "They're ready to take turns." Teaching children under five that their turn ends whenever another child wants a toy is the wrong lesson. Instead, parents should protect a child's right to have her full experience with a toy and trust another child's ability to wait. It's okay to say, "I'm not done yet."

You may decide the no-sharing-required philosophy won't work in your house, or you may need to adjust it for circumstances. When my younger daughter arrived at preschool, there was a "you don't have to give up your turn" policy with regard to the monkey bars on the playground. Every child was allowed to hang from them, one child at a time, until the playing child was done—the theory being, in part, that the child would exhaust her arm strength before too long had passed.

Back and forth my kid would go, back and forth, dangling from one arm, then going back and forth again—for the entire outdoor play period. Others would wait patiently and never get a turn at all. There seemed to be no limit to her strength or her interest, especially if she knew others were waiting. They had to change the rule to "once across and done."

That worked, too. You may feel that you have a child who, given a no-sharing policy, would remain at a particularly desirable toy for hours, racing back there after meals, falling asleep there in the evening, and waking only to shriek "I'm not done!" (I might know that child.) So for your family, some toys might come with time or use limits, or turns with all toys might last only until bedtime. What's important is to find a successful approach that you can feel happy and confident implementing.

The concept of "long turns" and having a right not to share is mostly for children under five. We expect our elementary-school-aged children to behave more equitably, especially with respect to household shared property. Allowing a thirteen-year-old a twelve-hour "long turn" on the only household computer without engaging him in a conversation about the needs and feelings of other family members is clearly not going to work.

But when it comes to the thirteen-year-old's own device, particularly one purchased from his savings, while you might limit his time on it, you probably wouldn't require that he share it with his younger sister. You can extend that idea to other personal property, no matter how reasonable the proposed sharing sounds. To take an example from *Siblings Without Rivalry*, an older sister may not be ready to share a shirt from her closet, even if it's outgrown. We all get attached to certain objects or even just to the idea of what's "ours." That's normal. One possible family rule there is that she doesn't have to share her things until she's ready.

So, what about the mystery item in the garage, the one left untouched for months (or even years) until unearthed by a sibling? If the ownership is unquestioned, the policy least likely to blow back in your face is to support that ownership, which is black-and-white and can be understood by even the youngest child. "He's right. It's his if he still wants it. Son, if you decide that maybe you've outgrown that Thomas the Tank Engine, your sister would like to play with it. But if not, it's still yours."

As for the Capitals hat of unknown origin? If you have a large family of children, you won't be surprised to hear that this is a problem we confront regularly. For most identical items, we label immediately upon acquisition. But sometimes something gets by me, and there we are, at 6:55 a.m., trying to leave the house when the disputed hat appears on someone's head. Experience tells me that if left to resolve this without help, three of my four children will come to blows, and even the fourth might be pushed to the limit.

What do I do? Often, I can make an educated guess about whether the hat wearer took the hat from his own cubby, or picked it up wherever he found it. I know which children are most likely to have left a hat in which part of the house, car, or larger universe. I investigate a little, see if I can find other hats and narrow it down. Then I just put it out there: "Look, you know where you got the hat. If it's not yours, give it back. If you can't agree on whose hat it is or who can use it today, give it to me and wear another hat."

We live in New England. There's always another hat.

PERSONAL SPACE

When it comes to the battle over personal space, there are really two things at play. First, there's the question of whether a child wants to interact with a sibling or be with her at all. Second, there's the space itself—the territory. Children can fight over either or, more often, both.

While a complete non-intervention policy over most disputes often results in a tacit favoring of the older, more powerful child, leaving children to work out space disputes is likely to favor the younger of the battling pair. We hit this when one of our daughters was twelve and beginning to want the space to grow into her teen-aged self, and the other was a young-for-her-age eleven, struggling a little bit to find her own footing. They fought constantly: over their bedroom, their friends, their behavior in front of the other's friends, how tall their older brother was and whether the younger child's fifth birthday had occurred on a Wednesday. If one said, "It's cold out," the other said, "It is not."

At the same time, it was clear that my younger daughter admired her older sister. She wanted to be with her, even while she resented being excluded. Anywhere our big girl went, her little sister followed, out of affection, desperation, and a sheer need to poke the beast. Finally, the twelve-year-old took to getting up at 5:30, before the rest of the family got up at 6:20, in order to have some time for herself.

One morning we were awakened by furious shouting, slamming doors, and the noise of feet pounding through the upstairs and down the hall to our room. "She got up! She got up on purpose and I was holding the bathroom door open and she ran under my arm and got in the shower and she turned it on and it's not fair!"

It took a long time to calm the house down from all the rude awakenings, but later, I found my younger daughter's alarm clock. Sure enough, she had set it to 5:29.

This isn't an uncommon dynamic between an older and younger sibling. If one wants to be alone and the other wants to be together, the one who wants to be alone might not be able to find any space without your help. Little brothers and sisters can be incredibly persistent. It's not really alone time if you're spending it in your closet with a five-year-old standing outside banging on the door (and while some kids will eventually go away, some really won't).

"I was the little sister knocking on the door of my brother's room," said Shumaker. "I was the kid who wanted company, he was a loner type who loved his private space. But when he granted me access, and we played together, I was on top of the world." How can we help our children begin to respect another's need for alone time on the one side, and open themselves up again to their siblings on the other?

"I think parents need to make some decisions around what territory children can be possessive of," said Shumaker. "If a child has a bedroom, they should be able to say if they want another child in it. Or maybe they should be the boss of their bed or a little closet." Other parents suggest designated "alone time," like right after school. "Children may not like being temporarily banished," said Shumaker, "but just like they can handle waiting for a toy, they can handle this." To make it easier, she suggests asking an older child when she feels like she might be ready to play with a younger sibling. In our family, playing with a little brother or sister can sometimes be a way to get some extra video game time, and we intentionally choose games that require cooperation as well as competition.

After the morning incident, we realized that our girls needed us to guide them in working this out. We found calmer moments to get them to agree on some ground rules that would give the older girl some space while not giving her the right to toss her sister from their shared room on a whim. We endured many complaints from the younger daughter when she was excluded, and even more from the older girl when she couldn't be indulged. Sometimes, especially when our older daughter had friends over, we took that chance to spend time with our younger girl alone. Eventually, as our younger daughter started to accept the need to give her sister some space, our older girl came around, and they were able to start doing things together again.

When Things Get Physical

Before you had children, you probably could have told me exactly how you'd handle an incident of hitting, biting, or kicking between siblings. Intolerable, you might have said. Hands are not for hitting! People are not for hurting! You, of course, as a parent, would draw a nice clear black line.

Now that you are that parent, you know things are more complicated than that. You know that one child can provoke another into a physical response, that you can't believe anyone when it comes to a disagreement over what constitutes an "accident," and that sometimes they really are having fun pinching and poking—but sometimes they aren't, or sometimes they're having fun until suddenly one isn't. You know, in short, that blame can be hard to assign and that the line is much fuzzier than you ever imagined, but that it's still important to draw it. It's just much more difficult than you thought it would be.

Most sibling conflict, even when it gets a little physical, is minor within the grand scheme of things, even though it may not feel like it at the time. Rivalry is normal and even healthy for kids. Sibling

aggression, though, is different. At its worst, it's a form of family violence, and one that should be taken seriously (and that requires professional help). For most families, though, it's more a question of
keeping things from ever getting out of hand without losing your
mind in the process (as you surely will if you get involved every time
someone kicks someone else in the backseat).

How do you know when to intervene? You don't, most of the time.
Not for certain. There's the rare case when the bite marks on the
screaming baby's arm can be easily traced back to the beaming toddler seated next to him, but most of the time, it's all shades of gray.
You will come down like a bolt of lightning on the child accused of
pushing another child's broken arm, only to hear later that even the
offended child thought it was an accident. You will accept the "it was
an accident" explanation for the child who Rollerblades over the other
child's toes only to hear a tearful confession later.

You may not know what's really going on until they tell you, and
by then they'll probably be grown with kids of their own. Meanwhile,
here are a few strategies to make things easier.

Make it a big deal. Don't look the other way, not for any of it. Even
if they both say they're joking around. Even if you know there was
provocation. Get in there between them. Restate your family rules:
there's no hitting, no pinching, no holding someone's legs so they
can't roll off the back of the couch like they meant to, and no kicking
the person holding your legs. (It's okay if these aren't exactly rules
you've been over before.)

Or don't. On the other hand, depending on your family composition
and your personal history, you may choose to look the other way for
nearly all of it. My three youngest children do sometimes get physi-

cal, but they are all generally the same size and shape, and equally likely to attack or defend. Their alliances shift. No one is ganged up on; there is no constant victim or aggressor. I wish it were not so, but I get that there are just times when children who live together—at least, my children—roughhouse. Feelings get conveyed in pokes, whacks, and kicks that can't be expressed any other way. The older they get, the more they're able to work it out on their own, even with the occasional hip-check. I've largely stopped getting in their way.

Treat both attacker and victim equally. When all you know is that he said, and then she said, and then somebody did something and then somebody did something else and then there were tears, try this: treat them both equally. If there's an injury that merits snuggling and sympathy, gather everyone up. "Oh, that must really hurt where she hit you. Oh, you must have been so mad to do that. This is terrible! What can we do to make things better?"

Alternatively, if you're just frustrated with the lot of them, take it out on everyone equally with no consideration of blame. "That's it, playtime is over. You—empty the dishwasher. You—go upstairs and bring down all the laundry."

There are no innocents. There are exceptions to this—sometimes you're holding a hockey stick and you turn around and it catches someone right in the head—but for the most part, kids who are hurting each other or getting hurt were already doing something you've told them not to do. You cannot, for example, get hit by flailing arms if you aren't giving an unwanted "hug." If you're not lying across the back of the couch where someone is reading, putting your feet on that someone's neck, you're not going to get pushed off the couch.

Why won't they just keep their distance from one another during day-to-day life? Why do they get so rough? I do not know. Sometimes, your kids know the risks, and they do dumb things to one another anyway, and then someone gets hurt. It's hard to cope with, and it seems as if it ought to be easy to know what to do, but it's not. If everyone involved feels terrible afterward, you can at least feel secure that you're on the right track.

Pure Deviltry

Sometimes there is no conflict. Sometimes, there are just children, using their powers for evil with time-honored techniques such as repeating everything a sibling says, scooching over on the couch until a sibling is squashed up against the arm, touching the cookie a brother is eating, or walking up behind a sister and putting cold fingers against the back of her neck.

This morning two of my children argued for ten minutes over whether their school was closed for Rosh Hashanah in 2015. Other classics include "who's taller," "who's faster," and "my hockey team could beat your hockey team." Mostly, this is just background noise. If I get involved—some of these are factual questions, after all: "I could just measure you" or "Look that up"—they'll move on to one of the other countless recurring disputes, like "Who found the big chocolate bunny that Easter two years ago when everything was outside?" or "Whose green tie-dyed Frisbee from the craft thing we all did on summer vacation is stuck on the roof of the shed?" So I try to ignore rather than intervene.

But a bickering backdrop can be hard to put up with, or worse, it can start you off on a mental hamster wheel: *Should I stop them? When should I stop them? How should I stop them?* In his book *"Mom, Jason's Breathing on Me!,"* Anthony E. Wolf has an answer. His advice? Stop them as soon as you're annoyed, and without taking sides or addressing whatever they're squabbling about. *You do you*, which might mean you tune them out, and might mean you bring the hammer down every time. At our house, that sounds like "Both of you, stop that right now," and "I'm going to pull the car over until the two of you work this out." Every so often, I see another car pulled over to the side of the road for apparently no reason, and I look in the window, and I see a couple of kids waving their arms and a parent with his or her head down on the steering wheel. I always give a little wave. Solidarity.

What to Say

Whether it's real fighting or just general bickering, I find it helps me to have actual, go-to phrases I can employ rather than shrieking the first thing off the top of my head, which is rarely constructive. Most of them I didn't make up—I collected them over years of reading and writing about parenting, and years of trying to improve the sibling situation at our house. I've nailed down the origin of some of my favorites, several of which I use so often that they provoke eye-rolling from my kids, who know that what I really mean is "I get that you're upset, but I am so not going to be helpful." Some are from *Siblings Without Rivalry*:

> *I have confidence that you two can work it out.*

> *It's your whatever, and it's your choice whether to share it. If you can, that would be great, but if you can't, that's okay, too.*

And from *"Mom, Jason's Breathing on Me!"*:

> *That sounds really frustrating.*
>
> *Gosh, that must be really annoying.*

(Sometimes I suspect both of these are themselves somewhat frustrating and annoying, but sometimes they invite a child to keep talking until she comes to her own solution or has emptied out her feelings. It's important to remember that *you don't have to go in there.* She is frustrated, she is annoyed. You don't have to be.)

When my kids were younger, the language was more about teaching than leaving them to sort it out. A few go-tos from *Peaceful Parent, Happy Siblings*:

> *Looks like we have a problem. We can solve this.*
>
> *Can you tell your brother how you feel?*
>
> *Do you think your sister likes that?*
>
> *What did you hear your brother say?*

I reached out to my community of parents, and I asked them: what are your set-piece sayings when it comes to battling siblings? Quite a few people offered variations on "If no one's bleeding, I don't want to hear about it." Here are the best of the rest:

> **You can be mad, but you can't be mean.**
>
> —*Jessica Michaelson, Austin, Texas*

God willing, you will know each other a lot longer than I will be around, so figure it out.

—*Andrea Hoag, Lawrence, Kansas*

Why are you telling *me* this? Sounds like you have a problem with *him*.

—*Karen Smith, Glen Ellyn, Illinois*

If you can't agree on it, no one gets it.

—*Rob Jones, Westchester County, New York*

It doesn't matter who started it.

—*Jeremy Shatan, New York, New York*

I was a sibling once. I know how it goes. I don't need the whole story. I trust you can work it out without me.

—*Bernadette Noll, Austin, Texas*

Who are you people and what are you doing in my house?

—*Deb Amlen, New York, New York*

When It's Time to Extract Yourself

I've been drawing from my daughters' rough patch throughout this chapter (the alarm clock story in the "Personal Space" section occurred about halfway through). I suspect it could have been a lot shorter if I'd started writing this chapter earlier in the process.

I was used to brokering multi-sibling bickering and shifting rivalries. We had worked with our kids on negotiating conflict for many years, not as some sort of organized perfect-parent plan, but just over the process of growing up in a big and somewhat complicated family. We had sat down between them during fights and taught them to consider one another's perspectives. We had modeled finding solutions to disagreements over space or objects. We had taught them alternatives to physically expressing anger, like yelling "I am so mad" and "I don't like you right now" or retreating to a safe space. When things went wrong, they had the tools to at least begin to look inside themselves and ask, *Why am I angry? What's really wrong? What can I change about this, and what do I have to live with?* I thought we'd reached the "no need to intervene" stage.

The sudden and continuous running fight between my daughters, though, felt like something new. It didn't feel like a run-of-the-mill little kid spat. It was vicious and it broke out at almost every opportunity, which is to say every time the girls (who shared a hockey team, a school, and a bedroom) were together. It was so constant, so loud, so abusive, so often physical, although in a minor way—tearing things out of one another's hands, slamming doors in faces. I didn't know what to do. In general, they'd all gotten along pretty well before. I'd never seen anything like this.

It wouldn't be putting it too strongly to say that I panicked.

I took it all personally. Sometimes I sided with my older daughter, especially if she wanted to be left alone. I, too, notice that her younger sister is not a person who lets you be alone when she's in the room. She hums, she sings a little, she moves noisily. She likes people to know she's *there*.

And sometimes I sided with my younger daughter. Why did my big girl have to be so mean all of a sudden? Why could she not include her sister in things like baking cookies with her friend? And the *bossiness!* I, too, would make everyone late for hockey practice if I had my older daughter yelling at me like that.

But mostly I was just so angry at them both, particularly on the day when I drove them for more than five hours to compete in a hockey tournament, which their team won—a victory they celebrated by dragging me into their loud, furious, pushing-and-shoving argument in the hallway outside the team locker room. I'm not sure I've ever been angrier or more embarrassed. And I just didn't get it. How could they act this way? Did they not understand how lucky they were to have each other?

I should step back here and tell you that I am an only child. That I had a sister, who died before I was born, and in spite of having had a great childhood with my loving and fun parents, I believed that siblings were something I always wanted. That we adopted our younger daughter into our family when she was nearly four, because I'd always wanted a big family, and that we chose to adopt a little girl, back when it was an amorphous choice instead of the inevitability we now see, in part so that my older daughter would have a sister.

This is not, any of it, even a little relevant when it came to helping the eleven- and twelve-year-olds in front of me find a way back to their previously loving relationship. It is, however, why it took me so long to get this right.

The hockey tournament proved to be something of a turning point for the girls. They, too, were embarrassed. Some of their teammates took them to task; others were, at a minimum, irritated by the fuss. In the car later, they were able to talk about some of what was bothering them beyond each other, things to do with the team and other changes. They had been listening to us. They admitted taking out frustrations on each other that couldn't be safely released anywhere else. They promised to try harder. In retrospect, I can see that they meant it.

But I couldn't let it go. I ended that five-hour late-night drive still fuming. I swore I would never take them to another tournament. I talked about it endlessly, conversations not centered on "What should I do?" but "Can you believe what awful little jerks they were?" At home, I started to berate them for fighting all the time, even when they weren't. "Come to the general store," I'd say, "if you can keep from fighting long enough in the car to do it." "Don't let the girls sit together," I'd say in a restaurant. "I can't take it." They had been so horrible! They were ruining our lives! Everything was awful, and I could not imagine what I was going to do about it.

Underneath it all, I was frightened. What if this never stopped? What would it mean for our family's long-term happiness if two of us couldn't stand to be near each other?

It was about then, a little desperate and a lot miserable, that I (while wondering whether I was able to write a book about happier parents at all) started to work on this chapter. I read research studies, I talked to parents about how their own children fought and how they kept their own emotions in check when they handled it. I consulted the old books on my bookshelf and ordered new ones. I called the authors of those books and other experts besides. And I realized, slowly, that what I was seeing between my girls wasn't some huge, family-destroying Shakespearean drama, but just ordinary sibling stuff that I needed to approach in an ordinary way.

They were getting older, and they needed to find a new way to live with one another. They needed to push each other away in order to find their way to a relationship that wasn't just dictated by all that forced togetherness. And I needed to let it happen.

We had done enough conflict resolution. I didn't need to get in between them and make sure they heard and understood each other. I certainly didn't need to take sides. I needed to back off. *If you see something, don't always say something.* I let them bicker without starting in on my "you girls always ruin everything" speech. I let most of the still-regular arguments about who could be in the bedroom or who had been first to set up at the table to do homework play out without my stomping over to join in. If I had something to offer I said it to them afterward, separately. (To the older: "Thank you for not engaging with your little sister when she was mad about her chores earlier"; to the younger: "You know you weren't really upset with your sister but at yourself, right? Let's try to find a better way to handle that.") I recited the words of Rob Jones, a father of two and one of five siblings himself: "They get along well, and they fight well." *There was nothing wrong.*

And things were, rather suddenly and very distinctly, better. Not perfect, but better. As I put the finishing touches on this chapter, they're still better. They still argue over the right to be alone in the bedroom and whether the younger is intentionally eavesdropping on the older and her friends (she is). But they've returned to where they were before, mostly getting along fine, frequently doing things together, occasionally helping one another out and just generally being sisters. When my younger daughter broke her arm the night before school started this year, she begged her sister to come to the hospital with her, and my older daughter dropped her plans for pre-packing the perfect backpack and got into the backseat to try every possible distraction for the long drive to the emergency room.

It turned out okay. I won't lie to you—I really didn't think it would. But it did.

Increasing the Joy

Addressing the conflict is only part of increasing your family happiness when it comes to siblings. We don't just want them to be able to fight fairly (and ideally fight less). We also want them to grow up as close and loving as their personalities allow. The goal isn't just not-so-bad. Some of that comes naturally, just with proximity and familiarity. All their lives, your siblings will share experiences no one else has (among other things, being raised by you). They'll have a history and a bond that's unique. But we don't want to rely on happenstance to build that into a strong lifelong relationship. How can we actively encourage the good times that really count?

ACCEPT THE NEGATIVE

Ironically enough, feeling happier about your children's relationship means accepting some of the bad—in particular, their negative thoughts and words about one another. New big brothers and big sisters will often say they "hate" the baby. Older siblings will "hate" one another. They have entire dossiers of why their sibling stinks, including every crime ever committed by the one against the other and a whole lot more besides.

"Accept the feelings, but not the behaviors," says Shumaker. "Don't be scared of the jealousy and the fear and the desires. If we're honest, adults feel those things, too, especially about new babies. Accept the emotion—and don't say, 'Oh, I know deep down you love the baby'— and they'll grow to like and love each other a lot faster."

Accepting the negative emotions, and allowing your child to express them to you without registering shock and horror, also defuses them. Resenting a new sister, or furious anger at an older brother, can be big feelings for small people. If your child can say "I hate him!" to you and not be kicked out of the family—or even get a response like "It's so hard when the baby needs me and you want me, too," or "I know, my brother used to leave me out when he had a friend over, and it made me so mad"—that means it's okay to have those thoughts, and it's possible to get past them.

LET RELATIONSHIPS EVOLVE

People, even children, change. My daughters were having a lot of negative feelings about each other (to say the least). I needed to learn to let them have and express those feelings without making things worse. When I left them to work out as much as they could together, I also helped them see that the feelings were both okay and transient.

KEEP THE FUN RATIO HIGH

Christine Carter, author of *Raising Happiness: 10 Simple Steps for More Joyful Kids and Happier Parents*, suggests we actively establish a measurable goal for good times. "Positive interactions between siblings need to outnumber negative ones by about five to one," she writes. She bases her theory on our human tendency to remember negative experiences more readily than positive ones, and on research into marriages and high-performance work teams that shows that when positive actions and words outweigh negative ones at about that ratio, all kinds of partnerships are more successful.

So without adding things to your schedule, do try to ensure that your days and weeks include plenty of time for siblings, no matter what the age gap, to enjoy one another. Offer them extra time with something they like to do together that you usually limit (in our case, that's video games). Make sure there isn't always a friend over when all siblings are free. Instead of bedtime, establish "kidtime," when all siblings need to be in shared bedrooms, upstairs, or however your house divides into kid and adult territory, and leave them to it for half an hour or so before starting the nightly routine or telling older kids to turn the lights out.

Encourage the kind of family storytelling that turns bad times into funny memories. My oldest son once accidentally swung his tiny sister's face into the corner of a bathroom cabinet, resulting in a fantastically colorful black eye that started out as a lump the size of a Ping-Pong ball. He was eight years old at the time, and he thought he had dislocated her entire eyeball. We still laugh about it. Vacation disasters, very silly arguments, the time one child was accidentally left at the grocery store—those can all become family lore. I suspect "the hockey tournament where we almost killed each other" will end up on that list, too, eventually. It doesn't necessarily have to have felt good at the time to become a good memory later.

GIVE THEM SIBLING TIME THAT ISN'T FAMILY TIME

Make sure your children have time together without you. Encourage their collective independence. Send them in pairs on "missions" in the grocery store or as a pack to the movies. Drop them off at mini-golf or the library. On vacation or at an airport, challenge them to try something with each other, but without you. Remind them to look out for each other, and not just older after younger, either. Make sure they're all in this together and, as they grow up, support any effort they make to stay that way.

On their *Happier* podcast, sisters Gretchen Rubin and Elizabeth

Craft often talk about how their parents financially supported their relationship by paying for them to visit one another once Gretchen and then Elizabeth (who is five years younger) had moved out of the house. They credit the plane and train tickets they couldn't easily afford with helping them develop a close relationship as young adults and, later, as adults.

SEE THE GOOD TIMES

Our children don't have to be happy to be together every minute of every day for things to be pretty good. If children spend, as one statistic I cited earlier in the chapter suggested, on average ten minutes of every hour together fighting, that still leaves fifty other minutes. That's not too bad, really. When you stop looking at the ten minutes (the trees), you can see the rest of the hour (the forest). Your job is to appreciate the forest even though your inclination is just to cut down that one tree.

SOAK UP THE GOOD

Just sit and watch and absorb while your kids are making brownies together. When your younger child asks the older for advice about a school activity, relish their ability to help one another. Even if they've ganged up against you, appreciate it. They've got each other's backs. That's what you wanted. Revel in it.

four

SPORTS AND ACTIVITIES: FUN FOR EVERYONE, EXCEPT WHEN THEY'RE NOT

L et me first say this about your child and sports and other non-school activities, like music, chess, or dance: if your child participates in any extracurricular beyond the most introductory level, it is all but certain that you will, at some point, do something you would once have thought was crazy.

You will drive a twelve-year-old ten hours in a single day to compete or perform.

You will serve family dinner in the car three nights a week for three months straight.

You will spend more than your parents spent on your first bike for a costume, instrument, or piece of equipment, even if money is tight.

You will allow your child to skip school for a game, show, or match.

You will wonder if you're crazy to even consider doing otherwise, because you will be surrounded by other parents all doing the exact same thing.

When you do your first crazy thing, when you open that gate, maybe you will think, if you think about it at all, that it's not you. That something has changed in youth sports and other activities, and that fighting the onslaught of new, expensive opportunities along with more and longer practices and seasons is like fighting the tide.

You're right. It's them. But it's also a little bit . . . us.

What Goes Wrong, or How the Fun Was Lost

If your child's sports and activities are contributing to your sense of being overloaded and unhappy, the most likely culprit is also the most obvious: there are too many of them, and they're overwhelming your family time, not to mention your own. There are other possibilities, too. You may really dislike the process, location, or parental expectations for some things. Your child may not really be engaged, which means that every session or practice becomes a battle. Or the timing could simply be off, making something that isn't in itself too much or too hard feel really, really difficult.

For most of us, though, the most obvious issue is the place to start. Many middle- and upper-class families put significant amounts of time and money into sports and activities for children. More than 90 percent of American kids now engage in organized sports at some point during childhood or adolescence. They spend more time on those sports and other activities, too—unsupervised "free" playtime has decreased for all children since 1981 and most significantly for the children of better-educated parents.

At the same time, the time parents spend with their children has increased, but not necessarily in obviously fun ways. In their paper "The Rug Rat Race," economists and parents Garey and Valerie Ramey looked closely at time-use diaries from 1965 to 2007 and found that the amount of time parents spend chauffeuring children to and from activities as well as organizing and attending those activities is up, in particular for kids with college-educated parents. Children with less-educated parents, they wrote, spend most of their free time playing with friends and relatives in their neighborhood, unsupervised by adults, while for the better-educated adults, supervision is the name of the game. Sociologist Annette Lareau calls this "concerted cultivation." Parents who can do so devote significant time and effort to their children's activities, enrolling them, scheduling them, preparing their equipment, and getting them from place to place. Meanwhile, married parents, busy dividing and conquering in the name of their children's development, spend less time than ever with their spouses: just 9.1 hours a week in 2000 compared to 12.4 in 1975. That's 171 fewer hours a year. That's a lot.

Some of this activity benefits our children. There's the obvious: they're exposed to different ideas and ways of learning, and they try out new things. Activities and sports tend to retain a certain ruthlessness that's missing in many classrooms: there are winners and losers and place ranks and chairs. Competitive activities give children space to try and fail and lose and build. Then there's the research: children who are more involved outside school engage in fewer risky behaviors, like drug use, delinquency, and sexual activity, and their participation has been linked to more opportunities for career advancement, as well as higher grades and graduation rates.

The key word there is "some." Kids who participate in some after-school activities are better off than those who, usually because of lack of resources, do none. But as far as I know, there is no research suggesting that a child who does gymnastics and Kumon and Suzuki violin and soccer and robotics has an edge over the child who is deprived of robotics, or that twelve months a year of soccer are better than four. When did it get so hard to draw that line?

It's not your imagination. Sports and activities really have changed since your childhood. Not only are there more options, but even the familiar choices seem to have gone mad. A sport you remember involving a short season of one or two practices during the week and a game on Saturday has morphed into one with two practices and a skills session during the week, two or more games (possibly involving travel) on the weekend along with several tournaments, off-season play, and the opportunity (or expectation) for players to participate in dedicated camps over holidays or work individually with a skills coach. The once-a-week music lesson, with daily practice and an occasional recital, has become one individual and one group session a week, with an expectation that parents will sit in on the lessons and practices as well as purchase the CD in order to play the music being learned on an eternal loop at home and in the car.

For some of us the simpler options—the recreational sports program, the music teacher down the block—are still out there. But the commoditized versions of sports and activities are seductive in so many ways, and in many communities, they've almost fully eclipsed everything else, extending their reach younger and younger until smaller programs can't compete and pulling many families into their wake. The travel associated with youth sports has become a $7 billion recession-proof boon to the economies of hosting towns. Of all trips taken in 2012, 27 percent were for the sole purpose of attending a sporting event, with some 53 million young athletes traveling for the sake of sport.

Parents, of course, could say no to all this, but there are reasons, some good and some more dubious, why we don't. For starters, our children don't come to us and ask, "Can I play soccer four nights a week, practice through dinner time, and do my homework in the car while we drive to the three games on the weekend, including a four-hour round-trip away game that starts at eight a.m.?"

Instead, "Can I play soccer?" starts with a cute little weekend team. The kids are outside, not at home in front of their screens, and if you're having to stand on the sidelines more than you might like, well, if you were both at home you'd be trying to entertain a preschooler, not settled in over your own book or hobby. It seems win-win.

But after the cute little weekend team, things change. One parent helpfully invites your child to play in a post-season league, or your child tells you that "all the players who are any good" are trying out for the local club. The friend she played defense with is doing a soccer camp next summer; can she go?

And maybe the club team seems like a great plan. Then the enthusiastic coach adds an extra tournament, and the home club decides to host one, to bring in some money. The games start on Fridays, the better to get lots of teams involved, which means missing school and work. That's not the call you would make—but the team is small. If you say no for your daughter, they have little chance of winning the first games. Or maybe the team is big, and a child who misses the first games is out for the tournament as far as the coach is concerned. And don't forget—your child cares. This is her team. She's loyal. You've taught her that it's important not to quit, that we don't skip practices and games just because we feel like it. Suddenly, you're down the rabbit hole.

Soccer is its own form of madness, but nearly every activity you can name has grown its own extremes. Children can compete locally and nationally in spelling bees—or in bees for geography or history.

There are math bowls, chess bowls, and a seemingly endless array of robotics competitions and science fairs; there are theater and improv and art competitions, comic book–writing workshops, community orchestras, choirs, and bands. Some of this may sound familiar, but as in soccer, the frequency, intensity, and expectations have changed.

"It's tough to say no" to a child who thinks she wants to move up a level in an activity, says Sarah Powers, a mother of three in Southern California, who grew up as a dancer and then taught studio dance for many years. "Bigger studios are adding younger and younger 'companies' that train for performances and competitions, and there's extreme pressure put on girls to join. They feel very left out if they don't—they're not going to the competition, they're not eligible for solos, they don't have the sweatshirt with the logo." These "higher levels" are professionally packaged to be very appealing for our kids, and they're money-makers for the adults on the selling end.

But before we absolve ourselves of all parental blame for sports and activity scheduling, consider that parents are the drivers, literally and figuratively, of all this madness. The seasons wouldn't extend, the summer camps wouldn't fill, the studios wouldn't be in business, if we weren't buying into it all. We get involved ourselves, maybe in our child's success or maybe in the community that forms around these activities. This isn't necessarily a bad thing—if it's making you and your child happy, and not taking something away from the rest of your family.

That is the million-dollar question. Our children's sports and activities can contribute to their happiness, and to ours. They can be a source of joy and pride for the whole family. Or they can take over our lives, spreading like kudzu into every area that's not concreted with other obligations and sometimes managing to invade those. How do we strike a balance that's right for us?

Making It Better

A happy family life that includes sports and activities for your kids is one that works for both or all of you, most of the time. One survey (from HopSkipDrive, a ride service for kids) found that 35 percent of parents described managing their child's school and extracurricular transportation arrangements as more stressful than filing their taxes. Unless you're a tax accountant, that's not a good sign. And if your kids aren't getting enough playtime and downtime, they're probably not benefiting from their extracurricular activities as much as you think. High schoolers participating in fifteen to twenty hours of extracurricular activity a week have more emotional problems like depression and anxiety, sleep less, and report higher stress levels. That's not a recipe for happy teenagers, or happiness for the families they live with.

There's not some master amount of activity that suits everyone. But there are things to keep in mind as you make decisions for or with your child. Many sports and activities snowball as children get older, leaving us with a sense that things are out of our control—but that isn't necessarily the case. As I'll explore later in the chapter, parents who push back against the pressure to conform to outside expectations about how children will participate often find that there's more give in the system than they expected or that they're happier helping their children find a way to explore an interest off the beaten path. The mistake many of us make is to equate the activity itself with fun and happiness and not consider how its various demands will affect our child, our family, and ourselves.

Protect Your Sanity

You can't possibly predict everything, but when you start thinking about signing your child up for anything, whether it's violin or soccer, go ahead and project wildly into the future. Think first just a little down the road: What obligations are there this season? What expectations do coaches or instructors have? Will there be other families or children indirectly depending on yours? Signing up for a small Lego robotics team, for example, means committing to the competition and possible success, which leads to more competitions. A big team may have room for some absences; a small one will rely on every member.

If there's an end-of-season event, do you have to be part of it—and do you really want to? When Sarah Powers signed her daughter up for ballet lessons at four years old, she expected children in leotards, following simple instructions without too much structure, once a week. That's how the class went, but as the end of the session approached, a recital was announced, with accompanying extra rehearsal times and fees. "Most people just do it," she said. "Your kid gets excited about the tutu, and $200 later, you're keeping a four-year-old happy at a four-hour-long recital." Powers is, as she put it, "aggressive about protecting my own sanity." There will be lots of recitals if her daughter continues in dance. The family can skip this one.

Look at how an activity will impact your whole family, including you and younger siblings. Ever since Powers found herself playing cards with a preschool-age child while trying to entertain a toddler in a tiny waiting room outside of her oldest child's music lesson, she's thought about what the other children will do during an activity— because unless you drive and pay a babysitter, or have two babysitters, that's how these things work. "Softball has a playground," she says, so they like that, and the new music teacher has a play space for siblings. "I don't really do the iPad thing," she says. "It would make it a lot easier, but I'm not sure it's important enough to plug everyone else in."

Be realistic about the time commitment. "An hour of soccer takes us two and a half hours," says Lisa Damour, the author of *Untangled: Guiding Teenage Girls Through the Seven Transitions into Adulthood* and the mother of two girls, thirteen and six. "It takes us forty-five minutes to find your stuff and transition you into the car and get you there, and then forty-five minutes to get away and get home and get you cleaned up. It's supposedly three hours a week, and we do have three hours a week, but do we have seven and a half hours a week?" Maybe they do, she says, but doing that math right makes it easier to make that decision and to work with it.

Protect Your Child's Sense of Self

It is a piece of the madness of many of the most popular children's activities that instructors or coaches expect you and your child to put their thing, be it dance or violin or baseball, "first." When a conflict comes up, they tell you, a real dancer/violinist/team player would know what to choose, even at seven years old.

That can too quickly lead to a child and family who have chosen— and dropped the conflicting interests aside. As important as it is to keep a grip on your scheduling madness, specialization is another possible route to unhappiness through your child's sports. "I see so many girls whose identities are all wrapped up in soccer," says Damour, who is also a consulting psychologist at a girls' school in Ohio. "They tear their ACL, and then they lose everything." Their friends, their social life, their free time, has been all caught up with the team, and now it's gone, at least temporarily. "It sneaks up on you," she says. "You sign up a six-year-old, and all of a sudden you're overwhelmed, and then it blows up and you have a teenager with an identity crisis. No one plans for that."

You can't design a childhood around the risk of an injury, but you can look at every activity as just a piece of your child's bigger life, and talk and act accordingly. The big music or dance studio may be incompatible with another commitment, but a smaller one might be more understanding. Less sought-after activities, like cartooning classes and after-school a cappella groups or squash, might demand less time and commitment.

You also can't control how your child thinks of herself, but you can control the way you talk about her priorities with her, and how rich her life is outside of even something she's passionate about. Most kids won't get an injury that ends their ability to sit at the piano, but they might realize, suddenly or gradually, that they're ready to move on. You can help protect their happiness, and yours, by helping your child keep eggs in a lot of baskets, even if they seem to have found a passion. Encourage kids to continue to try new things, maybe by joining an activity with a friend or sibling or even a parent, and to develop skills in multiple arenas.

What if Your Child Wants to Quit?

It's hard to be happy when you're dragging a child somewhere she doesn't want to go or negotiating minutes of music practice with someone who is shouting, "But I don't *want* to play the violin!" What should you do when your child wants to quit something, whether it's a sport she's played for years, a musical instrument, a class she just signed up for, or a team midseason?

This is a very family- and child-specific dilemma, but there are a few generally accepted practices.

No quitting in the middle (mostly). Many parents say they won't let a child quit "midway," whether that's a season, a month of lessons, or a class session, and especially not if there's a commitment to others involved. But there are exceptions.

"I let my son quit a really rigorous travel football program midseason in eighth grade," says Annie Micale Webb, a mother from Philadelphia. "I finally realized I had to listen to him and honor his real distaste for the whole thing. Sticking with his commitment to the team (what I wanted) was going to be physically and emotionally too much for him. When I stopped standing my ground only for my own preconceived notions and really listened to my child, I knew letting him quit was the absolute right thing."

Suz Lipman, a mother in San Francisco, let her daughter quit high school mock trial early in her third season. "She was very unhappy, and we knew from her previous two seasons how very much work it was. Her high school team went to state and national championships. So when she said she really wasn't into it anymore, had nothing else to gain, kind of wanted to play outside and have more free time, we agreed. It was early enough for the team to recruit other kids."

Kids do the quitting. The whining child often talks about quitting, and might even ask, "Can't I just stop going?" When there's any kind of a relationship involved, with a coach, a studio teacher, or an instructor, many parents who are willing to let a child quit will tell her that she can choose to do it, but she has to do it herself.

Putting the onus on your child makes her a part of the decision-making process, which is especially important if she started the sport or activity young enough not to have made a real choice. It might not have occurred to her that she had a choice, and giving her the power to stop can become a way to help your child think about what an activity means to her and what it would mean if it weren't part of her life. She might still decide she's finished (so this should never be an idle threat on your part), but it can't be done on a whim. When Huntington, New York, mother Denise Schipani's son (now thirteen) was eight, he told her he wanted to quit piano after two years of lessons. Schipani told him he could talk to his teacher about it; at the next lesson, he asked her if she was going to do it for him. "I said, 'If *you* want to quit, *you* have to talk to her about it.'" He didn't want to do it himself, and he didn't suggest quitting again. "I suspect he was looking for an easy way out, and it's not my job to give him that," she says. "I think he was testing out the idea," she says, to see how it felt for him and how his parents reacted. When it didn't fly, he let it go. "He also became a better player," she says, as did his brother, now fifteen. Both boys enjoy playing because it's become something they're good at, she says—and the family just invested in a new piano.

No quitting when you're down. There's a right time to quit—after a season or session, after some thought, after talking it over with your parents and the right other people—and there's a wrong time: after you don't make the top team, lose out on the solo, or don't get first chair.

When kids are disappointed, they say a lot of things. That's not the time to let them act on them and quit—or, for that matter, the time to let them sidestep their disappointment by switching to a different league or trying out for a different youth orchestra. And if you're the one pushing the move, or if you're gaming the system by letting your child go to a bunch of different tryouts in order to take the best spot she's offered, I suspect you've lost sight of why your child is playing. Your actions are also making other parents and children unhappy when orders and teams are constantly reshuffled (making it clear who "made" it last). Even if your child doesn't complain, constantly switching studios or soccer clubs is hard on a kid, and never having to deal with not being at the top of her activity doesn't help her grow.

Go with your gut. Kids start things early, and sometimes it's time to let sports and extracurriculars go. *People, including children—especially children—change.* Evolving isn't necessarily quitting. When Laura Hudgens's twelve-year-old son chose not to play baseball after playing for six years, she knew it would be hard. "But it took up most of the summer and prevented him from doing other spring and summer activities he loves that my husband loves, too, like camping and canoeing. We let him make the decision, helping him see the pros and cons, and also that whatever he decided there would be some regret." That's been true, the Berryville, Arkansas, mother says. They both miss the baseball community. "He gave up something he loves in order to do other things he loves. But ultimately we all feel good about his choice."

Sometimes, though, your gut will tell you this isn't the right time for your child to quit entirely. Jenni Levy, a mother in Allentown, Pennsylvania, says that when her daughter wanted to quit dance in fifth grade, it felt wrong. "Our sense was that she was anxious about being 'good enough.' She tried to quit everything that year." Levy and her husband didn't push their daughter to keep up the level of dance she'd been doing (four or five classes a week), but told her she had to have at least three hours a week of physical activity. After a year with one hip-hop class and tennis lessons, their daughter went back to dance. "In August before sixth grade, she said, 'I want to take ballet again' and signed up for four classes, and that was that." (She's now dancing at a high school for the arts.)

Consider a different approach. Marjorie Ingall, a mother of two in New York City, says her husband finally let her daughter quit flute in fifth grade. "They fought about it a lot," she says. But after her daughter quit, "she liked to noodle around on it, picking out songs, as long as no one pressured her. And she brought it to summer camp, where she jammed with friends. And then she got to high school, and suddenly there is jazz band! And two really great, supportive teachers! And tons of encouragement for noodling!" It was the Suzuki method their daughter hated, and the pressure from her parents. Now that it's fun, she's stuck with it.

Ellen Spirer Socal, a mother on Cape Cod, tells her own story. Her mother let her quit piano lessons, and she regrets it. "My teacher was very focused on the recitals and piano competitions. I was capable of playing just fine at home or during a lesson, but I froze up in front of an audience and was terrible at playing from memory," she says. The night before a competition, with Ellen in tears, her mother called the teacher and said she wouldn't be competing. "I never went back to piano lessons," she says. "I wish someone had thought of getting me another teacher to learn to play for fun and not to 'perform.'"

Music might be different. While I know many adults, myself included, who think we wish we hadn't quit playing whatever we played,

I suspect that what we really wish is that we *knew how* to play—without all the hours of practice and mastery entailed.

But it's exactly those hours, and the resulting mastery, that makes some parents argue that music isn't something a child can quit. Music, they say, doesn't really become fun until you reach a certain level, and it's unfair to a child not to let them get there. It's also an education in itself. There's a small but significant association between music study and academic achievement, and many music educators point to the ways reading music is akin to language learning and requires an understanding of mathematical patterns. For some families, music is mandatory.

"We said up front that everyone studies an instrument until he or she is eighteen," says Sarah Stewart Taylor, a mother in Hartland, Vermont, whose three kids, now eleven, eight, and six, each started music at around four years old. "It's just what we do. No questions asked. So whenever kids wanted to quit, I could always say, 'Okay, you don't want to play cello anymore. Which instrument do you want to take up?' and they would always think about it and ultimately decide they didn't want to have to start from scratch. Now they never talk about quitting because they've gotten to the point where they see progress and it's fun or at least satisfying. But there were a lot of rough years when they were young, a lot of tears and shouted demands to quit," she says. "The experience has kind of transformed our parenting though. 'Because it's just what we do' is an answer I use for a lot of things now."

When children whose families have made music a daily choice get older, at least some appreciate where their effort has led. Many switch instruments, armed with their solid basics; others apply the skill to choir, orchestra, or band and find themselves very at home. And, realistically, some parents who said the same thing as Taylor when children were younger find themselves allowing their teenagers to give up an instrument when it becomes clear that there simply isn't enough time to fit it all in.

How do you know when that's the right way to go? There's no absolute knowing, and both sides have backers. If pushing your child is leading to great unhappiness for either of you, it's time to either stop pushing or find a way to continue that leaves room for joy in the challenge. *Decide what to do, then do it.*

Accept the Gift of Failure

If your child dances, plays an instrument, or competes at anything from robotics to chess to sports, congratulations. You've just given them what Jessica Lahey calls "the gift of failure" in her book of the same name. Our society worries a lot about little kids getting participation trophies and being celebrated for "just showing up" in the name of self-esteem, but any parent of even a slightly older child who tries out for a spot on a team or an orchestra or signs up for a competition or audition knows that all of that ends very quickly.

To compete in anything is to risk losing, and your child will lose. She won't make the team or get the solo. She'll make a mistake that costs her the match. Her team will play hard but lose the game or the meet or the tournament. She will be sad. Will you?

You can be happy when your children aren't. Realistically, yes, you will be unhappy. You'll be disappointed for your child, and you'll be right there with her in her own disappointment. But you'll stay a whole lot happier if you keep your eye on the larger picture. Competition and disappointment are part of the package. Here is your activity- and sport-specific mantra: *It is not my job to do anything. In fact, it is my job to do nothing.* Hug your child, let her feel her pain, don't try to push her past it, and, above all, don't try to "fix" it—not if it's a team tryout and you might be able to change the result, not if you think there really might be room for one more in the recital, not if you've got video on your cell phone and you're sure you can convince the ref that that puck went in the net.

Ben Sasse, a former wrestler, the US Senator from Nebraska, and the son of a University of Nebraska wrestling and football coach, wrote about this form of failure on Facebook:

> This is *good* scar tissue. The growth happening underneath these scars is precious, and will serve your son or daughter well. From this experience, your child will be able to acknowledge the success of others, even at personal cost. Your child will know what it means to work on a team to the benefit of others before self, what it means to take direction, to accept responsibilities, and to put forth their very best, leaving it all on the field/court/mat.
>
> And your kids will know how to respond when even their best isn't enough.

This is hard advice to follow. When my older son was in third grade and had been playing hockey for four years, he tried out for the next season and was placed on a team, exactly as he had the two previous years—except that it was the fourth of the four teams for his age group. The lowest team. The "red" team. It included at least one child who had never before played the game, and our son was, to say the least, crushed.

It pains me to admit it, but my husband, with my support, made at least one call (and maybe more). Really? Couldn't our son, and the other young player who'd been on a more competitive team both of the preceding years, be moved up? Maybe they wouldn't develop as well on this team! Maybe their spirits would be destroyed by this! Couldn't we somehow fix it?

Fortunately, we couldn't. Because if you ask my son, he'll tell you what happened. He was bummed. He felt the failure in a big way. He cried, he cried some more, he abused himself and his abilities, out loud and surely in his head. He said he wouldn't play, that he was done with hockey, this season and forever.

And then he had a great season with that team—one of the best he remembers, in terms of fun and locker room camaraderie and really enjoying the game. Maybe, for him and the other children on the coed team, there was something to be said for shifting gears and spending a season on a team where it really was all about learning and supportive teamsmanship and getting out there and playing hard. Nobody expected them to win. It was enough that they played the game. Meanwhile, he worked—on his shot, his skating, his plays. He still didn't succeed every time he tried out, but he's now on his varsity high school team.

What you want now isn't always what you want later. We all hope that our kids will learn something from their chosen sports and activities, and when it comes to sports, one lesson tends to be about losing. We want them to become resilient, learn to stay tough, and come back to play another game. That, more than ball-handling skills, is what we foresee them using when they're our age and the chips aren't falling their way. They can't learn that if we don't get out of the way.

Don't Be *That* Parent

Once your child is on the ice, the court, or the stage, the rest happens without you. This, to me, is the most magical thing about sports and activities, especially when our children are young and demanding. You get them there, and, unless you're a coach, the rest progresses regardless of what you do next. You can run an errand, or read a book, or answer emails. If you have another child with you, you can do something focused on that child.

Or you can watch, as many of us do, particularly if it's a game. You can cheer from the sidelines or enjoy watching your child take (or resist) instruction from someone else. You can appreciate watching your child exist as a person in the world without you, a part of a class or a teaching pair, or a team that doesn't involve or require you. And afterward, you can pass that appreciation on to your child, with words like "I love to watch you play" or "Class looked challenging but fun today."

Stop there, and research shows you're increasing the odds of happiness for both you and your child. Children enjoy sports more when their parents aren't part of the pressure that's a natural part of competition. Bruce E. Brown, who has coached in youth sports for more than thirty-five years and now runs a coaching consultancy with Rob Miller, asked hundreds of young athletes to answer the question "What's the worst part of a game?" The answer they heard, again and again, might surprise you: the worst part of the game for many kids is the ride home.

Why? Because their parents have tips. They have commentary. They have "constructive criticism." And they have the power to shift a game from a fun piece of a kid's day to a disappointment and to make a kid feel as though her worth depends on her performance. Suddenly, it's harder to bounce back after a loss or enjoy being a part of a win, and even harder to get back out there next time, try out for another team, or sign up for another season.

Ask a parent why he signed up a young child for a sport or activity, and you'll hear all the right answers: we want them to learn something new, to explore, to have a chance to practice and improve, to play, dance, or sing with others, to be capable of getting out there and playing or performing or accepting a challenge on her own.

But as they get older, we often lose sight of the fact that the sport or activity is about your child's growth, her learning, and her ability to be part of something. We want to jump in and make it the "best" experience, make sure she "gets the most out of it," assess the teaching or the coaching or the playing time or the group or team placement. But none of that contributes to what you first hoped your child would gain here. When you put yourself front and center in your child's experience, you take something away from your child.

If your involvement in your child's activities is eroding your relationship, neither of you will be happy. Many children aren't playing soccer or the violin with the goal of being the best, or even the best they can be. They're doing it because they like it. They enjoy the game or the challenge or the music or the camaraderie. When it comes to sports, 90 percent of kids tell surveys that they would rather lose than not play, 71 percent would play even if no one were keeping score, and 37 percent dream of playing with no parents watching at all.

Happier parents make sports and activities a source of joy and pleasure for their kids by behaving like supportive parents, not demanding coaches or crazed fans. Know why your child loves what they do, and keep your attention on supporting that love. Before the performance or the game, remind your child to have fun. Afterward, tell her you enjoyed it and that you hope she did, too.

Respect That They're Not You

It can be difficult to let a child quit something you yourself love. "Our daughter told us she wanted to quit travel hockey when she was twelve," says Dori Gilels, a mother of two in Missoula, Montana. She plays hockey herself, along with her husband and son, and both kids started to play at four. "We really wanted her to continue, but she finally had the courage to tell us she didn't love the sport as much as we did."

Neil Lloyd, a father of two in Chicago, has been a musician all his life (although he's a lawyer by day). His children, now sixteen and fourteen, started lessons early, but never fell in love. His daughter stopped playing the viola at twelve; her brother does the minimum to fill his school's music requirement. "As a musician, it was kind of heartbreaking," he says. "I tried saying things like, 'If you stick with it just a little longer, you'll have it for the rest of your life.'" For now, it looks as though his passion won't be shared, except that his daughter just joined an African drumming group. "We'll see," he says.

Protect Your Family Values

Where do your child's sports and activities fit within the spectrum of what's important in your family? When extracurriculars conflict with family relationships, traditions, religious practices, or important values, what choice will you make for your children when they're young, and how will you guide their choices as they get older?

Friends of ours whose two youngest sons played hockey with our older son keep the Sabbath, observing quiet and family time from sundown on Friday through sundown on Saturday as part of their Christian religious practice. That's twenty-four hours during which hockey is often played (among many other things), making theirs a difficult choice as their four sons got older.

Conventional wisdom would suggest that those boys might have found themselves on less competitive teams, or at the end of the lineup, because of that family observance. Sometimes they did. One son was excluded from the invitational pre- and post-season tournaments by his coach. Sometimes they found themselves on teams with coaches who did accommodate them, but made it clear that they were annoyed and unhappy about it. And sometimes things went right. When the family moved to New Hampshire, two of their sons tried out for the high school's varsity hockey team.

Before the team placement decisions were made, says mom Rebecca Goff, her son Matthew went to the coach with his freshman brother by his side "and told him they wouldn't be able to play in any Saturday games."

"We tried to be very respectful," said Matthew Goff, the older of the two and now a student at Dartmouth. "I think we both knew there was a distinct chance that expressing our belief might mean we didn't make the team."

The coach (who is now my older son's coach) put both boys on varsity and then moved all the home games to times after sundown on Saturday (not unusual for high school, when games are often in the evening). "The following year he not only scheduled home games later on Saturdays but also asked the away game coaches to schedule their Saturday games for after sundown," Rebecca Goff said. The practice continues for their youngest son, who made the team as a sophomore.

The prevailing norm in many communities is that children's activities take precedence over all else. "Important" games or competitions are scheduled on Fridays, requiring children to miss school and parents to miss work. Tryouts and auditions are declared "no excuses"—skip the family reunion or Bat Mitzvah, or the spot will be taken by someone else who will. And there is no spring break in athletics, often even when school policies say otherwise.

But parents and older children can still make choices, and your choices don't have to be the same as those of the people around you. *You do you* is a lighthearted mantra, but it's also a very important one. If something about a child's sport or activity intrudes on something else important, it's time to speak up. You may find that once you say no to any practice scheduled to go on long past bedtime, others agree and things are changed. Or your decision might be accepted without comment. Or you might find your child or family excluded from some things.

All of those results are fine if you've made the choice that works for you and your family. Three Goff boys attend or have been accepted into excellent colleges. The fourth is a successful high school student. More importantly, they're a strong and connected family, with young adults now making their own choices about how their values affect their lives—the kinds of choices all of our children will face one day.

"I have often had people ask how I am able to take an entire twenty-four-hour period off and get everything done and not stress out about it," Matthew Goff, now a student at Dartmouth College, told me in an email. "In response, I have always told them setting aside the Sabbath every week is exactly what gives me the sanity to get everything done in the first place."

And the coach who excluded one boy from his extra teams? Years later, says Rebecca Goff, "he told our family how much he had grown in respect for our family and our convictions." They're still in touch.

Keep Sports and Activities
in Their Place

One of the joys of being a modern kid from a fortunate family is that you get to do a whole bunch of stuff for fun that most adults don't get to do at all. As far as I'm concerned, that's a big mistake by us grown-ups—see the final section in this chapter, "Find Your Own Thing." But there you have it. Adult people drive you around and pay for you to run and jump or learn drums or sing on a stage, and then they cheer and clap. With any luck, everyone has fun, and then everyone goes home.

That's not always the way it works. When we start to take it too seriously, the fun goes away quickly, and if you're dragging your kid to a "have to" practice instead of helping him get somewhere he wants to go, no one is happy.

For most children, a sport or activity is not a ticket to college. When it comes to sports, as Mark Hyman, author of *The Most Expensive Game in Town: The Rising Cost of Youth Sports and the Toll on Today's Families*, says, "If you want to get a scholarship for your kids, you're better off investing in a biology tutor than a quarterback coach." In most sports, fewer than 10 percent of kids go on to play in college, and even fewer get any kind of sports-related financial aid—only around 3 percent of that 10 percent. The odds of "going pro" are orders of magnitude smaller. But an astonishing 26 percent of parents with high-school-age children who play sports hope their child will become a professional athlete one day. The percentages are even greater among less-educated and lower-income parents: 44 percent of parents with a high school education or less and 39 percent of parents with a household income of less than $50,000 a year are dreaming of the bigs and the majors for their kids. A lot of money and time is spent on those dreams.

This is a game, an activity, an art, a joy, and just one piece of a happy life. Sure, we want our kids to take their commitment to the cast of the school musical or their soccer or robotics teammates seriously. And we hope they'll learn some things about dealing with other people, about failure, about the need to work hard to improve. But parents are happier when we treat our children's favorite pastimes, no matter how blown up they may be by the youth soccer industrial complex et al., as just that—*their* favorite pastime. That means we talk about it as fun and we don't worry too much if things go wrong. We might be at every performance if they're rare, less so if they're not, and we know it's okay if we don't make every game.

When the adults in their lives keep things in perspective, children learn to do the same, and that tends to make everyone happier. Maybe our children do need sports and activities to round out a college application eventually, but spending four years devotedly and happily tending the school's saltwater fish tank is better than four miserable years on the debate team. Ask yourself, and your child—if this was just for fun, would you still do it? Would you do this much of it? Would it take this much money and time?

If the answer is no, think again.

Embrace It (and Make Your Own Fun)

Who has not been made crazy, on a particularly mundane-seeming day, by the clichéd appearance of the phrase from poet Mary Oliver: "What is it you plan to do with your one wild and precious life?" There it is, mocking you in an appealing font over some form of inspirational image while you contemplate your planned weekend of driving children to various games, competitions, or rehearsals all over the state. *What will you do?* it demands, and some part of you thinks, *Is this it?*

How's this for an answer? *Yes.*

Yes, this is it. Would you really want to do something different? Would you want your child not to have chosen this thing that he loves? Would you want someone else to be there for his big day, whatever that is? Isn't this really where you want to be, even if it's in the car at five a.m. on the way to the state finals?

Of course, we carpool when we can, and we don't need or want to go along every time. But when you do, embrace it. Welcome the car time with your child, the joy of watching whatever it is, the pleasure of seeing your healthy, happy child getting to do this fun thing. "You're really not going to get to do this for that long," says Andrea Montalbano, author of the Soccer Sisters series for middle graders. She played soccer herself through college and now has two kids who play in Massachusetts. "We pulled into a tournament in New Jersey recently, and I grabbed my daughter, and we took a picture in the parking lot. I don't get to do this with my mom anymore. I try to treasure it. There's no place I'd rather be."

Think about the reasons you love this for your kid or your family, not about the slog. In her book *Flight of the Quetzal Mama: How to*

Raise Latino Superstars and Get Them into the Best Colleges, Roxanne Ocampo describes her family's decision to enroll their young son in a debate program that required a three-hour round-trip on Saturdays: "It wasn't convenient," she says (an understatement), but it was "a great investment in Emilio's future." Because their family had collectively decided that success in the highest levels of academia was a goal they would all work toward, they "stepped up" and made it happen.

Once you have made it happen, find a way to make it fun—for you. I knit during hockey games, and I love the feeling of doing something I enjoy while my kids do the same. And when we travel around the state, I make those trips worth my while. They know that if I drive, we might skip a team meal in favor of a good ramen place or taco stand. They know they'll be spending time in the local bookstore and that if the town sports a fancy grocery store like Whole Foods or Trader Joe's (our area has neither), we'll be there. Also I control the timetable, the radio, and any snack stops. The result is that hockey becomes a series of road trips that, at least most of the time, are fun for everyone in the car (so much so that another kid often tags along). I miss it when the season ends.

Find Your Own Thing

Here's an idea: sports and activities aren't just for kids.

There are improv groups, arts-and-crafts classes, and adult leagues for team sports. You can take surfing lessons, painting lessons, or piano lessons. Can't swing a babysitter or rely on a partner? For solo endeavors, there are online groups, courses, and instruction videos. Many a real community has formed around a virtual writing or crafting community. Keep chickens. Be a beekeeper. Invest less time worrying about whether your kids have found their passion and more time finding yours.

Spending too much time on your child's activities and not enough (or none) on your own pulls on your happiness. In my research, parents who were still enjoying a hobby or activity from "before kids" tended to be more satisfied with their lives, and when their kids were older, they also felt happier in their parenting. "One of my daughters is a swimmer," says Jamie Wilson, mother to eighteen-year-old triplet daughters and a twenty-year-old son in South Carolina. "Her coach was starting a Masters Swim team," she says, and she joined because she was once a swimmer who had quit the sport in high school, and she was now looking toward an open-water charity swimming event six months away. That was four years ago, and Wilson hasn't stopped swimming since. "I was having so much fun," she says. With times that qualified her for national meets and a team of other adults all sharing her interest and enthusiasm, "I became obsessed. When your kids are getting older, you need something of your own, because if you're still spending a lot of time helping them do things they could do themselves, you're really not helping—you're hurting." Nothing prevents you from doing all the planning and packing for your teenager's swim meet like being away already at a meet of your own.

While "returning" to an old passion might feel easiest, and even more justifiable, finding something new can also spark your old urge to learn, develop, and improve. We're adults now, and we can decide to adopt a hobby or sport that intrigues us, or even one we dreamed of as kids, and if we want, we can bring our kids along. Having kids who join in your activities, rather than the other way around, also correlates with life satisfaction. I was the kind of child who saved up money for trail rides at a local park, and when I signed my older kids up for the riding lessons I'd always wanted, I signed up, too. Now, as I've mentioned, we own a barn and run it as a family business, and working around the farm isn't optional.

But just the fact that you could bring your kids into your adventure doesn't necessarily mean you should. Your "thing," whatever it is, might be entirely new, entirely frivolous, and entirely for you. Before Jamie Wilson rediscovered swimming, when her children were very young (the triplets were three and her son, five), she took up the guitar. "I was at home with the kids, and I wanted to be there," she says, but at the same time, the energetic Wilson needed something more. While her peers were shepherding their preschoolers to Suzuki violin, she scheduled her own music lessons, which gave her the push she needed to set up babysitting and ignited her drive to improve. "I played every night for seven or eight years," she said, and eventually began to write and perform her own songs (you can find her on Spotify as Jamie Twang). Her kids, she said, needed her, but they didn't need all of her, all the time.

If we want to raise grown-ups (and we do), we have to make this grown-up thing look good—for their sakes, and for our own. Find something fun, and give yourself permission to do it.

Don't think you can fit that in? Consider this rant from Madeline Levine in her book *Teach Your Children Well*:

> If you're willing to give up your life, interests, friendships, and profession so that your child gets to see you week after week passively sitting in the bleachers watching whatever game he's playing; if you spend night after night sitting next to your child, helping with homework or overseeing her efforts instead of going out with a friend or your spouse; if money goes to prep course after prep course, tutor after tutor instead of to a family vacation or even a weekend away for

you and your husband, then . . . [y]ou have taught your kids that the moon and stars revolve around them and that the needs of adults, adults charged with the responsibility of taking care of and supporting a family (and often taking care of aging parents as well) can't hold a candle to a twelve-year-old's soccer game or a sixteen-year-old's math test.

Don't do that, and you'll all be happier.

five

HOMEWORK: MORE FUN WHEN IT'S NOT YOURS

Our family's homework travails began when my oldest son changed schools for second grade. In his old school, he had no homework; in the new one, he had some—one worksheet of math problems a few nights a week, and a weekly spelling list and test. The American Academy of Pediatrics recommends no more than ten minutes of homework per grade per night, and he should easily have been able to complete the work within that time.

He couldn't. It wasn't that he couldn't do the work. He just . . . didn't. He twirled his pencil. He balanced his chair on two legs. He gazed into the distance, contemplating the specks of dust glistening and drifting in the sunlight of the window. He didn't complain or even seem particularly unhappy (and he did not then, and does not now, have attention issues). He sat there, pencil in hand, work on the table, and did other things. Leave him alone, and later, you'd find him on the floor under the chair, zooming the pencil around airplane style. Sit with him, and he'd engage you in constant, non-homework-related conversation about the pencil, the dust, the view out the window, the political situation as he understood it.

If this sounds rather charming, it was (now in high school, he's still charming). It did not, however, get the job done, and that didn't make anyone happy. We consulted the teacher, set timers, adjusted the workload, found ways to direct his attention back to the task at hand, but he didn't change much. In third grade, the work increased (slightly) and so did the time he spent with it. Not on it, because for at least 50 percent of the time he and his homework spent together, no one could say he was "doing" homework. It drove us crazy. Why could he not just zip through the math problems, which were nothing he couldn't easily do, copy the spelling words or whatever, and be done so he could do something else?

Meanwhile, the parents around us were having different homework struggles. Perfectionist children who couldn't be persuaded that they'd done enough on their State Fair poster by midnight, frustrated tantrums over fractions, twins in different classrooms with entirely different homework loads, family dinners ruined, and younger siblings tugging and distracting parents trying to help struggling older kids. Then there was the mother of one child's classmate who would call to see if she could pick up our child to come play.

"After homework," I'd say.

"What homework?" she'd ask. According to her kid, there never was any.

All of this added up to substantial amounts of misery for everyone involved—and our pencil-twirling oldest turned out to be a piece of cake in comparison to one of his younger siblings. Homework was hard on everyone.

Surely, somewhere, there were children who went home, did their homework without comment, and turned it in the next day—or children who were blissfully homework free. If that's the case in your family, you can skip this chapter (or save it for later). Homework isn't a universal problem, but when it's a problem, it feels overwhelming. Some parents described teachers complaining about the homework. It was undone, poorly done, not turned in, not up to potential. Then there were the parents who were complaining right back. Homework was stressful, homework interfered with play and family time. Children were too worried about homework, or too confused, or needed help but then insisted their parents were "not doing it right."

Is there any way to salvage some parent and family happiness out of this? Because in general, parents, students, siblings, and even, I soon learned, many teachers are united in one belief: homework sucks.

What Goes Wrong

Our homework didn't make our parents' lives miserable. In many cases, it barely appeared on their radar. Those of us who finished school at the end of the twentieth century can look at our own children and see their time in school as similar to our own, in classrooms where boys and girls are at least nominally equal and college is often the goal. For many of our parents, that wasn't the case. Their high school experience was very different from ours. Most of our mothers weren't necessarily expected to excel in rigorous subjects, and they might not have been expected to go to college at all. High school, as an institution, evolved very rapidly. Unless they were from wealthy families, their parents (our grandparents) were probably the first children in their families to even attend high school, and not finishing wasn't unusual. In 1910, just 9 percent of the population graduated from high school; by 1940, that percentage had increased to just over 50 percent.

That democratization of secondary education was uniquely American. Immigrant parents would have had even less experience with the classes, activities, and homework that were becoming a standard part of adolescence here, let alone with the process of applying to colleges that follows. So for generations, instead of shepherding a child through a familiar experience, parents either struggled with what it means to raise a child with a new set of expectations or stepped back and let those children handle it. Hovering over homework, or school in general, wasn't part of the picture.

But when our generation of parents sees our children embarking on the path from kindergarten and beyond, we're seeing a process we know intimately, and we want to help. Oddly, though, much of our "help" is less than helpful. Both individually and as a society, we've upped the ante for upper- and middle-class kids by packing their schedules with enriching non-school activities. Our parents didn't have to concern themselves about whether homework could get done in the limited space between violin, soccer, and Kumon (oh, the irony). We've also pushed schools, especially in affluent communities, toward more academic rigor. Kindergarten is no longer just for playtime, and recess along with music and the arts is rapidly disappearing from the lower school schedule. In high school, electives like photography and metal shop lose out to extra academic offerings thought to be more impressive to college admissions officers, and those classes often involve additional homework.

That means that if you suspect your own children have more homework than you once did, you're probably right. While there's no evidence of an enormous nationwide increase in homework load, data on two groups of kids suggests a significant uptick: homework for nine-year-olds went from no homework at all to some, and while the national average homework load for high schoolers has hovered at less than two hours a night for decades, students in high-performing (and high-income) schools reported more than three hours. (It's worth noting that homework itself is not correlated with student performance.)

Those small-sounding changes have made a big difference for many families. If you're the parent of a nine-year-old, or a younger child who has been assigned to bring in four interesting facts about marmosets, you know that—as we discovered when our oldest hit the homework roadblock for the first time—the difference between "none" and "some" is more than just "significant." For some children, it's the end of the world, or you'd think it was, as you watch them rolling around on the floor and screaming in protest over five math problems that could easily be done by now if they'd just get over it.

"No" homework is no homework. "Some" homework can change the family dynamic, turning parents into taskmasters and evenings into stress-filled power struggles, or at the very least demanding accommodation where once there was just free time. Even that's harder than it sounds if, for example, pick-up from the after-school program is at six p.m., there's still dinner to be made and eaten, and the assignment is "read and discuss the story of Johnny Appleseed *with a parent.*"

For older students, that two-hour national average probably includes two ends of a bell curve: none or very little, and "tons." When researchers asked 4,317 students from ten high-performing high schools in upper-middle-class California communities to describe the impact of homework on their lives, those students reported averaging just over three hours of homework nightly. (They added comments like: "There's never a break. Never.") More than three is a whole lot more than two hours (and that was the average, meaning that some children were finding themselves sitting down, as my own high school sophomore son, once that pencil-twirling second grader, now does, for four to five hours some nights).

Whether it's some homework, more homework, or piles, the homework that causes stress for students also causes us stress as parents. One small study found that stress and tension for families (as reported by the parents) increased most when parents perceived themselves as unable to help with the homework, when the child disliked doing the homework, and when the homework caused arguments, either between the child and adults or among the adults in the household.

In my own research, homework appears among the top four of anecdotally reported stress points for parents, and in our survey, we found that reporting higher rates of homework seems to nip away at our feelings of satisfaction as parents, and even more so if we're reporting regular arguments with our children about it. When our children are younger, all that homework (again, especially if we're fighting about it) also makes us feel less effective as parents. The more homework our younger children have, the less in control we feel over the situation and that makes us less happy.

For many of us, homework is the first point of conflict with our children when we see them after school and work, and the last point before they (or we) head off to bed. *Do they have any? How much? When are they going to do it? Can they get it done before practice/rehearsal/ dinner? After? When is it due? When did they start it? How long will it take?* Even parents who are wholly hands-off about the homework itself still need to know how much, when, and how long if there are any family plans in the offing. We can't plan anything, start anything, schedule anything, without keeping homework fully in mind.

How to Get Happier, Homework and All

Getting past the homework barrier on the way to a happier family is complicated, because the things you can change aren't easy to change, and the things you can't change can be particularly hard to live with. There are three major potential trouble spots when it comes to homework.

First, and arguably easiest to change, is your approach to the homework as a parent. We tend to want to focus on the grades and the results, but the homework that goes out of the house is far less important than the homework that's coming in and what happens when it gets there. When our involvement with that is out of balance, it contributes to our unhappiness.

Next, there's how your child approaches the homework. If your own approach to homework is out of whack, these two things are probably deeply intertwined, but it is (and should be) a separate question. Teaching your child to manage her homework herself in a positive and productive way is part of your job as a parent.

But even if you achieve homework nirvana on the first two fronts, another potential roadblock looms: the homework itself. The homework your child is getting might not be working for your child and family for various reasons. It could be too much or too little (common when a school is trying to learn to work with a child's learning challenges). It could be unclear or dramatically different from what your child expected when she signed up for a class. It could just be a poor fit for your kid right now. If any of those things are the case, you, and your child, have a stark choice. You can work toward change (knowing that it may never happen) or you can learn to live within a difficult situation for a year or more.

Our Attitude Toward Homework

The simplest change you can make around homework to increase your own happiness is, of course, to change how you feel about it. Without being utterly heartless, one thing is simply true: it's not your homework. You could, legitimately, fully disengage. You could walk out of the room when homework appeared and explain to your children that you are out of the homework business. If the result was that no homework was done, and the school complained, you could respond by saying that you will fully support the school in any discipline it chooses to impose for the failure to do homework, but you are going to keep your family focus on other things.

You probably won't, but you could. (Even if you did, as long as you're in the house when homework is happening, you're still going to get caught up in the drama.) Just considering the possibility, though, should open you to this proposal: your children's homework should not, as a rule, make you unhappy. Even if it's hard. Even if they're frustrated or miserable. Even if the whole things seems grossly unfair and mismanaged. *It's okay to be happy when your children aren't.* You can do whatever you're going to do to help them through their struggle without getting dragged into the stress.

If that feels impossible, you're not alone. Janet Rotter, head of the Studio School in Manhattan, has spent more than forty years in education, and she has watched homework evolve. "Homework has become this end-all and be-all," she says, "sometimes even coming before schoolwork itself. People—adults—will say to you, 'Oh, I couldn't possibly see you this weekend. We have a lot of homework to do.'"

"It used to be between the child and the school," she says, but now she sees teachers putting "a lot of pressure on parents to help kids do it." That, as you probably expect, is not Rotter's way. The Studio School puts the onus on the children entirely to manage their school and homework lives, from being the ones to call and explain an illness or absence to taking control of what supplies they need and asking their parents to help them get them. Instead of expecting parents to involve themselves nightly, this school asks the parents to get out of their children's way.

That, says Rotter, is a difficult transition for many parents. "We have these fantasies of what's going to happen if the homework doesn't get done," she says. "The child will get in trouble. The teacher will be mad at him. She'll be mad at me. She'll think I'm a terrible mother."

Those, she says, are thoughts you have to let go. "Homework is a vehicle for helping children learn how to do work away from the teacher without someone making sure they did it." Instead of being "the homework police," she asks parents not to remind their children but to ask, instead, what the children think they can do to help themselves remember. "It's really about what you do when you don't want to do something, about giving up pleasure," she says of the child and homework. "They have to learn how to learn, and we have to really let the process unfold."

Our job as parents, she says, is to (brace yourself) "teach the children that not everything revolves around their homework. There is more to life. We as parents don't base our worth on whether or not that homework gets done."

When it comes to school and homework, we parents have become confused about the goal. We think we want our children to "achieve" and "succeed"—but those are the wrong verbs. They're too easy for us to take over and run with.

Instead, our children need to *learn* to achieve and succeed themselves. Think of it like basketball. The goal of the game isn't getting a ball through a hoop. If it was, we could get a ladder, or lower the hoop, and then all go out for ice cream. But no, the goal is to learn to get the ball through the hoop as best as a player can and to figure out where you belong on a team, how to follow the rules, and even ultimately whether you really want to be on the court. Without those things, there is no game.

If we're too emotionally involved in our children's school and homework, we make ourselves and our children suffer. Suddenly, what's important isn't our family, our relationship, or who we are together and separately but what's in this one essay or on that report card. Most of us prefer to believe that the pressure around homework for our children, which makes us all unhappy, is external. It comes from the school, from society, from the college application process.

Too often, according to our older children, we're wrong. In the study of 4,317 students from ten high-performing high schools in upper-middle-class California communities, researchers invited students to answer open-ended questions about homework and stress (as well as complete a survey). Although the schools they attended were responsible for the homework loads they faced, many said the real pressure came from their parents, and a perpetual message that if they didn't do the homework perfectly, they wouldn't get the grades and they wouldn't succeed.

Jessica Wolf has been one of those parents. The mother of a high school junior and a college senior has seen a lot of kids through the college admissions process as a college essay coach in Montclair, New

Jersey. She wants to "consciously dial back on the freneticism" around the process with her younger son after her relationship with his older brother suffered during high school, so she doesn't look at the grade portal (an online tool that allows parents to see a daily progress in classes). She lets her son tell her what he wants to tell her and reminds him that, if he needs help, she has his back.

"It's very, very difficult," she says, to stay hands-off. Hers isn't a community where parents take a backseat on schoolwork. "I was at a dinner, years ago, with a bunch of other women, and I guess we all had kids in the same class. At eight thirty they all got up, and one said, 'I've got to get home; my kid has a paper due,' and everyone was like, 'Yep.' I remember one saying, 'I'm practically going to have to write this myself.'"

"For some parents, that's all they talk about, that's all they worry about," says Rotter. "They act as if the homework is more important than the child." Denise Pope, a senior lecturer in education at Stanford University and one of the researchers who led the study described above, suggests that those parents might be falling into the "trap of parent peer pressure" that Jessica Wolf describes. "It's really up to us to say the opposite." Pope advocates spending the time you might otherwise spend on nagging about grades talking about other aspects of life and being a voice of reason, especially if your child is a perfectionist or is discouraged—and even if she seems fine.

Grades aren't permanent. Success isn't permanent. Failure isn't permanent. Some people march straight through high school, college, and graduate school. Others take different paths. Don't just highlight one route in life and make sure that even a child who's driving herself hard toward socially accepted "success" knows (as you do) that there are many roads to happiness.

How Your Kid Does the Homework

It is very, very hard to be happy while one of your children is clutching your leg while you try to make dinner, forcing you to drag her around the kitchen while she wails, "I can't do it! I need help!"

Trust me, I know.

Ordinarily, it's a truism that the only person we can change is ourselves. In this case, though, it's our job to teach our kids not how to do the homework itself—as in, how to add and subtract or write a summarizing paragraph—but how to get the homework done without our being a regular part of the routine.

It's important to be clear on the goal with homework. Don't think "getting it done well," think "becoming capable of getting it done well without help." That can be tough. It's easier to help get it done (especially if your child is begging for help, or the kind of "help" where someone else does all the work) than it is to say "I know you can do this," and let them do it, even if it takes a while, and even if initial results are far from perfect. *What you want now isn't always what you want later.*

When your child understands that the responsibility for the homework is his, you'll be much more able to be happy and at ease during his regular homework times, and not just because, "Hey! You don't have any homework!" If the expectation is that you will be deeply involved in the process, from getting him to sit down with your endless nagging to rushing to the rescue in the event of a compound fraction to checking the work to make sure that it's done, done right, and packed up and ready for school, then your child can take all his negative energy around homework and dump it right on you.

Suddenly, it's your fault he has to do it. It's your fault if it's hard, or if he's not doing it well, and it's your fault if it's not done or forgotten.

Not only is he failing to learn much, if anything, from the homework process, but you're the bad guy. This isn't going to make you happy now, and it isn't going to lead to greater happiness later.

It's never too late to straighten out who is at the helm (your child, in case there was any confusion) when it comes to getting the work done. Here's the message we want them to soak in:

- You're learning. It's okay to make mistakes while you're learning. That's how you improve.
- It's less work in the long run to try your hardest.
- That doesn't mean it has to be perfect.
- Your best work is good enough.

If you've sat next to your child and helped the homework happen in the past, lay it out: "You're in second/fifth/tenth grade now—you sit down and start working, and I'll be nearby if you need help." You want to send a message of expectation and belief in your child's competence and ability. "Take an interest," said Julie Lythcott-Haims, when they ask for help. "You can help them interpret instructions, you can help them procure materials, but when they're turning to you and saying, 'I can't, I don't know,' you have to say, 'Yes, you can. This is the homework assigned. Your teacher thinks you can do it, and I do, too.'"

This is true of daily work, and it's true of the kinds of big assignments that have many parents whipping out the glue guns. Helping your child learn to do a big project (as opposed to creating a successful project) doesn't mean leaving a second grader to do her own Web search on "penguin mating." (This is, in fact, a very bad idea.) You can help make a plan, teach techniques that make presenting easier, and troubleshoot when, say, the papier-mâché scale model of Epcot's Spaceship Earth proves too heavy for the proposed drinking-straw base. The goal is finding the line between supporting and doing, and staying firmly on the cheerleader side in all things school-related, whether it's student council election posters or long division.

This will not necessarily be a fast process. I don't mean to make light of how challenging that change may be for your child and, by extension, you. One of my children has struggled with school; she doesn't believe her best is good enough because, for so long, her best was so often objectively wrong in terms of calculation, spelling, or grammar. She's a hard worker and she likes to get her work right, so she would prefer a holding hand. We endured the "but I need help" tantrums for years, and in many cases, we got her help, in the form of a tutor or additional time with the teacher after school, but we didn't give her the help ourselves—because when we did, we became either the bad guy (forcing her to sit there and work hard while she grew angrier and angrier) or the patsy (explaining every step of the way until there was nothing for her to do but hold the pencil).

If that first night of math homework without your help takes your sixth grader three hours, sit tight. What took three hours the first time might take two next week and half an hour the week after that. If it doesn't change—if your child is truly struggling without your help—then you've both learned something valuable that's far better learned now than later: something needs to change. Maybe that's the homework or the class. Maybe your child needs additional help (but not the kind that masks whether she can understand the material). Maybe she's in the wrong class. It really is better to be able to follow, understand, and do well in grade-level math than to be constantly out of one's depth just because one's parent or older sibling was always in the advanced class.

With most children, you can help a little ("quarter" means "fourth") and step away, but with others, there's no such thing as a little help. For us, even the slightest indication that we might involve ourselves in our daughter's homework, like a willingness to spell a word, sent us spiraling back to the beginning, with her refusing to do anything without one of us sitting by her side. That meant we had to be absolute in our refusal to help (and whenever we had guests of any kind, it meant they thought we were somewhere between crazy and cruel). If you're in a similar situation, you'll need to spend some time being absolutely hands-off (and by "some time," I might mean years).

That's okay. It's fine to send a child to school with homework that's incomplete or done wrong—in fact, it's what you're supposed to do. Too often, homework is useless from an evaluation perspective, says Doreen Esposito, the principal of PS 290, a K–5 school in Manhattan. "Many times, parents are doing it for them, or tutors are doing it with them." Teachers, she says, need to know where their students are independently. Letting the homework go back in the backpack without your eyes first helps them do just that, even if you happen to have noticed a problem. *If you see something, don't always say something.*

But what if the homework is graded, and what if those grades matter? Here's another ticklish spot. In most of the country, nothing about a child's marks has any lasting impact until ninth grade. That means it's easier for most of us to let the chips of various homework failures fall where they may.

If your child's grades matter—if you live in New York City, where students apply to middle schools or charter schools, or are in some other way in a situation where the numbers are going to make a difference—then you probably look at things differently. You're in a tough spot, right there at the intersection of what's culturally wrong with homework and how parents are making it worse. Most of us won't have to deal with the ramifications of a child making mistakes with long-term implications until they're in high school, when college and adulthood feel closer, children are more competent, and it's easier to see why they need the freedom to screw up (although not necessarily easier to watch).

On balance, you want your child to do the homework. When you look back and tally things up, nearly everything you teach her around homework (including the things you teach by what you do, not by what you say) should be in service of the larger message: she makes mistakes while learning, does her best, and doesn't freak out if her best isn't perfect because she knows it's good enough.

If sometimes you find yourself in a place where you're doing more to help than you want to, don't beat yourself up, but don't slide further and further along the slope, either. If you can, talk with your child about why you're more involved and how that can change. This might be a time to go on to the next section and start advocating for homework change—sometimes teachers haven't fully thought through the implications of a homework grading policy.

How Your Kid Does Homework Now Isn't Necessarily How She'll Do It Forever

Every situation is different, and every child is different. Even with the best of intentions, it's unlikely you'll quickly find yourself out of a job when it comes to homework—you still need to help them learn how to do their best work efficiently and effectively. So what can you do that helps them move toward that goal? Encourage your child to make some conscious choices around homework instead of doing it "whenever." Offer help with when and where, not how. Ask things like "When are you planning to get your homework done?" with, you know, bonus information—"You've got soccer from four to five and Holly is coming over for dinner." Especially at the start of the year, let the kid make the choices, then help assess. "Hey, your teacher keeps writing that she can't read your math homework. Let's figure out how you could make it neater." "Hey, you left the homework until after soccer last week and weren't happy. Maybe a different approach this week?" (I've even had my kid record a message to their future self, saying, "Don't wait until bedtime to do the math!")

Then let them figure it out, and don't judge the results. It's easy to slot your kids into categories when it comes to homework—the organized one, the slacker, the hard worker. But those things don't always hold true. The organized one will forget something big, the easy-A-maker will fail, the slacker will suddenly get interested. If you haven't made those roles part of their identity, it's easier for kids to let themselves see things differently, to get past mistakes if they've made them, or to get excited about a new class or project.

People, including children—especially children—change. Kids grow. They evolve. They're supposed to be learning how to do this stuff—and that doesn't just mean algebra and the ABCs. They're learning how to sit down, how to do hard stuff, how to do something they don't want to do, to plan, to think, to try again.

They learn some of that from homework. That doesn't mean we have to like homework. We just have to get out of the way and let them do it.

The Homework Itself

Sometimes the homework itself really is the problem, and once in a while, changing that is easy. When my oldest son was in third grade, his school tried out a program that required the children to complete their homework online. There were many problems with this scenario (our dubious rural Internet connection at the time; the trouble it caused with his younger siblings, for whom just touching the keyboard was a coveted privilege), but the largest was that he could not type, and the assignments took him forever. We gave it some time, in the hopes the bugs would be worked out, but after a long night of hunting and pecking to meet the requirement that he copy (by typing them into the particular homework program) sentences including his spelling and vocabulary words, I finally got in touch with the teacher. "Oh," she said. "It would be fine if you typed the sentences for him."

"But the assignment is to copy the sentences. That's the whole assignment."

"Yes, but it's fine if you do the typing."

"If the assignment is to copy the sentences by typing, and I do the typing, whose homework is it?"

To her credit, she laughed. That was the last such assignment, and the homework program itself lasted only a few more weeks. It just wasn't effective for the kids at that age, and it took parents and teachers working together to figure it out.

It's rarely that simple. In general, whether you wish there were less homework, or more homework, or different homework, giving things a little time to shake themselves out before you take action is a good plan, especially at the beginning of anything new (and that's a fine time to work on your and your child's perspective on homework—it's homework, and it's not a matter of life or death).

But what if, after a little time has passed, you feel like the homework is a problem overall? Or what if one assignment, one class, or one teacher has your child (and you) all tied up in knots? It is possible for you, or an older child, to make some changes in homework—

sometimes immediately, sometimes in the long run—that might make everyone happier, if you approach it right. But you can't do that until you understand what the homework is, what it's for, and who has the power to change it.

What Is This Homework, Really?

The first thing we as parents need to do is assess our child's experience of the homework against, well, reality. Does sixty-four math problems sound like madness? Ask your child to reach out to a classmate and be sure she got the assignment right before you join her in freaking out. (We once discovered, after much drama, that only the even-numbered problems had been assigned.) Of course it's crazy that she's expected to write five researched pages on a given topic by tomorrow morning—but is she sure that this assignment was given out this afternoon? Kids make mistakes. They also procrastinate, and some are prone to adjusting the truth to make themselves look better (at least one of mine frequently "kinda" knew about the reading). And in some cases (as with my pencil twirler) it's simply taking your child longer than it does anyone else's.

One more thing to consider as you try to evaluate the work your child has been assigned is whether he's more capable than you (or he) thinks. That may look like a huge page of math problems, but a kid who has been practicing addition facts in class may be able to knock them out in less than two minutes (in fact, that may be the goal). More complex endeavors may be well within your child's grasp, perhaps combining the things he has been learning in the classroom in new ways that will stretch and challenge him, but truly are doable—doable, that is, in a manner suited to his age and experience, not yours.

When my two youngest children were in fourth grade, they were assigned to prepare a five-minute-long speech from a biography, to be delivered, not read, from notes on index cards, in costume and in character and with at least one prop. I thought it was impossible, particularly for my daughter, who can have trouble telling the important facts or events in a book from the details. But various circumstances meant that even though we intended to help, we couldn't.

They did fine—because they were, in fact, ready for this project, and their teacher knew it. Madeline Levine, a clinical psychologist and author, suggests that if, as a parent, you find yourself classifying an assignment as impossible rather than challenging and getting ready to don your superhero cape and leap in, you should stop and look more closely. It may be out of your child's comfort zone, she said, but if you break it down into chunks, is it within their "capacity zone"?

When kids pull off something that's a real reach for them, that's a happiness booster for both of you. If I had helped with my daughter's report, it would have included much less information about the ponies and horses Elizabeth Blackwell, the first woman to become a doctor in the United States, owned as a child and maybe a little more about her medical career. But that didn't matter. The right question isn't "Can she do this the way I'd do it?" but "Can she do this at all?"

What Is This Homework For?

The goal of that oral book report wasn't that my child learn the "right" things about Elizabeth Blackwell. It was that she take information from written sources and present it aloud to her classmates. Often, the homework's objective is pretty simple. For younger children, in math, it's usually practice. Teachers want those simple facts to become automatic. The same goes for spelling. Sometimes an assignment that seems like busy work, like copying the spelling words out four times each, is an effective, if not particularly inspiring, learning tool.

With projects, book reports, and similar homework, the goal—along with the more obvious educational content—might be learning to manage time or to plan ahead or divide a big project into smaller pieces. Teachers might assign reading to allow the teacher to move faster or to be ready for class discussion.

Understanding what the homework is meant to accomplish can be key to working with a teacher toward an individual, short-term change if it's one particular kind of homework that's creating a problem. If, for example, the goal is for a child to read every night but your child spends so much time watching the clock and adding and subtracting minutes that no reading can get done, maybe she could check a box instead of entering a number. If the teacher has asked that you set a timer so that a child can work toward speed on a page of math facts, but your child is made frantic (as one of mine was) by the ticking away of the seconds, maybe she could use an app or flashcards to practice.

You don't, of course, want to make your child the exception to every rule. Sometimes tests are timed, sometimes homework is no fun. But especially in the lower grades, teachers are often willing to work with parents if a type of work is causing an issue.

Who to Talk to, and What to Say

Oona Hanson, a Los Angeles parent who became interested in homework policies while advocating for her own child, and eventually obtained a master's degree in educational psychology and became involved in school governance, suggests that regardless of whether you think you'll be advocating only for your child or seeking larger changes, you start by talking to the teacher about what you've observed, not what you think.

"Describe what is happening with your child," she suggests, and don't put the teacher on the defensive with phrases like "He loves your class, but . . ." Work from the assumption that you and the teacher both want what's best for your child, but don't assume anything else. When she described her daughter's concerns over a packet of homework that came home every week in kindergarten, the teacher quickly told her not to let the child worry about it. The real goal was just to take something home at the beginning of the week, then bring it back at the end. "She said, 'She can do as much or as little of the work as she wants.'"

Should you ask around before you approach the teacher? Yes—and no. Tapping a friend whose child is also in the class on the shoulder at a soccer game and starting up a conversation about the homework is great, as is placing a phone call (to another parent or child, not the teacher) to clarify the night's assignment. A quick spout-off on Facebook, though, is a bad idea. "When parents get on social media and then they start texting each other, everything gets blown out of proportion fast," says Anita Perry, a former teacher in Devens, Massachusetts. "Suddenly the principal is involved and it's this big enormous problem," when reaching out directly to the teacher could have led to a simple resolution.

Similarly, your kitchen table complaints aren't going unheard, even if you didn't press "post." "First and second graders are very honest," says Perry. "They come in the next day, and they say, 'Mommy said this homework was stupid and I don't have to do it.'"

Beth Rabin, a Los Angeles mother of twin daughters now in high school, first contacted a teacher about homework when one, then a fourth grader who normally loved school, began to really be "dragged down" by her homework.

"I observed for nearly two weeks," she says. "I made sure I had good data, and then I went to her, and I just said, this is what's happening. This is how long it's taking." The teacher's response was to suggest a reduction in homework in an area (vocabulary) where her daughter already had strong skills. That didn't eliminate the most challenging parts of the homework, but it did lessen the amount of time spent on it.

Sometimes, teachers genuinely don't know how long an assignment takes a student or how it plays out in the family. Your suspicion that a younger teacher, particularly one without a family of her own, might not have thought about the homework in the same way as a teacher with more experience or a family does may be correct. One seventh-grade teacher wrote me an email saying that when she first started, at age twenty-one, she never really thought about how homework would impact a family. "My understanding was that I should assign homework every night. I did that until last year, when a parent made me see things differently. I just was following what I thought I 'should' do as a 'rigorous teacher.' I thought I would get in trouble if I didn't assign homework each night."

Years after the fourth-grade homework incident, Beth Rabin realized that each of her twin daughters was spending eight hours a weekend outlining a chapter in a particularly dense textbook for an advanced placement course. Again, she observed, and again, she got in touch with the teacher, this time with a question as well as a description of what was happening. How long should the outlines take? Two hours. Eight hours was indeed a problem. "To her credit," says Rabin, "the teacher asked around," and found that some students were able to get it done in two hours, while others were not. Rabin's daughters and some of their classmates needed to develop more of the skills needed to do the task; the teacher worked with the girls, suggesting strategies for doing the work as well as managing the time involved.

It's important to remember that the solution may not lead to perfection—Rabin's daughters still spent more than two hours on that assignment—but it might be enough to reduce a child's stress and, by extension, your own. Rabin's daughters are stretching to achieve something that might be easier for some students. Some assignments take some students more time than others; some classes are designed to require more, or more challenging, work at home; sometimes students take on a course load that's more work than they realized. Sometimes the right course is just to accept the homework and move on to managing it and helping your child find her way to success with it. Sometimes, you'll want to take your advocacy further.

Most teachers really are receptive to a parent approach about the homework, but some aren't—and some genuinely aren't able to make the changes you were hoping for because they're working within a set curriculum or with a school- or district-wide policy. That means your next stop is with school administrators, and maybe beyond. Principal Doreen Esposito says PS 290 changed its homework policy partly as a result of parent advocacy.

"It started with a concern over inconsistency," says Esposito. Some teachers in the upper grades gave a lot, others relatively little. At a meeting of the leadership team formed among teachers, administrators, and parents, one parent with experience in the area offered to present the research around homework. He did it, she says, in a non-confrontational way. "What he said was consistent with experiences I had had," she says. "Some of the homework we sent home seemed to have no purpose, yet parents were fighting with their kids to get it done."

If some parents weren't happy, many teachers weren't happy, either. "Homework is busy work for teachers," she says. They have to show that they're looking at it, yet it's often not useful as a way to evaluate students. "If it isn't done in class under the right conditions, you don't really know where they are independently."

In 2016, the school moved to what they call "home-based learning" rather than "homework": projects, practice, or curricula designed by students in consultation with their teachers to enhance or deepen their learning. She ticks off a list of the qualities the teachers hope the home-based learning will develop: creativity, curiosity, perseverance, independence, problem-solving, responsibility, collaboration, self-direction. Home-based learning, she says, "allows kids to reflect on their work and create their goals, and to make that connection at home."

But working toward that kind of big change isn't easy, and it isn't fast. Here's one final thing worth remembering, even if your actions seem to be leading nowhere: sometimes change is gradual, and sometimes we're contributing to it even if we can't see it. The parent who brought in the research about the homework did so after his daughter had a particularly difficult fifth-grade year, but by the time the new program was implemented, she had graduated.

And sometimes, after you've done everything you're willing to do, the homework still will be a real pull on your family's happiness in a way you don't feel you can tolerate. After four years in a public school with homework expectations that consistently made her son miserable, New York City mom Julie Scelfo moved him (and subsequently his siblings) to a school with a different philosophy. His first school, she says, expected parents to have nightly involvement in the homework, handling things like "grammar and punctuation and spelling" at home, and the homework began in kindergarten with weekly packets and just kept increasing from year to year. Some families would welcome the invitation to be such a big part of a child's education, but it wasn't working for Scelfo.

"I was a working parent, with three little kids," says Scelfo. "I tried to sit with him. I tried to be patient, but I couldn't always do it." Then, when her son was in third grade, she found him struggling with an assignment that probably needed her help, "and he hit himself, and he said, 'I'm so stupid,' and something just snapped in me," she says. "I thought, 'What am I doing, trying to force him into this?'"

At his new school, the expectations around homework are very different, and they fit the family's lifestyle much better. "The school is really about giving responsibility to children," she says. "They're supposed to make the call if they will be absent or late. The school tells parents, stay out of the homework unless the child asks. Don't say, 'Did you do it?' Don't say, 'When will you do it?' Don't ask if it's done. They take all those lessons out of the sphere of the parent."

Your child's school, and his homework, really do have a big impact on both your and your family's happiness. If you're able to put the resources into it—and that's not a small consideration—finding a way to make a big change in the classroom or the school may be what it takes to make a difference in the homework itself.

Who Should Do the Talking?

So far, we've focused on how parents can advocate for our children around homework—but there does come a point when our children should advocate for themselves. They can use time-honored strategies—making an appointment, going to talk to the teacher—

but there are also routes open to the young, naive, and enthusiastic that aren't open to their elders. When my oldest son was in eighth grade, he and a group of friends entered the Verizon App Challenge, which invited students to develop a smartphone app that would help other students. Their app would have allowed teachers to evaluate how much homework was being assigned to a given student overall, rather than focusing on only a single class. As they said in their presentation, "If a teacher says you'll have half an hour to an hour of homework a night, that sounds reasonable. But if you have six classes, that's three to six hours of homework."

Their idea won the state and regional rounds, although it was not one of the two apps selected to be developed in the national competition. The effect on the school of having five of their students win national honors (and a check for the school's science education department) for an app that attempted to make their homework more manageable, though, was dramatic. My son and his classmates, who graduated that year, only saw a slight benefit. His younger sister is now in the same middle school, with many of the same teachers. Although she's a very different student, it's clear that those teachers are making more of an effort to coordinate large assignments and even nightly work.

The big play—creating a committee, doing a large data-gathering project, making a funny video about homework, or even engaging in protest—is an option for kids. But usually, you're going to need to help them start exactly where you would start—in a meeting with the teacher—whether the problem is that they're not understanding classroom lectures enough to do the homework, they want to talk about why the homework is what it is and what it's for, or they just want to convey how challenged they're feeling.

Helping your child do this is a little different from getting ready to do it yourself. For starters, an email—the first recourse at nearly every age—is unlikely to be an effective tool for children and teens, for one simple reason: it's too easy. It's easy for a child to dash off and too easy for a teacher to disregard—or say no.

It's much harder to look a teacher right in the face, describe a problem, and wait for a response—and this is much more likely to lead to a positive result. Most children need pushing to do this, and some might even want to write down a few notes about what they want to say. If your child is open to it, talk to him about how the teacher might respond, and how he might feel and then respond himself. Children who are really frustrated in a class might fear tears, and that's understandable. You can practice saying something like "It's okay that I'm crying; it's just because I care about this. But we can still talk and figure something out."

Finally: Sometimes You Will Do Things You Said You Would Not, and That's Okay

Six or seven years ago, I walked into my friend Suzy's house to find her seated at her table, surrounded by scissors and construction paper, painstakingly gluing tiny squares onto a piece of poster board. Seated next to her was her nephew, Forrest. Forrest, a high school junior, had moved in with Suzy a few months before. He was a good kid, but he had been living alone with his dad and had struggled in his last high school. He was determined to make a fresh start and get himself into college, and Suzy was determined to help him.

Suzy dotted glue on the back of a tiny square, carefully lowered it onto the paper, and whacked it into place with her palm.

"It's the stupidest assignment," she said, dotting glue onto another square. "It's a roman mosaic or something. He has to glue all these on tonight." *Whack.*

Forrest, next to her, was surrounded by books and probably four or five hours of academic work. It was early evening. "I'm just going to get him started, at least," she said.

Suzy is not particularly artsy. She was having no trouble, as far as I could see, in imitating the work of a teenaged boy. And her younger daughter had been all through elementary school with my oldest son. I knew that while Suzy might help build a set for the holiday concert, she certainly wasn't sitting at home redesigning her daughter's second-grade poster biography of Abraham Lincoln. This wasn't like her, but looking at the books around Forrest, and knowing how hard he was working to succeed in his new, more academic environment, I didn't have any trouble following one of my mental rules: never judge a parent (or an aunt) whose children are older than yours. Sometimes, you do what you swore you wouldn't do.

"Sometimes," though, is an important word. If you're stepping in on every project, if it worries you that that second-grade biography trifold board "looks like it was made by a seven-year-old," if you're stenciling or pasting on backgrounds or using scrapbooking scissors with wavy edges every time the word "project" comes up, then it might be time to begin following the steps for extracting oneself from homework involvement or going cold turkey on anything involving poster board.

But sometimes you'll do it. Sometimes, you'll find your sixth grader, who decided the lettering on the traffic safety poster should be white and the entire poster colored around it, sitting there with a marker at eleven p.m., carefully filling in all that space, and you will get a second marker, and you will sit down, and you will help. Sometimes the phone will ring just as you're sitting down with your laptop or leaving for work, and it will be your child, frantic, who has forgotten one page of the big Emily Dickinson folder she spent all weekend putting together, and it's a required page, and it will be a slow day and you will have some time and you will drop it off.

And sometimes you won't. You won't be home to help color, you'll be in a meeting when the frantic text about the forgotten page comes through, or you'll remind both of you that you told her to pack up her backpack last night, and while you are sorry that her rough draft of her *Robinson Crusoe* essay is on the kitchen counter and now she's going to have to stay in at recess and rewrite it, these things happen. Sometimes you'll be able to choose when you help, and sometimes circumstances will choose for you, and it will all work out fine in the end.

Forrest graduated from a small college last spring and is working his first job running construction sites. He's a lovely, independent young man who doesn't run to Suzy with small problems or expect her to call his boss for him if he's late for work, which he wouldn't be, anyway, because jobs are scarce and this is a good one. Occasionally he brings home his laundry.

As far as I know, he's never again been asked to make a roman mosaic out of construction paper.

six

SCREENS ARE FUN,
LIMITING THEM IS NOT

I n your children's eyes, screen time is already fun. Who are we kidding—adults like their screens, too. In this case, it's not a question of making something fun. That's covered. But making screens a part of a happy family life means finding a screen-use balance that leaves plenty of time for everything else, and ensuring that maintaining that balance doesn't itself lead to unhappiness.

Every year, a new set of data emerges alerting us to what we already know: we—parents, teenagers, children—spend a lot of time watching or interacting with screens. Some of the latest numbers show parents—*parents*—of children ages eight to eighteen reporting an average of more than 7.5 hours a day of personal screen media use outside of work, although it's important to note that some media use is concurrent with doing other things, or even counts double—surfing the Internet on a tablet while watching television, for example. Teenagers (using the same standards) report a little under nine hours of non-school-related screen time, and tweens (eight- to twelve-year-olds) about six hours a day, again excluding screen time spent on work, school, or homework. Younger kids appear to watch and play less: parents report that children five to eight spend about 2.5 hours a day on media; two- to four-year-olds, 2 hours; and children under two, about an hour.

So much of our conversation around screens and kids is about setting limits, but those numbers suggest that while we're good at limiting the screen time of children whose time is easily controlled, the minute children become more able to access screens themselves, the game changes. If the goal of limiting young children's media usage is to teach them to set reasonable limits for themselves later, it looks like we're failing. In fact, it looks as if we can't even limit ourselves. Yet, in that same survey in which parents reported a whopping seven-plus hours of daily personal screen time, the majority (78 percent) also cheerfully declared themselves to be "good role models" when it came to media and technology use.

I think we can safely say that we're serving as role models, yes. The "good" part of that, though, we might want to question.

This is a large part of what makes the screen time piece of the parenting puzzle so very difficult. Ask a few hundred parents to name their top three worries about their children at any given moment (as I have), and complaints about some form of screens, media use, or "SnapFREAKINGchat!!!!" will pop up in the top five overall. We know we want to do something to manage the technology that has come so recently to surround us. We know that while some of what we do online is great—we learn, we connect, we read, we expand our thinking—some of it leaves us cranky and wondering where the last three hours went. Our kids face the same struggle, but figuring out what sites or gadgets or activities belong on which side of that line is hard and constantly evolving as screens, media, and our children themselves change. It's hard to feel happy and comfortable with our choices when the ground is always shifting under our feet.

What Goes Wrong

What's happening here? For starters, different is always scary, and in no single area are our children's lives more different from our own collective childhoods than when it comes to screens. The amount of media that's available for our consumption now is truly overwhelming, but it may be the change in the way we communicate that's most disturbing to us. Where we hung out in person, passed notes in class, sent letters to pen pals, and spent hours on the phone, our children are hanging out online, posting, texting, messaging, and photo-chatting. The evolution of our civilization is reflected in changes in the way we interact and exchange information, and we are, as individuals, dependent on how we master those skills. It's only to be expected that big changes in how we communicate, changes that make it hard for us to teach our children to do as we have learned, would be disturbing.

When Common Sense Media asked more than one thousand parents to describe their concerns around screen time, most fell into two categories: worries about what the children *aren't* doing (face-to-face conversations, reading, playing outside) and worries about what they *are* (spending too much time watching or playing, using social media, accessing pornography or violent content). Both of those mirror fears older generations have long had about their children: *What are they doing that we didn't do? What will they lose if they don't do as we have always done?*

Add a bonus challenge similar to the one offered by junk food— much of this stuff is designed to be much more exciting and alluring than its real-world counterpart—and then factor in that final element of our own difficulty in handling technology, and you have a recipe for a problem that seems almost designed to suck the fun out of life.

Finding a comfort level with that kind of uncertainty is hard. It means that we can't focus on the apps, gadgets, or sites themselves, all of which can and will change without notice. Instead, we must make choices and set limits, based on deeper family values, and then teach our children to do the same, or admit we're muddling along with them in the same struggle. We are trying to help our children master something that many of us have not mastered ourselves.

Happier Tech for Grown-Ups

It's impossible to write about screen time and a joyful family life without first considering our own screen use. Often, we're ambivalent about it. We set our own goals around our phone use: We'll turn it off an hour before bedtime! We'll take a walk in the woods without it! We struggle with when to return email, how to put our full attention on what we're doing, how much time to spend on social media, and how we feel after a bout of Facebook or Instagram. When Manoush Zomorodi's *Note to Self* podcast on NPR created a project designed to help us manage our information overload, more than twenty-five thousand people joined in.

Some of us are perfectly happy with our screen time. Smartphones and the Internet have been game changers for parents. They've replaced the physical village with a virtual one, which may not be able to babysit, but can answer most questions far more quickly than we can reach a doctor, our own parents, or even a knowledgeable friend. Many of us do our work at least partly online, which enables us to be physically present in our children's lives in ways our parents could not. If we struggle with a particular parenting challenge, we can connect with a community of similarly affected families no matter how rare the issue.

But for many of us, there is a downside: because we can always be connected to a world outside our homes, it gets hard to disconnect. We appreciate the blurring of the line between work and home when it allows us to take a quick call in between innings; we resent it when we feel compelled to respond to a boss's email rather than read bedtime stories. We love sharing our own photos, but when our house is chaos and we're spending spring break snowed in with norovirus, other people's beach pics don't help.

Deciding how we want our family to interact with that digital world means first deciding what we want from it ourselves. It means thinking about what comes first when your attention is being pulled in multiple directions, and why. We're not likely to nail this on our first try. But if we keep the following things in mind when it comes to our own adult screen use, we can pave the way toward a happier family tech experience overall.

GIVE YOURSELF REAL OFFLINE TIME

Many of us carry our phone everywhere, toting it around the house, laying it on the table next to our plate at meals, balancing it on the toilet paper holder in the bathroom. Even if we feel like we're not constantly looking at it, we probably are, and having it always at hand means it's always the go-to in even the smallest moment of downtime.

That is, as I like to tell my kids about some snacks, "not a healthy choice." And it is a choice. Even if you have a job that requires you to be reasonably accessible, or if you have children with a caregiver who needs to be able to reach you, it's okay if it takes a little while. If it's possible for you to turn off your phone during a root canal, you can also do it during a yoga class, a half-hour walk through the park, or a deep-concentration work session. During the evening, and on the weekend, let yourself travel back in time to before your phone was a constant companion. Leave it at home to go to the beach or even the grocery store. Plug the phone in wherever it goes and sit down with a book for an hour.

Make a conscious decision about whether you want the phone at every opportunity, and find ways to make it easier to leave it behind, or to use it only for the purpose you intend. I carry my phone in case of emergencies on horseback trail rides, but I keep it wedged in a strap around my waist that's hard to access, and I put it in there hoping not to take it out until I'm back in the barn. When I run outdoors, I use a similar strap, and I turn on a podcast or music before I start—because I know that if messages pop up, and I can see them, I'll be stumbling along trying to text at 4.4 miles per hour.

The more often you set the phone aside, the more often you'll want to. It's wonderful to know you can reach a friend, entertain yourself, or get help in an emergency at the touch of a button, but it's equally wonderful to know that your time and attention are your own, to give as you choose. What did you do for fun in 2006? Next time you have a few minutes, instead of picking up your smartphone, do that.

ALL OR NOTHING IS BETTER

Let's say you're going to have to work some at home this weekend—two hours on Saturday afternoon. You could do that in a couple of ways: you could shut yourself into your closet for two hours and emerge with the work done, or you could sit at the kitchen counter and work one minute, then answer a kid's question another minute; work two minutes, spend two minutes getting the knot out of someone's hair; work another minute, get up and make someone a sandwich; work five minutes . . . you get the picture. By dinnertime, you're fried, and no one has had any fun.

The first method is going to be a lot more effective.

Every time we switch tasks, we lose time to the switching process. *Decide what you're going to do, then do it.* That in-between state is frustrating for us, and it's frustrating for our kids. Psychologist Catherine Steiner-Adair, author of *The Big Disconnect*, asked one thousand kids how they felt about their parents' smartphones, and the most prevalent answer amounted to "excluded." Kids know when we're not all there, and they don't like it.

You won't always be able to get it right, and even if you do, things will come up. I try to remind the kids that it's the phone—which may look to them like the reason I spent the first period of the hockey game in the parking lot—that makes my job flexible, which is the reason I can drive them to a Friday afternoon tournament game in the first place. It's good for kids to see how you balance responsibilities, too.

DON'T SET A DIGITAL DOUBLE STANDARD

Someday, if they don't already, your children will have their own phones, laptops, and tablets. How they use them will reflect how you've used yours. If your phone has been a regular presence at the dinner table, theirs will be, too. If you regularly look at a screen instead of at them when they're talking to you, they will someday do the same.

The two rules above—give yourself time offline, and all or

nothing is better—establish standards you'd like your children to use later. We don't want our kids to be on their phones during family meals. We want them to be able to set the phone aside for a conversation with the people who are with them in the room or the car, or even at the grocery store. If they've grown up watching us use a phone as a tool, not a constant companion, it will be easier to teach them to do the same. If we've told them we will be spending the next forty-five minutes managing work emails, and then we will put our laptop away—and followed through—then it will be easier, later, to say something like "Please finish texting with your friends and then join us for miniature golf."

It will also be easier to accept reasonable screen time and phone use from your teens. It's fun to be able to text your friends a picture of your hole-in-one under the swinging dinosaur tail, whether you're fourteen or forty. This isn't to suggest that you have to follow the same rules and limits around screen time that you set for your children, or even your teenagers. But if you share family values around how and when you connect or go online, setting those limits and keeping them will come more naturally than if you try to persuade your children to do as you say, not as you do.

IF YOU CAN DO IT OFFLINE, DO

If you value what you'd consider non-digital activities, like reading and writing, yet you tend to do those things in digital ways (ebooks and email), maybe it's worth making a concentrated effort to show your kids how much time you put into those things by removing them from your gadget (where, as far as your kids are concerned, you could be playing the latest addictive game) and bringing them visibly, ostentatiously, back into the physical world.

In other words, why not read a book or paper magazine, and sub-scribe to the paper version of your local newspaper or a favorite na-tional publication? Send a card or a letter to a friend? Draw a few pictures, write in a journal, doodle on a grocery list?

Reading an actual book in the evening or on a plane or at the beach is one way to counteract that sense of imbalance we sometimes have about the ways our devices consume our waking hours. A physi-cal book does not contain within it the siren song of email or social media. Notifications from various news sources will not drop down onto its pages. And your children will know, without a doubt, what you're doing. You're reading. Quietly engrossed in the printed word.

You might find you prefer it. I do, although I don't mind reading ebooks and in fact use the larger iPhone so that I can read on that screen if an unexpected opportunity presents itself. Many children and teenagers say they prefer physical books, too—64 percent of teenagers told a (surprised) British marketing research firm that print books were their favorite, while just 16 percent preferred ebooks (the rest were indifferent).

Printed newspapers and magazines have another strength: they are themselves alluring. If you want to raise a child who's informed by the *Dallas Morning News* or the *New York Times*, the constant arrival and departure of physical copies of those is the best possible recipe. The front-page headlines and images are designed to evoke curiosity, and the presence of all the available topics, from sports to crime to human interest, as well as the ever-shrinking comic pages, increases the odds that a curious child will pick one up. The same goes for magazines. If you want to raise a *New Yorker* addict, the covers and cartoons are the gateway drug.

CONDUCT AN ANNUAL SOCIAL MEDIA AUDIT

Want your kids to have good social media practices later? Start with yours now. Somewhat dubious statistics suggest that most parents put a picture of their newborns on social media within the first hour of the child's life. That's followed by milestones and candid shots and family photos and funny stories and more (to the point where some childless friends may find subtle ways to say "Don't show me more like this").

There comes a point, though, when your children might prefer that you shared less. When researchers studied 249 parent-child pairs distributed across forty states, they found that, for the most part, kids and parents agreed on what tech rules families should have: don't text and drive; don't be online when someone wants to talk to you. But while children ages ten to seventeen wanted rules for how their parents shared things about them on social media, their parents, for the most part, didn't even put that on the list. We don't even think about it. When Karen Lock Kolp's Facebook page popped up a video she had posted of her son as a four-year-old five years earlier, imitating Gandalf the wizard declaring, "You shall not pass," she reshared it immediately and called her then-nine-year-old to see.

He was humiliated. "Please," he said, "do *not* share that again." Since then, she asks first, posts second.

If you're prone to posting things on social media now that your child might not appreciate later, balance your desire to share with future searchability. Send the video to a few friends instead of putting it up on YouTube; keep bath-time photos in your personal cloud. I once, during my time as the editor of the *New York Times'* parenting and family column, received an essay from a writer about her concern that her infant son's penis was too small. The writing was good, the topic probably one with which many parents could relate—and yet. I explained, as gently as I could, that I was rejecting the submission on behalf of her future teenager. There are some things that don't belong in the *Times.*

Keep in mind that even young children can feel exposed when their lives are too public. Your six-year-old might be a little surprised, and a little resentful, if a neighbor asks if the tooth fairy returned the tooth she took last weekend—thanks to your post about the resulting tears. Your eight-year-old will be mortified if the rabbi or pastor asks if she's going to do better on her spelling test next week. Some family things should be kept in the family.

REMEMBER, YOUR FUTURE DRIVERS ARE WATCHING

One last thought about you and your phone—if you aren't putting that phone aside while you drive already, start doing it now, in a big, loud, pointed way. "I'm putting my phone in my bag because I'm driving!" you should say. "I'm not answering my phone even on the hands-free because I'm merging onto the highway!"

Pull over to send a text. Have a child read you texts and type replies if you really must be in contact while you drive. Pull over to set up a new podcast or audio book, or to have a conversation that involves anything more than just "Yes, we're having trouble finding a parking place."

Don't touch the phone while the car is moving.

Why? Because that toddler in the backseat will be the driver in the front seat one day, and he is watching and learning from what you do far more than from what you say. You may think you can glance down at your phone real quick and then back up at the road (you're wrong). But do you want your sixteen-year-old to do the same?

If you don't want them to do it while they're driving, you can't do it while you're driving.

Kids and Teens and Screens: Limits That Leave Room to Grow

We're parents. We set limits; that's what we do. If we haven't actively set them, it's often because our unspoken limits haven't been pushed up against—yet. Screen time is not an exception. When I first began drafting this chapter, I thought I'd be considering two perspectives. Call them "the case for limits" and "the case against limits." But there was a catch, and a big one: I couldn't find any parents who didn't have any limits at all. Many initially said they didn't have limits, and I presume those are the same parents who respond to surveys by saying they don't set limits on either content or time spent online.

But dig a little deeper, and it's quickly clear that "no limits" is a fiction. "No limits" means no set rules, not a household online Wild Wild West. Some parents said they had no set limits, but that they did put a stop to watching or playing if they perceived that it had gone on too long. Others limited passive but not active uses, or had no limits on certain games and shows "as long as chores and homework were done first." Parents might allow iPad games and interactive books mixed in with everything else in the toy box but limit television, or allow unlimited television (on the theory that it would get old after a while) but not gaming. They might not restrict a teen's use, but still require that the phone stay downstairs at bedtime or turn off the Internet at a certain hour. And even the very most permissive of parents limited content, with violent first-person shooter games having age limits and porn off-limits entirely. Show me a parent with "no limits," and I'll show you a parent whose child hasn't tried to download *The Many Faces of Death*. The question isn't whether you need limits. It's how specific and spoken those limits will be.

We're right to set boundaries in this area. Children need structure in their lives, and providing that structure (even if it's just a sense that we're not going to let them watch or play for "too long") helps them feel like part of a steady, secure, predictable system, which makes almost everyone happier. Technology is specifically designed to make all of us—young children, teenagers, and parents, too—want more. Limits help us combat a force that's larger than we are.

But while we should be looking for the right limits to use with our family (more on that later), we shouldn't be panicking over letting our children, even very young children, watch and play in moderation, and in ways that work for us. Even the American Academy of Pediatrics recently revised its guidelines away from suggesting "no" media for children under two. Some screen time with age-appropriate material is fine for kids.

On the other hand, research on whether some media can actually benefit children, usually by teaching them something they did not know before, is limited and somewhat inconclusive, but that's okay, too. If you're the parent of a baby, toddler, or preschooler, and you just need a break to take a shower, you don't need that break to actively teach your child Mandarin Chinese. You just need to be able to take it without guilt—and you can. A little bit of video, designed to let you catch your breath, regain your patience, shower, or have an uninter-rupted conversation with a friend, will have no observable effects on your child's future.

For children at every age—and even for yourself—don't think of your technology rules as limiting something dangerous. Instead, think about them as protecting something valuable: the time you and your children spend, together and separately, doing other things. That time does need protection, because there is an entire industry dedicated to pulling you and your kids away from reality and into a world populated with advertising, consumer messages, and in-app purchases. Remember, too, that protection is not enough. Your goal is not only to control the ways your children interact with screens, but to teach them, as they grow, to control themselves.

Setting Limits for Happier Screen Time

The "right" rules and limits look different for different families. Ask your peers what they do (as I did) and you're likely to get answers that range from a total ban (usually for younger children) to "we just yell at them when it's too much" (heard especially from parents of teenagers with smartphones). There are a whole lot of ways to get this right, and a clear need for our policies to evolve as both our gadgets and our children change. We're not working toward an absolute, but toward a balance that blends technology with everything else we want to do in life.

Like nearly everyone else, I've wrestled with the question "What kind of limit should we set?" against a constantly changing landscape of what, exactly, we were limiting. I set our family policy long ago, when my oldest child was eight and his younger siblings five, three, and three. I had the first iPhone, but it was far too precious to allow little hands to hold. iPads didn't exist. I was limiting a desktop computer, a portable DVD player with limited battery life, a Nintendo system, and satellite television—and yet, the policy I came up with then still works for us today.

As much as I'd like to tell you that our screen-time policy reflected much deep thinking about our family values and our future, it did not. Instead, it was entirely based on how much I hated the begging and negotiating that had begun to surround any kind of media time. *Can I watch a show? Can I? Can I? Why not? Can I? Just one? Just part of one? Can I play my DS then? Just for a few minutes? Can I? Why not? Can I? Can I?* Our younger daughter even had a special abbreviation for "Can I": *Ki? Ki watch? Ki play? Ki? Ki?*

I needed a rule that would let them answer the question for themselves. My goal wasn't really to lessen their time with video games and screens, which was in a fine place, but to lessen my involvement with it. I considered time limits, but how would I track them? If each child had an hour on the single computer, how would that work if three kids wanted it an hour before bedtime? If everyone had an hour of TV a day, would that end up being four hours, or would I be banishing children who'd used their hour from the room with the TV? I knew I'd be forever setting timers and repeating "It's time to get off" and giving warnings and dealing with "Just one more minute" and "I'm almost done."

So instead of "how long" limits, we set a black-and-white "when" limit: nothing on weekdays, open season on weekends unless things got out of hand, with any complaints or whining about a "turn it off" request being met with an immediate removal of the next day's privileges. I was willing to be hard-core about that (in part because I was always happy to have an excuse to turn the screens off entirely), and I think it only took twice before they figured out that I meant it. When school breaks and summer vacation rolled around, we kept the same clear rules and found an unexpected benefit: with clearly defined times when video entertainment just wasn't available, the kids always had an expectation that some days they'd be doing other things.

Those rules have worked for us for eight years, and they're largely working still. I might not have sat down with our family values in mind when I came up with the weekends-only rule, but I turned out to hit upon the one thing about screen time that mattered to me most. My kids internalized the idea that there should be a limit, and that they should know what it was and stick to it. (Amazingly, in all this time, we've only had a child sneak screen time once.) Having established rules contributes to our family happiness, and mine: everyone knows what to expect, and even when technology changes, the rules are simple enough to stay the same. We also tell children when they've had enough, if we need to (it's amazing how many hours a child can spend with a screen over the course of a rainy Saturday).

When our two older children were able to buy their own phones and laptops, we asked them to respect the rules regarding games and television, and they do. So far, we haven't had to limit their phone time—which doesn't mean we won't. They've had the experience of realizing they've frittered away a day they'd meant to spend doing something else with time online, and they don't like it. They have learned (slowly) that the limits in place on other media help them do other things they love or just things they need to get done. I encourage them frequently to apply that knowledge to their phone, to keep their notifications off so that they control when they choose to engage, and to be aware that time spent scrolling Instagram doesn't usually feel good later and is often a sign that you're not feeling great in the first place.

Don't imagine that this doesn't mean I'm not driving along telling my daughter to put her phone away and to tell me about her day at school, because I am. But they use an app that tells them how much time they're spending texting and scrolling (it's called Moment, and I use it, too), and they are slowly coming to see the value in leaving the phone across the room when they do homework or in their pocket when they're out with the family. The limits they've been following for years have set the tone for limiting themselves.

But as much as I like our rules, they're not for everyone. When you're trying to set your own family tech rules, you'll consider both your own preferences and the age and needs of your kids, and you'll need to be open as things and kids change. In this case, *you don't have to get it right every time* translates to *you don't have to get it right the first time*. You're allowed to make adjustments as you go—in fact, you'll probably have to. Here's what you should be thinking about for younger children and middle graders in a household where media access is largely through devices controlled by parents, and what you should consider later, when the children possess media access points (phones, tablets, laptops) of their own.

Tech Limits for Young Children

WHAT'S OUR PROBLEM WITH MEDIA (AND DO WE HAVE ONE)?

Parents of young children who aren't happy about the household's screen time tend to have one of two problems. Either the children are watching or playing too much, or they're begging and pleading too much. Even when the screen time itself isn't an issue, the negotiations around it can make anyone crazy.

If neither moderating nor negotiating screen time is an active problem, you may not need to codify what's working. You probably already have what amounts to an effective policy, even if it's just "you can watch when I say you can." Don't mess with what works, even if part of the reason that it works is that it works *for you*. If you're good where you are, there's no need to change to conform to someone else's ideal.

Our oldest child, as a preschooler, regularly got up at five a.m. His infant sister kept us up nights, but often slept in the mornings, from four until about eight. On the weekend, one of us would get up with our son, give him a tray of breakfast, set up some form of video or television long enough to maximize our sleep, and then stagger back upstairs. If he watched a full three hours of television at that point we counted it a victory for our health and sanity, even if the American Academy of Pediatrics, which recommends no more than an hour a day of media at that age, might have thought we needed more limits.

If what you're doing isn't working, take the time to think about what the problem is. Like me, you may feel that your kids aren't watching or playing too much—but you yourself are spending too much time and energy negotiating over every minute. If that's the case, setting a limit might not change your kids' overall screen time, but it might save your sanity.

ARE YOU IN CONTROL?

One of the first questions you should answer as you consider what's happening with your family and screen time is this: who's the decider? Do you choose what, when, and where they watch or play, or are you more likely to be giving in to their requests (or demands)? When your children are young, most of their media choices should really be your media choices. If, by any chance, you don't feel that's true—if you're feeling at the mercy of your child's begging or insisting or weeping or tantrums when it comes to what, or how much, she watches or plays—then know that you can take that control back. If you set a limit, and you stick to it, eventually that limit will become routine.

This may take what feels like a lot of time, and it may require removing a phone, tablet, or laptop that your child has come to consider "his." But it is far easier to regain your sense of control over your child's media at this age now than it will be later. If the transition to "off" is a trouble area with toddlers or preschoolers, try using the technology to help you wherever you can. In one small study, parents found that turning off continuous play on videos or digital players, using a DVR with only one show recorded, or taking advantage of tools that cause digital gadgets to shut down after a certain amount of time can ease transitions. You can also install limits on computers or video-delivery services, and even set your house Wi-Fi to turn off at a certain time.

Here, as with nearly everything, giving in to whining or repeated requests only invites more of the same next time. You might even consider, as we did, making any demand to extend time or change the limit grounds to take away the next watching or playing session, especially if continual whining for more screen time has really become a drain on your ability to enjoy your family time. It's fine to be what your kids may consider unreasonably harsh in this area, especially while you're making changes to limits. Did I mention that there is no evidence that some digital media use harms kids? There is no evidence that *no* digital media harms them, either.

DO YOUR KIDS KNOW THE GOAL?

Limiting screen time and ending the begging is only half the battle. What you really hope to be doing is establishing a baseline for how much is enough, and teaching your children to make their own decisions about that later and stick to them. So talk about why you're limiting screen time and making healthy media choices. If your child's school has a media education program, or the pediatrician asks them about time spent online, use that to your advantage. Would your child want to tell her doctor or teacher that she spent six hours playing a video game or watching a cartoon? If she wouldn't, why not? Our kids often have a sense that they need limits—make sure that instinct becomes a concrete belief in the importance of moderating time spent on screens.

WHAT'S IMPORTANT ENOUGH TO PLUG THE KIDS IN?

Let's not indulge any illusions around the benefits of screen time—for adults. It really is a free babysitter, even if not one that lets you head out for a night on the town. When you need them to be distracted, you can achieve it, so take time to consider how you want to use that power (and keep in mind that for most children, especially young children, the magic wears off with overuse). Will you offer a device or video on an airplane? We did and do. At the grocery store or during errands? We didn't and don't. There's a lot to be seen, learned, and experienced while shopping. In the car? Long trips were a yes for us, but we never used a video for anything under an hour. Car time is great talking time. Setting a precedent that it's watching and playing time now is probably something you'll regret later. At the doctor's office? In general, this was a no for us with an exception. Research suggests that video games can work as pain relievers under some circumstances, and they certainly relieve anxiety for many children. When a shot or a scary procedure is in store, the tablets come out.

At a restaurant? When our oldest son (now fifteen) was a toddler, we decided that, because we love to eat out, and we expected him to learn to enjoy that experience with us, we wouldn't offer him any distractions at the table beyond a book, crayons, or small toys. That was sometimes difficult. We left a lot of food behind when his behavior was disruptive, and I spent a lot more time than I would have liked dividing my attention between a good meal and a picture book. At the same time, we had close friends who simply brought a DVD player to restaurant meals. They ate and talked; their child ate and watched.

I admit it, we mocked them.

But that child is now fifteen, too, and is a lovely human being, not overly attached to devices, not at all inclined to watch *Dora the Explorer* during meals, and every bit as delightful and successful at being a person in the world, and in restaurants, as my son. This makes me a little resentful, and I'm still inclined to say that videos shouldn't be used as a pacifier in a situation in which a child should learn to behave. But as long as you're not always offering a gadget instead of doing the harder work that teaching a child what's appropriate in a public place entails, it's all going to come out in the wash.

DO I WANT PARTICULAR TIMES OR DAYS TO BE ENTIRELY TECH FREE?

You may be willing to allow your children to use gadgets and media pretty freely for an hour a day, or to let them watch a daily TV show or play games for a certain amount of time or after doing certain tasks. But if there is a time of day, like before school, when no form of media use will work for your family, or a time when certain uses will conflict with what you or others need to get done (one child gaming while another does homework, or children watching television you dislike nearby while you're making dinner), then build that into your policy.

DO I WANT TO DISTINGUISH BETWEEN TOYS AND TOOLS?

Some media uses are passive (watching videos), some active but in ways that don't require much thought or creativity (many video games), some are nominally educational (a category to be regarded with suspicion, unless a child is actually doing homework), and some are creative (meaning they encourage the creation or production of something—a game, a video, a song, a poem—that did not exist before). When your children are old enough to understand that difference, you can shift your screen time limit to allow them to use screens as tools (eventually you will have to do this for homework in any case). If children want to write or code or read using a device, or if they have an app that allows them to measure or identify constellations or design a T-shirt, that's a form of screen time you'll want to encourage (in moderation). If you're lucky, they'll find they prefer creating to using the creations of others.

HOW INVOLVED DO I WANT TO BE IN ENFORCING THE POLICY?

One reason I chose our weekends-only policy was that even the youngest child could distinguish a weekend from a weekday during the school year, and my older kids could remind the others the rest of the time. One parent told me that his children are allowed a minute of digital media for every minute of reading. My mind boggled. I saw that as involving an astronomical amount of monitoring; for them, it works.

WHAT ABOUT SCHOOL-PROVIDED TECH?

Some schools provide a tablet or laptop to each child as long as they're a student at the school. Those schools also usually attempt to limit what can be done on the device, but it's the rare child who can't get around those limits, and the Internet access the devices provide creates the opportunity to do a lot of watching videos and messaging under the guise of "homework." Kids with school-provided tech will need to develop the ability to monitor themselves, but you'll need to discuss with your child how you'll help her focus on schoolwork when distractions beckon, and how your policies will be enforced when you can't realistically quarantine the gadget. While they're learning, consider having them do any online homework in a public space, where you can easily glance over and see what's on the screen—even if it means quieting other distractions. A little quiet never hurt anyone.

WHAT'S RIGHT FOR MY KIDS?

Some children will stick to limits more easily than others—and some are just less interested in various forms of media. Many families have different limits for different children, because "not too much" works for one, while another needs "one hour a day, two on the weekends" because she will max out that time. In families like mine, where unequal treatment would create disharmony (oh, how mild that sounds, compared to what the actual result would be), the tech rule may be set to the lowest common denominator, with exceptions granted when appropriate.

DO I WANT TECH TO BE A REWARD?

Many families allow tech after chores and homework are done, as a prize for good behavior or grades or as a trade-off for other desired activities (usually reading). Others worry that setting up tech as the ultimate goal of reading or finishing other tasks discourages an appreciation for reading in itself, or glorifies the tech above all other forms of fun. But families who do use the "reward" policy are happy with it—and it gels with the way many adults use everything from television to social media to games as a reward or a way to wind down when the work is done. "My kids have a weekly chart of responsibilities we created each worth one minute of playing time," says Alexai Perez, a mother of three in Florida. "We also hand out consequence slips, which deduct two minutes of playing time, for noncompliant behavior after being asked and reminded once. We add up all the minutes (usually works out to about an hour or an hour and a half of earned time). They get to use their time playing on the weekends only after daily chores are completed."

Teaching children to monitor themselves in this way can help them do the same as teenagers, although you will probably need to suggest it to them and help them stick to it, maybe by holding a phone until homework is done or showing them the kinds of tools adults use to keep their technology in a "work" mode until they've met their goals.

IS THERE CERTAIN CONTENT I WANT TO AVOID?

Some programming or games might be acceptable in some homes, but not in yours. Violent or sexual content is an obvious place for limits, but you might have other household no-goes. Some toddler programming might grate on your nerves (for example, the whining of PBS's *Caillou*). Many families actively forbid tween sitcoms from networks like Disney and Nickelodeon (as one friend told me, "We blocked Disney and Nick on the TV because it made her obnoxious"). The day your daughter puts her hands on her hips and dons an unfamiliar cutesy expression and tone before declaring, "You're a big fat meanie!" and flouncing off may be the last day for certain shows at your house. Some parents even forbid all television on the same grounds. Another friend, during the same conversation, said, "We stopped letting them watch TV one day because we realized that they were bigger jerks when they did." *You do you.* My children know certain shows can't be watched within my hearing, because the plots and performances drive me wild, and worse, from their perspective: they bring me into the room to comment on the gender stereotyping, the dumb choices, the way the characters treat one another, or just the sheer stupidity of it all.

Apparently this isn't as much fun for them as it is for me, which makes this a rule we can all agree on.

WHAT HAPPENS AT OTHER PEOPLE'S HOUSES?

Tech rules obviously differ from house to house. Few parents object to their children coming home after a sleepover having used far less media than they might have spent time with at home, but when it's the other way around, some worry. Whether you'll talk to the other parent is a separate question (and unless you're very close and the play is frequent, I would address nothing other than the question of scary TV and movies or age-inappropriate games). But will you expect your child to adhere to your rules at someone else's house? Erin Brown Croarkin limits her eight- and ten-year-olds to an hour a day, weekends only. "They cannot have it at a friend's house if they have had it at our house," she says. "Right now, they are honest."

I don't expect my children to take our rules elsewhere (other than those around appropriate content), but I do ask that they follow other house's rules and ask their friends to follow ours—and not spend a friend's visit, or a visit to a friend's house, online unless they're online together.

WILL MY CHILD CHEAT?

If you don't feel that you can trust your child not to try to get around the media-use rules you set, it's even more important to set rules that are easy for you to monitor and enforce. Consider things like whether your child is frequently alone with the opportunity to use digital media (including an iPad or gaming device), and how likely you are to use other forms of monitoring, like checking the timing of DVR use or looking at browser histories, in order to know what's happening when you're not looking.

Consider, too, what you might do if your child does cheat. When my younger son was eight, he ordered a game for his Nintendo device that he was incredibly excited about. It arrived on Tuesday. Tuesday! *Days* until the weekend, when he could use it!

That night, after bedtime, I walked into his room and caught him playing. He was, I think, genuinely remorseful, but he still lost game and device privileges for the entire next weekend (as well as all other media use). That same child has given in to temptation a few times since, and we both learned that he needed external limits for a while. I held the devices, controlled the passwords, and reminded him of the consequences. When he got older, we gradually loosened up so that he needed to rely on his own willpower again, but it's something he and I talk about more than I do with his siblings.

DO I HAVE SAFETY AND PRIVACY CONCERNS?

Prepare to discuss your family rules around things like logging into multi-player online games, using a parent's email to sign into websites, use of the desktop camera, and sharing of passwords. And, of course, as your child joins different gaming or social platforms, you'll want to revisit those rules, as well as any family rules about what can be shared online.

THE TWO-HOUSEHOLD QUESTION

If you parent with a partner but maintain two separate households, this question becomes even more challenging. Even partners who live together need to take time to agree on a policy and how it will be enforced. When you and your child's other parent aren't on good terms, this can become one more thing you don't discuss or don't agree on.

"My almost-six-year-old gets about twenty to forty minutes on weeknights. Friday nights are pizza and movie night. And she gets an hour or two on Saturdays and Sundays," says one mother. "My struggle is that she gets a lot more at her dad's house. I already feel like I'm pretty liberal, although I will take it away if she starts getting cranky or bratty. But I can see the impact of her coming home from Dad's after an entire day of screens. And there's not a damn thing I can do."

Parents who think their child spends more time with digital media in a second household might try working with the child to set an overall limit—one that covers both houses and allows most of the screen time to take place there without turning you into the bad guy. Many schools and pediatricians' offices talk about limiting screen time, and parents in a tough co-parenting situation can turn this to their advantage, maybe by helping the child create a chart that echoes a limit suggested by some other source, and talking about how that three-movie marathon last weekend was fun, but might mean it's a good idea to do other things this weekend.

Of course, especially with younger children, the parental benefits to a child taking some screen time can be considerable, and if you're losing all of those to an ex, you're bound to be frustrated. While the situation evolves, you may just have to let what happens there stay there, while you focus on setting the right balance in your own house.

Setting a Family Media Policy for Preteens and Teens

Your control over limits—and how much control you should have over those limits—shifts again once your children have their own devices and particularly their own phones or networked tablets, which aren't even limited by their ability to access a wireless network. The age at which that happens differs widely from family to family. In ours, children are required to purchase their own devices (using savings and their allowance) and, if the device is a phone or a networked tablet, pay their share of the family data plan. My oldest did this at thirteen, my next oldest at twelve, and as I write, I'm allowing my eleven-year-old a much freer hand with spending her allowance in silly ways (in-app purchases, nail polish kits) to ensure that she's not able to afford a phone before I think she can handle one.

Just because the kids purchase the devices (which includes laptops) doesn't mean the devices don't still have to adhere to our rules, but it's around the point when a phone is acquired and homework begins to be done online that many families find limits need to evolve. What worked when you controlled access points loses its power once a child can do more for herself—witness the jump from two to three hours of screen time for younger kids up to six hours and more for eight- to twelve-year-olds, who are more likely to have their own devices or at least more able to work the remote. Older children need to respect the limits you've set, which means they need to believe in the importance of the rules and in your ability and willingness to enforce them.

MAKE SCREEN BALANCE A FAMILY GOAL

If you're lucky, you've been having conversations about why you limit screen time all along, but if you haven't, start. If you yourself struggle to set limits, own the challenge. Show your teenagers the apps you use to help resist the siren song of social media while working, and describe the temptation to answer emails (easy!) instead of drafting notes for a major project (hard!). Describe your own goals around screen time, and then ask them to talk about theirs. They might re-member a vacation when you spent too much time working (which, while not screen time, can feel like it to a kid), and those memories can fuel a conversation about why it's important to establish times when you're in the online world and times when you're not.

The following questions can help you start that conversation, but remember the decision about what rules and limits your family should follow belongs with the adults, not the teenagers. Sometimes, you'll need to tighten things up, and rein back in use that's become too much. Other times, you may listen to a well-reasoned proposal for a loosening of the rules. Do listen to your children on the topic of screen time, but don't give up your authority. Our kids need our honesty and our guidance. You may still be evolving in your own tech use, but you know a lot that they don't about balance, relationships, and what's truly important in life. Screen time is just another area in which all of the usual challenges play out.

What is the screen for? It's a good question—what do you want to do with your phone? What do you want it to help you do? What do you want from the computer or the television? Distraction, entertainment, background noise? Connection? Information? Is what you're doing with the screen consistent with what you hoped you'd do? Is it helping you to be happier or better or to reach a goal? Or is it getting in your way?

By the time they're in their tweens and teens, most of our children have thoughts of their own about how they want to interact with screens. Many of their schools have digital manners and media literacy discussions, as do pediatricians and physical education or health classes. As well, they're part of the same ongoing cultural conversation that we are. They know we're all, as a society, working to balance life online and off, and they probably have stories about kids who spend too much time on their phones or gaming. What they actually do with their phones and devices may not appear at first glance to fit in with their feelings about kids who do nothing but text and Snapchat all day, but then, aren't we the parents who spend seven-plus hours a day on personal screen time? This stuff is hard, and there's no point in pretending it isn't. Talking about the things we want our devices to help us do and feel in the real world helps us keep our daily small choices about when and if we pick them up in line with our larger goals.

Even once you've agreed on the family values that are reflected in the ways you use technology, the devil is in the details. Homework certainly isn't "screen time," but is texting? How about watching a YouTube video your friend sent as a link? What about watching the video your friend made or making one yourself? Here are some questions you can use to start a discussion with your older child, whether it's a dinner-table sit-down or a few assorted car talks. Their answers can help you work together to set a formal family media policy, or just talk about what is and isn't working at your house.

> How much television or video or any form of screen watching or playing would you consider reasonable on a school night?
>
> Do you want to consume, or do you want to create?
>
> When is the latest you think you should be sending or receiving a text?
>
> Is it hard for you not to look at your phone while you do homework? What would help?
>
> What are some things you like to do on the weekend? How much of that time do you want to spend on watching things and video games?
>
> Should that be different if you have a friend over?
>
> What will you do if you get a text that's scary or sexy or otherwise worries you?
>
> When your friends are angry with one another, how do you see them using their online connection? How will you use yours?

It's also fine to share your worst-case scenario concerns. If there's media coverage of a particularly outrageous example of poor online behavior, talk about it. Say, directly, how you'd hope your child would behave, even as they're shrieking, "My friends would never share nude pictures/live-post a rape/create a Facebook group for misogynist content about a women's sports team." Of course they wouldn't. But when they do, you want your children to hear your words echoing in their ears as they refuse to join in.

Where do the devices go at night? There's a conventional right answer on this. Late-night device usage can interfere with sleep, both because of the light and because as we become more and more tired, it can become more and more difficult to turn off temptation. We also make bad choices at night. We're our worst selves, saying the things we least want to have said, to the people we least want to hear them—not a good time to be on social media.

All of this is prevented if the devices, whatever they are, don't go to bed with us. Holly Buffington Stevens, a mother of a seventh grader and a ninth grader in Atlanta, requires her kids to leave their school laptops and phones in the charging cabinet in the kitchen when the family heads (admirably, all at about the same time) upstairs for reading and bedtime. "Same goes with friends when they sleep over—we take their phones before bedtime. I'm always amazed by the number of texts my kids receive from their friends relatively late at night."

I think that's an excellent requirement, and I even went so far as to create a big public charging area for our many and varied family gadgetry—but at least as of this writing, we don't require our kids to use it. Some do, some don't, some vary. I use my phone as an alarm, and so does my husband. My daughter reads on an iPad at night (new settings allow you to adjust the light emitted so that it should not interfere as much with sleep). Sometimes my kids use a device as an alarm clock, too. We talk about late-night texting and surfing, and we periodically check to see if there's a problem.

I recognize, though, that it's a heavy temptation, sitting there, all night. I'm not wholly convinced that ours is the right choice on this one. It's just what works for us now, which is sometimes the best you can do.

Should you keep tabs—and how? After all these conversations and choices, you're still far from done. You and your child have to live with the plans you've made, and if you've imposed any limits, you have to consider whether and how you'll check on your child's compliance. These decisions are all about building trust, but sometimes you need to trust—and verify.

How we do that monitoring, though, varies greatly and isn't necessarily what you'd expect. Relatively few parents rely on outside tools such as parental software controls or tracking programs to oversee their children's lives online. I've explored many options for either limiting or monitoring various screens, only to reject them for two reasons: first, I haven't found any that wouldn't be fairly easy for a child to thwart, and second, I want my children to rely on their own self-control instead of mine. It's tempting to imagine I could outsource this whole digital media thing in favor of yet another device or app that would enforce the limits I set, or fool myself into thinking I had an all-seeing eye on what my children were doing online, but there are no shortcuts for doing the hard work of teaching, talking, and, sometimes, enforcing.

Instead, we must focus on our own ability to talk to and guide our children in what might seem like a new world but is in so many respects just an extension of the same culture we've always inhabited.

That's good for children (many experts, like Catherine Steiner-Adair and Devorah Heitner, advise against depending on external monitoring) and it's good for parents. Parents who are actively involved in talking with their children about usage, content, and sharing describe themselves as more confident in their parenting abilities, which is generally correlated with overall life satisfaction. In this case, a sense of interaction and involvement—asking questions, offering opinions, and talking about what we all watch and play—makes us happier.

How that looks in practice varies enormously. Considerations include a child's age, his personality, and the social arena in which he moves. For most parents, the mentoring and monitoring process is an evolution, inevitably in the direction of less oversight (you won't be checking up on them when they're in college), but often with blips of more intense supervision, especially when mistakes are made. That evolution from parent monitoring to self-monitoring is an important one, and if you help them do it while they're still under your roof, that will be one less transition to manage as they move into adulthood.

ADDING SOCIAL MEDIA INTO THE MIX

There are entire books dedicated to the topic of tweens, teens, and social media. (I recommend *Screenwise*, *The Big Disconnect*, and *Social Media Wellness*.) For many families, it's a challenge, as kids experience an extension of their social lives with which we can't directly relate but which many are finding is, ultimately, just another piece of the familiar puzzle that is growing up.

Families make dramatically different decisions around children and social media, from four-year-olds who are "Instafamous" to fourteen-year-olds who have themselves decided to give the whole thing a miss. Whatever your choices, every time your child joins a new form of social media, that new platform should include a discussion of how your child plans to use it and a demonstration of the perils: "Look! Viral embarrassing YouTube video." "Look! That disappearing Snapchat, captured forever with a screen shot! I can do that with that text you sent about your secret crush on Emma, too, you know." "Hey, wanna hear about the time my friend Wendi's kid posted his brother's phone number on Instagram and said it belonged to Justin Bieber?" Discuss with your child if you're going to check in on her use of the new network, how, and when.

You can talk, too, about the things we can all feel when we're watching other people's carefully cultivated lives scroll by. We miss parties, we're not invited to things, we aren't taking a cool vacation, we don't look like that in a swimsuit. Be blunt about how people's shared images don't always match their lives. It may not feel kind to use an example from among your friends and acquaintances, but kids need exactly that kind of dose of reality. "You know Finn's mom almost never looks like that." "Remember, you were at that birthday party, and the birthday girl had a temper tantrum and left crying right after the cake." Remind them that you can look around and snap a beautiful Instagram image at any moment, no matter how much reality bites.

TEACH TECH MANAGEMENT

As your kids learn to self-monitor, they also need to learn to use their technology, but not to depend on it. That means understanding all the ways games and apps are set up to keep you coming back with notifications and alerts designed to pull a quick click (and that includes news, email, and messaging apps). Teenagers hate to be manipulated or told what to do—so make sure they know that's exactly what the grown-ups at their favorite apps and games are attempting. As cool and edgy as things online may appear, they're designed to make money and spread advertising. The real rebellion is in resisting the bait and making your own choices about what you want to do online and how. Help teenagers and older children decide which few things they actually need to flicker across the screen of their phone, and teach them to work and socialize with the phone facedown (and ideally silent) when that's appropriate. Show them how to set up their own "do not disturb" preferences as well.

RELAX

Finally, whenever you find yourself caught up in all the stress and worry that our new connected world has brought, remember: this Internet thing is fun. Cat videos. Instant access to that *Simpsons* scene where they're all in family therapy. That one friend you text with off and on all day long.

We can binge watch an old or new favorite TV show with kids on a miserable wet weekend, download movies instantly, order up a favorite song to spark dinner cleanup, send a kid a picture of an elephant wearing colorful Indian pajamas when he emerges from his algebra final. We can make a family video holiday card, turn a toddler shouting "Yo Mama!" into a ringtone, and find a used copy of *Anne of Green Gables* with exactly the cover ours had as a kid.

It's not "digital life." It's just life. Let your kids waste time. Waste some with them. Find a screen to share. Dare to believe that it will be okay.

seven

DISCIPLINE: THIS HURTS ME MORE THAN IT HURTS YOU

D iscipline, that fine art of getting children to behave in a way that meets the standards of their family and community, is hard. So hard that when I invited the 1,050 people who responded to my research survey on parenting to fill in an open blank with the answer to "what they enjoyed least" when it came to raising kids, the largest grouping of answers, just under a third, offered some variation on "discipline": "Enforcing rules, taking away privileges." "I don't like having to punish my children." "Discipline. I know it's important to have consequences, but it is still hard to discipline." "When I have to be hard on my kids to teach them right from wrong." "Having to make rules for them and stick with it." "Having to take stuff away for bad behavior." "Punishing my child, even though I know it's for his own good."

There's the minor stuff: run-of-the-mill issues such as reining in the child who would prefer to run amok in the grocery store, tear across the parking lot, skip the homework, and stay out late with her friends. Then there's the major stuff. No child, no matter how well and tenderly taught right from wrong, gets through childhood without blowing it big-time, and suddenly, the guidance that is everyday parenting does not feel like enough. There must be consequences. Time-outs. Lost privileges. Lectures. Grounding. And there will be recriminations—yours, at a minimum. Did you not teach this child right? Tell her not to draw on the back of the couch, bite her brother until he bleeds, put the dog in the wagon and push it down the driveway, use your iTunes password to spend $243 on in-app purchases, smoke pot?

Of course you did. Or you tried. And while tomorrow may be the day to review those lessons (and tonight the night to think about how you're conveying them), first comes the moment when the child who has really done wrong is standing in front of you, and that moment is hard. For that matter, all those little moments in the grocery stores, parking lots, and at dining room tables don't feel so great, either.

That kind of discipline—the things-are-going-wrong kind—is just one small piece of a much larger picture. Yet here we are, so many of us, all balled up about the same thing. I called one of my favorite thinkers on parenthood, Dr. Kenneth Ginsburg, to ask why. He's a pediatrician and an author. He's also a happy parent himself. "What's the first thing you would say," I asked him, "to a parent who told you discipline was his 'least favorite thing'?"

"Oh, no!" he shouted into the phone with his trademark enthusiasm. "You have to remember what the word means—to teach or to guide in a loving way. Not to punish, not to control, never to harm. Its root is 'disciple.' When you understand that your role is to be a teacher, everything changes." Those dreaded moments? Yes, they show up, he agreed, but most of discipline, he argued, is role modeling. "It's not a taking away. It's not punishment. It's guiding a kid to navigate the world safely."

In other words, if you think of discipline as an iceberg, what we dislike about it is just the 10 percent that's sticking up above the water. We hate the enforcement. But it's the 90 percent of what we do to teach our children how to *be*, both at home and in the world, that really matters. It's also that 90 percent that gives the pointy, frosty 10 percent strength. If we can shift our narrative around the 10 percent moments to make them just part of a larger whole, we might be able to feel better about discipline overall.

For Dr. Ginsburg, that change in how we think and talk about discipline is key to improving our entire approach. "We've got a cultural and a personal narrative around this that needs to change," he said. Not only is most of our job in this area positive, as we model personal responsibility and guide our children toward self-control, but even the piece we dread shouldn't worry us the way it does. We see the moment when our child doesn't live up to our expectations as a sign that our normal approach has failed—after all, if it had worked to teach them right from wrong in the first place, we wouldn't be having to enforce the lesson, right? But this is when we fail ourselves, because those moments, because children, whether they're toddlers or tweens or teens, don't get everything right the first time, and they don't learn just by listening. They learn by exploring, pushing the boundaries, and having things go wrong—and that last part, where things go wrong, doesn't really mean the larger process has hit a wall. Instead, big strikeouts are part of the game. Our job as parents isn't to prevent them from happening. It's to help our children see what happened and learn to navigate so that things go better next time.

Dr. Ginsburg isn't alone in seeing value and even potential joy in our children's most challenging moments. "The behaviors that are the most challenging, and that drive us the craziest, are actually telling us something really important," says Tina Payne Bryson, a psychotherapist and the coauthor (with Dan Siegel) of *No-Drama Discipline: The Whole-Brain Way to Calm the Chaos and Nurture Your Child's Developing Mind.* "They are telling us the specific areas in which our kids need teaching, support, and skill-building. Instead of focusing on what we need to *take away* from our kids for them to learn their lesson, think instead of what we need to *provide* for them to learn so that they become self-disciplined."

What Goes Wrong

Before we start trying to think about discipline differently, let's figure out how we got here. Had you surveyed a thousand parents a hundred years ago, or in any decade over most of the last century, it's unlikely that "what they liked least" would have coalesced around discipline. Our parents, and most parents before them, were largely in agreement about how children should behave, and how their parents should go about getting them to do just that. "Most people parenting teenagers now," Dr. Ginsburg said, "would have been raised by authoritarian parents. It's a high-rules, low-warmth style," he said, which isn't to say it isn't meant lovingly. "It's 'my house, my rules.'" Most of our parents would have experienced a similar style themselves. Adults who grew up in the middle class in the '50s and '60s often describe being disciplined at home and at school with a paddle, strap, ruler, or switch.

Corporal punishment isn't a necessary piece of the authoritarian style (spanking has been a matter of debate for hundreds of years), but few questioned the need for some form of punishment, even if it took the form of being sent to bed without dinner or missing an anticipated event rather than a spanking. As a general rule, people believed there was a clear connection between punishing a child and reducing bad behavior.

For most parents today, the clarity of that simple cycle of transgression and punishment is gone. In its place we have a better understanding of how a too-heavy parental hand can push a child away and even lead to an increase in risky behaviors later. But while there's a consensus among experts like Dr. Ginsburg about the balanced style of parenting that should replace the "my way or the highway" approach (more on that shortly), there's not a lot of societal agreement on what, exactly, we should be doing to achieve that balance. That can mean that we parents feel a lot of angry glares in public places when we don't do whatever it is we're supposed to do to control our kids. Many of us favor a "positive discipline" approach, which rewards the right behavior rather than reacts to problem behavior, but this can leave you at a loss when the only rewardable behavior available at the grocery store is that the child didn't actually flip over the cart.

But there's more to what makes discipline tough for us than our personal struggles. In many respects, we face a different disciplinary landscape than our parents. Technology is a part of it, as are changing norms about how people speak to one another, how they behave and dress in public, and how the people and institutions around us treat questions about discipline and authority. A few decades or less ago, a student who rolled her eyes at a teacher could expect a detention while a student who called a classmate "fat" would be met with a shrug; today those responses are reversed. Like it or not (and if you're asking, I think both merit a disciplinary response), that's the world most of us send our children out into. At the same time, being called out for misbehavior by a neighbor, another kid's parent, or a stranger was common for a child not long ago; now it's rare. One reason discipline feels more painful to us as parents is that more than any generation before us, we're solo. Add in the incredibly high expectations we have for ourselves, and you have a recipe for feeling inadequate.

Our children are also more supervised than any generation that came before them, which has shifted how we convey our behavioral expectations as well. Because we're usually with our kids, we rely heavily on the power of our "no" rather than teaching our children how to behave without our guidance, and for their part, our children lean on our presence. Because we're always available to smooth things over, they're less likely to have experienced the consequences of rude or inappropriate behavior in a public setting. Meanwhile, we expect our constant attendance itself to be enough to get the job done. We show up relentlessly, as though looking for a good attendance award, when we might teach our children more by being less present.

"We kind of want to professionalize child-rearing," says Ylonda Gault Caviness, the author of *Child, Please: How Mama's Old-School Lessons Helped Me Check Myself Before I Wrecked Myself.* "We feel like, if we have this input, we should get this kind of outcome. We're very organized and we've got Google Calendar and date nights with each child and we're doing all the things. But it's not just a formula you can plug in."

That doesn't have to mean we're not doing a decent job, even if it doesn't look like it every minute. The biggest thing that "goes wrong" when it comes to discipline is the nature of children and teenagers. Children push and test and forget and act on impulse. Teenagers do the same, with the addition of more freedom, more hormones, more knowledge, and on occasion even less self-control. They're being exactly who they need to be to turn into the adults they'll someday become, but that isn't necessarily easy for the adults who are trying to get them there. Looked at in this light, discipline, even the enforcement bit, is just parenting.

The last thing on my checklist of "why discipline is actually really hard" is that we get almost no control over when we need to bring it to the table. In fact, things nearly always come up at the hardest possible moment. A late commute after a long week at work during a month of stress over your father's health and the possibility that you may need to move the family halfway across the country for your partner's job? Why yes, thank you, that's exactly when your children will offer up their very biggest challenges. So often, when we feel empty of any ability to give, our kids force us to reach deep into our well.

We're muddling through a foggy landscape of societal expectations and changing norms, charged with reining in young people who are designed to resist at every turn. We can't control when we'll be called upon to produce some form of "discipline" out of our magic bag of parenting tricks. So what can we do to make this least-favorite aspect of being a parent better? Enough to make a big difference. We can take a cue from Dr. Ginsburg and start thinking about it differently, which might change our behavior not just when we're on the disciplinary "spot," but when we're off as well. We can shift our approach and adjust how much we let others second-guess us or get under our skin when we're not doing what they would do. And we can feel happier about how we express our approach, to ourselves, to others, and to our children.

Here's what we can't control: the result.

And that is why discipline can be so overwhelming, even terrifying. "Discipline" is both a verb and a noun. We use it in order to teach it. If your child reaches the age of eighteen without having ever eaten a fruit or vegetable, unable to do a load of laundry, and still putting soccer ahead of homework, college and adult life may involve some rude awakenings (or possibly scurvy). She'll cope. But without discipline, it's hard to successfully enter any part of adult life at all, and the worst part is, we can't know how much our children have learned until they've been tested by something we can't control. There are no guarantees. Everybody hates that.

But there is some really good advice. And if you can find a happy peace with this arguably most-challenging aspect of parenthood, you'll find that happiness extending into nearly every other challenge, because discipline troubles are a piece of everything that makes raising a family less fun, from miserable mornings to horrible homework to vicious vacations. Make this better, and a whole lot of other things fall into place.

Making It Better: Bring Your Best Self

Discipline may be the overall practice of teaching a child how to behave in the larger world, but for most of us, especially if we're naming it as our "least liked thing," what we're thinking of are the tough spots. Insisting that chores be done is discipline. Maintaining expectations for homework and public behavior is discipline. But what pulls us up short and makes us hold our head in our hands is what we need to do when the chores aren't done and the expectations aren't met and one child is kicking you in the shin while another is on the phone trying to explain how her friend ran out of gas on the highway on the way to the concert you said she couldn't go to. That's where the rubber hits the road.

Among the biggest challenges for me when it comes to that form of discipline is that I have to be the grown-up. Sometimes my children just plain make me mad. They look up at me and flat-out deny biting a sibling while I'm examining their distinctive tooth marks in a plump baby leg. They scream, "No! I no want p-butter!" And in waving their arms to make their point, they knock the plate and sandwich out of my hand. They saunter off to begin slowly making their lunch when I announce that it's time to get in the car for school.

I am human. I get angry, I get hurt, I get frustrated, disappointed, and upset. All of that is allowed, but when it comes to teaching my children to master their own worst selves at tough moments, I obviously can't start from there. Instead, I must first discipline myself. My hair is not on fire. *There is nothing wrong.* I can take the time to climb down off the ceiling before I do anything else.

This is difficult when you have very young children, particularly when their demands mean we aren't getting the sleep we require, doing the things we need to do to care for ourselves, or finding time for things we enjoy. It's also difficult with older children and teenagers, from whom we expect more, and who know how to push our buttons in very special ways. In fact, it's just plain difficult. Sometimes we'll find ourselves in situations with our children where it's easy to enforce our family rules or values warmly, calmly, and firmly. More often, we'll be doing it while dealing with a cascade of emotions within ourselves. Whether you've always struggled with a hot temper, a passive-aggressive streak, or impulse control or whether you've generally operated on an even keel, children can bring you to heights of rage you've have never before experienced, unless you're employed in a workplace where your colleagues intentionally drop your mobile phone into the toilet.

When I say as much to Dr. Ginsburg, he maintains his enviable calm. The problem, he tells me, is that we need to expect the tough moments. It's not *if* your child will do something that's over-the-top infuriating, disappointing, or even frightening. It's *when.* If you see even the worst-seeming problems as part of a bigger picture that's inevitably full of ups and downs, you can take a deep breath, pull your shoulders down out of your ears, and quiet the voices in your mind telling you that you have failed as a parent, or that this child is just like you and will screw up just like you did. "Look," he says. "It's not a tiger. It's almost never a tiger. A D on a test is not a tiger, shoplifting is not a tiger, an arrest for underage drinking is not a tiger." In other words, even the biggest crisis is probably not immediately life-threatening. You don't need that adrenaline-charged reaction your body is offering. You have time to deal with what's in front of you calmly, as an adult, helping a child to learn from her experience and go forward. Sounds good, right? Here's what I learned about how to get there.

RESPOND, DON'T REACT

It's hard to teach our children to try to do what we as adults are likely struggling with in the very moment of the teaching. Both you and your child need to master your immediate desires, fears, and emotions in a way that allows you to move toward your long-term goals, and you're supposed to be leading the way. The screaming child in the grocery cart who wants a lollipop doesn't really want to be screaming. She wants to be a happy, comforted child (preferably not in the cart, or at the grocery store at all, but with a lollipop). And we don't really want to be the purple-faced grown-up screaming back. We want to be peacefully at home with our groceries and a happy child (lollipop entirely your call). Getting from point A to point B takes discipline inside and out.

The more we struggle with disciplining our own response to our children's behavior, the more likely we are to be struggling with our children. There's neuroscience behind this. In his book *Hardwiring Happiness*, neuropsychologist Rick Hanson describes our brain's "reactive mode"—the place we go when we "feel apprehensive or exasperated, pulled in different directions."

A brain in reactive mode is not a brain that's thinking clearly. "Adrenaline and cortisol course through the blood, and fear, frustration, and heartache color the mind," he writes. "The reactive mode assumes there are urgent demands, so it's not concerned about your long-term needs." Your brain is offering a stress response better suited to fleeing a cheetah than to soothing either a child or yourself, and that doesn't help.

"If we're emotionally chaotic and reactive in discipline moments, we're making it less likely we can effectively teach our kids," says Tina Bryson. Our stress response activates our children's stress response in return. "When we are reactive, angry, unpredictable, our children's primitive brains are getting the 'threat' signal, and the brain cares first about safety. No learning can be done when kids don't feel safe."

When the parents we surveyed spent more time punishing, yelling, or hashing over the rules of the house, those parents (particularly those with younger children) felt less satisfied with their role as parents. When discipline feels like a problem, it becomes an even bigger problem.

The alternative to that "reactive mode" is a "responsive mode," in which our brains, not feeling disturbed by a sense that our safety, satisfaction, or connections are at risk, can remain at rest even in response to challenges. To keep our minds from snapping into reactive mode, we need to stop seeing our child's bad behavior as a threat to ourselves. If you can stay focused on the "teaching" side of discipline—the 90 percent—it's easier to get through these more difficult moments calmly, because they don't feel as fraught. You know that your immediate response here isn't some sort of ultimate parenting test, with a win-or-lose result ahead.

But that's not always easy to remember. The reactive mode often overwhelms us, especially when the disciplinary crisis is sudden, feels big, and comes at a rough moment. What can we do to pull ourselves out of what Dr. Hanson calls "the red zone" before we pull everyone else in, too? First, he told me, label it. "Just softly in your own mind put some words to what you're feeling," he says. "'I'm so mad, so freaked out, I want to hit that kid, I want to scream.' Name it as neutrally as you can." Then, he says, buy yourself some time. "We make mistakes when we're moving and speaking too quickly. Pause, slow down. Imagine yourself observing from the outside of a glass wall, or think of a video camera in the corner, recording this to play later."

Do the best you can to calm your body. "Exhale," he says. "It activates the parasympathetic nervous system. Lift your gaze to the horizon, which engages the circuits in your brain to take a panoramic view." Above all, he says, remind yourself how safe you are. *There is nothing wrong.* You're not denying the situation. You're just helping yourself calm it down. "We're very quick to move to alarm about our children and our partners," he says. "We go straight to 'everything's falling apart.' Take a moment to remind yourself of the actual possible consequences of what's in front of you. You're not sick, no one's dying, you're not going bankrupt, there's no terminal illness." Basically, everything is okay.

Take the time you need for this process. Your child can wait, in time-out, in her room, with a partner or an older child, for you to respond—not react—when you're ready. Forgive yourself, too, if you react before you can stop yourself. *You don't have to get it right every time.* If the situation merits it, bring your response to the table when you're able; if not, let things blow over. This is an area where most parents get more opportunity to practice than we ever imagined.

WHAT DO WE ACTUALLY DO?

If only, once you were ready to respond, you were all set with the formula that would lead straight back to the road to happiness for all, with a quick stop at the I'm-so-sorry-I'll-never-do-it-again service area.

Sadly, it's the nature of many of the most difficult discipline dilemmas that they're unpredictable, varied, and specialized. It's not just that your child is having a tantrum over cookies, but that you promised her cookies before her tonsil surgery tomorrow and now the bakery only has peanut butter cookies, which you can't get because your visiting nephew is allergic and everything else is closed. One child hit the other, but you know good and well that the other probably asked for it, even though you only saw the hit. The child caught at the party where there was alcohol has a plane ticket to compete with her team in the national debate championships tomorrow. You thought you'd know what to do in those situations—no tantrums, no hitting, no drinking—but it's never a nice, clear case of this-then-that.

When I complained to Dr. Ginsburg that the trouble with discipline is that it's impossible to know what the right thing to do is when things start going wrong, I expected enthusiastic sympathy, because Dr. Ginsburg is a dad, because he really gets the challenges of parenting, and because he is never not enthusiastic.

Instead, I got another swift correction. No, he said. We do know what to do—or at least, we know how parents should *be* and that can guide us to the best response. "There's a ton of research out there that shows that there is a right way to do this," he said, and he quickly offered up a primer on the four parenting styles—three bad, one good—that researchers have developed over the years. There's the high rules/

low warmth "authoritarian" style many of us experienced; the high warmth/low rules "permissive" style, in which a parent is more of a friend; the low rules/low warmth disengaged parent, who believes "kids will be kids" and "they'll figure it out"; and, finally, the ideal rules-and-warmth pairing found in the balanced, or "authoritative" parent, who provides firm boundaries around issues of safety and morality and warm, supportive guidance around everything else.

So while there may not be one right thing to do, there is a right approach. "We do know what to do, or at least how to do it," says Dr. Ginsburg. "Striking the right balance that includes attention to monitoring, while not smothering, is scientifically proven to matter." Happier parents of young children are more hands-on when it comes to discipline, stepping into an argument between friends to model listening and problem-solving, demonstrating how to complete a chore, or keeping a close eye on adherence to screen-time rules, but as children grow older, those parents are stepping back to allow kids a chance to show their self-discipline—and, if that doesn't go well, stepping forward to help, only to step back again a few weeks or months later. Dr. Ginsburg is quick to list just a few benefits of that dance: kids whose parents offer authority when needed and support the rest of the time have lower levels of depression and anxiety and lower rates of drug use; they're half as likely to be in a car crash; they start sexual experimentation later.

Of course, knowing how you want to *be* doesn't always tell you what to actually do, no matter what Dr. Ginsburg says. That's the balanced parent catch-22: we must be flexible but firm. We need to take circumstances and who our child is into account, but not to the point of compromising safety, morality, or our child's belief in us as a guiding light in a cloudy world. So, the bakery tantrum on the night before a scary surgery might merit a soothing compromise, the hitting child might get a pass this time, the child on her way to the debate tournament might not have to let down her team, but she might have just gained an unexpected chaperone.

When you're able to take the time to move into responsive mode, you're also more able to see your way toward that balanced style. You won't make as many mistakes around deciding what is really an issue of safety or morality that requires your close attendance (staying close in the parking lot, cheating on a test) and what's not (sibling nastiness, forgotten homework). You'll be able to be loving even when you're also angry and disappointed. You'll think through what should come next, and you'll be able to be happier with your own actions (although your child might not be).

Connect, Teach, Enforce, Repeat

Parents tend to be happier around discipline, even during the most difficult moments, when we have a sense that it's working. We feel more effective as parents if we can reassure ourselves, for example, that breaking the rules of our house has consequences. Ask a bunch of us for discipline advice, and one of the most common answers is some version of this: never threaten a consequence you won't carry out. We put a lot of weight on that word and concept—"consequences"—but what exactly do we mean by it?

The American Academy of Pediatrics says that effective discipline includes three things: (1) a generally positive and supportive relationship between parent and child; (2) a way to teach the child the right thing to do in any given situation; and (3) a plan for ending the behaviors you don't want. It's that third piece—the 10 percent of the iceberg, to go back to my earlier analogy—that gives us the most trouble, both because we don't like it and, often, because we feel that we don't know how to do it.

In some cases, we can let "natural consequences" run their course—the child who throws her cookie now has none—but with many of the expectations we set for our children, the natural consequences of their behavior are either distant or more painful for the adults than for the kids. Especially when our children are young, many of the behaviors we want to end are fun from their perspective—chasing the cat, spitting water out of a straw at a restaurant. We tell them to stop, and they don't. What then?

That point is, says author Joanna Faber, when many of us turn to "the threats, the warnings, the commands," it sounds to small children "like a Charlie Brown parent talking: wah wah wah womp wah." If we follow it up with a punishment—"That's it, then. You won't stop, so no television for you tonight!"—we put ourselves and our child on opposite sides, with her attention now on herself and what you're doing to her rather than on the behavior you were hoping to teach. For many of us, that's not a happy place to be, especially if it leads, as it often does, to a meltdown.

Faber's suggestion? Try to engage and connect the moment things start to go south. It's fun to chase the kitty or squirt the water, but here's why it's not fun for the kitty or the other diners. "Scolding, smacking, or putting a child in a time-out might stop him in the moment," she said, "but you're not here just to stop him in the moment." You're here, she says, to teach your child to make the right choices for himself, so offer that option first, even if it seems as if he should know better by now. Some things take a lot of saying.

If he still can't make that choice, make it for him: "It's too tempting for you to chase the cat right now, so I'm going to shut her in my room." "It's too hard for you to resist that straw, so we're going to give it back to the waitress." "I know I said we were going out to lunch after the game, but I don't want to do that anymore, so we're leaving."

The consequences, she says, "can look much the same" as any punishment you might have imposed, but using words that show that you understand your child's feelings, and that express yours, can make it easier to keep yourself calm and to allow the child a chance to apologize and make amends (even as you still remove the cat or the straw, or leave the restaurant). You may not achieve calm. You may not get a "sorry." You may, instead, meet with grumbling and complaining or shrieking and wailing, and all may not end happily. That's okay. They're hearing you. They're gradually connecting their behavior to your response. It's all part of the process, and you're all but guaranteed to get another chance.

That whole sequence of connecting, teaching, and then, if necessary, ending a behavior is one you will repeat again and again, especially with a younger child, so make your words positive ones, even if the behavior is anything but. "If I'm going to say it a hundred times," says Faber, "I figure it might as well be something I want my child to learn." Thus "Pat the kitty gently," not "Bad boy! Don't chase the kitty!" We want to teach our children, not give them labels to live down to, which means that repeating "Please put your bowl in the dishwasher" in various ways thousands of times over the course of a childhood is better than "You are such a slob," no matter how tempting the latter may be.

That kind of repetition is where a lot of us fall down. Consistency is hard, and it's especially difficult when we've become so accustomed to an on-demand world. When I run out of my preferred brand of coffee, I open an app on my phone, and in two clicks six more cans of French Market Coffee & Chicory, Restaurant Blend, are on their way. Why, then, do I have to tell you to put your cereal bowl in the dishwasher six times and then tell you I'm taking a dollar off of your allowance if you don't do it before you will comply? And why did you not take the spoon? And why—*why*—will we have this exact same conversation tomorrow?

Because that is the way this works, and the sooner we embrace that, the sooner we can get back to being generally happy in spite of it.

Most parents, says Bryson, "expect too much. Just because a kid *can* do something well, like control anger and handle disappointment, doesn't mean he can do it all the time." Those seeming setbacks can really set us off. When we feel that our kids have let us down, says Bryson, it triggers our parental fear that this is about our child's character, "when in fact, it's typically about a skill or an ability they don't fully have wired yet because their brain is still building."

When we accept discipline as a long-term teaching process, it gets easier. Instead of thinking, *I've asked him hundreds of times to do this and he still doesn't do it*, parents who are happier in their disciplinary role think something more along the lines of *I've asked him a hundred times and I'll ask him a hundred more and that's how we get there.*

"My oldest is eighteen," says Ylonda Gault Caviness, "and seriously, it wasn't until days before she turned eighteen that I was beginning to see that, oh, she heard me." Suddenly, her daughter was getting ready on time or putting in a load of laundry. "There were so many things that I thought, okay, I gotta just write this off, I've said it a million times, it's not going to happen." And then it did.

As Catherine Pearlman, a parenting coach and the author of *Ignore It!: How Selectively Looking the Other Way Can Decrease Behavioral Problems and Increase Parenting Satisfaction*, says, try not to let the crying and the complaining and the shouts of hatred bother you. "That's how you know it's working."

Maybe You Don't Have to Do Anything

As kids get older, the natural consequences of their actions are more likely to really bite them where it hurts. Even when it's not as serious as an arrest or expulsion, the results of something like being late for a team practice, rude to a teacher, or not turning in homework assignments can be enough to allow a parent to do nothing but sympathetically make sure the connection hits home. You are, of course, sorry that your child lost her place on the starting lineup, wasn't chosen among her classmates as a school ambassador, or lost the chance to move up to the honors English class. But no, you're not going to try to make it right, although you are willing to help her think of ideas to help herself.

With younger children, a different kind of "not doing anything" can be a genuine discipline strategy, and even a very effective one, if you can swing it. Most of us are familiar with the idea that rewarding a behavior you don't want with attention only reinforces it. (I hit my sister and now look! Daddy is sitting in my room talking to *only me!*) For many minor things, like tantrums over the end of screen time or whining about chores, the best thing to do is to do something else. If you get good at it, this is a strategy that can really up your happiness. *If you see something, don't always say something.* Sometimes, your kids are just being annoying, and it's possible to choose not to be annoyed.

Pearlman lays out a clear map for how this works. When we talked, she used a child's mild temper tantrum as an example. "Start by ignoring it," she told me. "Flip through a catalog on the counter. Put all your attention on that catalog, even if it's really hard. At the same time, you're listening, because you're going to reengage as soon as it stops—about something else. You're just going to go on as though there was no tantrum or whining or whatever." Later, she says, you "repair" if necessary—talk about other things to do when a child is upset, apologize if you wish you'd done something differently in the moments leading up to the tantrum, or invite an apology if your child's behavior was particularly egregious—but often, you just move on (particularly from something like whining about chores).

There are also times when a child is doing something you feel as if you should stop, like making a repeated noise to annoy a sibling, hopping on one foot in a circle around the kitchen, opening and closing a cabinet door again and again and again, or indulging a harmless habit like leg jiggling or hair twirling. You really can let a lot of this go. "Just because a kid is doing something doesn't mean you have to address it," said Pearlman.

This might be difficult at first, but as you get used to it, it will increase your own happiness enormously. *I don't need to do anything about that*, I say to myself as the child assigned to feed the dogs slams the bowls angrily on the counter. *I can just let that go.* The chore needs to be done, the screen time needs to be over, it's time for bed, etc. That I've got. The rest is just static.

Little Kids, Little Problems. Big Kids . . .

The core of discipline isn't the enforcement of rules, but teaching a child to absorb, embrace, and follow those rules on her own—to discipline herself. Discipline isn't just meant to create a happier, more harmonious family life, or to engage a child's help with the work of the household. It's intended to teach the child how to be an adult in the world, where we will not be able to retrieve our stapler from a colleague by hitting her over the head with even the lightest of plastic desk toys, and where our partners will expect us to do our part in loading the dishwasher. We discipline to raise our successful thirty-five-year-olds, who can get places on time, hold down a job, and raise families of their own.

That requires that we back off from constant monitoring and enforcement of most things as our children get older (although you are allowed to repeat the request that they put their dishes in the dishwasher for as long as it takes). It starts small, with things like leaving them to pack their own bag for sports and school, and to handle the consequences of the lost or forgotten item. It expands as older children are left at home alone, trusted with Internet passwords, or asked to obey household rules when no one is watching. And when our children make mistakes with those minor challenges (as they will), experiencing your disappointment and losing their privilege or access gives them a taste of what screwing up feels like, and what it's like to have to re-earn your trust and a chance to try again. Those things lay the foundation for the bigger challenges that come later, when you have a teenager at the wheel of a car, armed with a cell phone, her own hard-earned money, and the ability to do just about anything any adult could do in that moment, including a whole lot of things that are against your family rules and even against the law.

You're counting on the accumulation of all those years of teaching, both generalized (in our family, we are honest with one another, we respect the property of others) and specific (we do not send naked pictures of ourselves or others over mobile networks, we do not drink until we are old enough to do so legally) to help her stay safe and stay on the right path.

Sometimes she won't, no matter how hard you've tried to get this "right." And you won't even always know about it—in one relatively small study, 82 percent of high school and young college students said they had lied to their parents at some point during the past year about friends, money, parties, alcohol/drug use, dates/dating, or sexual behavior—exactly the areas where we worry about our children getting in over their heads. That's a scary statistic, especially when you think about the mountain of risky behavior their lies covered up.

One big irony here, again, is that as our children get older, "natural consequences" really set in, and that's exactly what we are afraid of. The potential natural consequences of drinking and driving or unprotected sex can be life-changing. The natural consequences of smaller failures in the school and activities arena also have real-world implications. Often, we're threatening our own "big" consequences in the hopes of helping to scare our children away from the even bigger consequences we can't control.

At the same time, the stakes feel higher for us as parents. These are our teenagers, not our forgiving toddlers. They can carry a grudge, hurt our feelings, and physically walk out of our doors. It can be hard to discipline them. Canise Herald, an Indiana mother of a fourteen-year-old, treasures her good relationship with her daughter, and says she's often easier on her than she thinks her own parents might have been. "You don't like making your kid mad at you." When her daughter was caught using her mobile phone in a way the family had forbidden, she lost the phone for a period, but otherwise "got off easy," in part because Herald and her husband just can't stay mad at their daughter for very long. Lightening up can feel like the most loving choice.

But when your daughter is arrested for underage drinking, or your son is caught cheating on a test, in the last months or years before you expect to send them off to college to handle so much of life entirely on their own, you will be angry, and shocked, and worried. How will you get them through the consequences the world is about to impose?

What can you do to convey your own disappointment and your lack of tolerance for what's happened? And how can you trust them when, in such a short time, you watch them head out on their own?

What you do next, says Dr. Ginsburg, is exactly what you'd do with a younger child who'd seriously broken your house rules. The only difference is that you have less time in which to see if it's worked.

"One of the consequences of blowing it in a big way is that your child loses your trust," he says, and that loss of trust has its own consequences. Your child may lose your permission to use the car or the family wireless network. She may need to return to telling you, in detail, exactly where she is, and when she's moving, and accept that you will be checking up on her in ways you were not in the past.

With a younger child, you can take as much time as you need to restore the privileges that are taken away after a major incident—for example, at our house, more than $200 in in-app purchases made when a child was given too-early access to the family account. You can talk about what happened, why the child was tempted, how he came to make the wrong decision, how he felt afterward, and how to keep it from happening again. You can talk about the restored trust at each step (the return of the screen privileges, access to the device without supervision, and eventually access to a new password).

With an older child, you may have to restore privileges more quickly, so that you can once again assess whether that child will be ready to take care of herself in a college environment. The same conversations should happen, but in a shorter time frame, because both of you need to see that your child is capable of doing better before she heads out on her own.

As for the external consequences—the real-world results of an arrest, or cheating, or a very large bill for some very virtual goods—Dr. Ginsburg says it's a parent's role to support a child through those consequences, to help her advocate for herself, to do all you can to mitigate any long-term or even permanent impact, but not to absorb them or find a way to make them go away.

It's likely you won't feel very happy when your child makes what feels like a massive mistake. You'll feel its weight on you; you will be disappointed in your child and for your child. It will be difficult to *be happy even though your child is not*. But you can return to the basics. You and your child and the rest of your family are safe and secure. You can, again, lift your gaze to the horizon and see the bigger picture. At some point, life lessons start coming from life itself.

A mother in Delaware who says her daughter made more than one suicide attempt in her early teens (the result of depression and a neurological condition) describes how the experience changed her perspective on discipline. "You have to really think about what is important to fight about when you have somebody in that situation," she says. For some children, the consequences the real world provides are more than enough to raise anxiety levels and can be overwhelming. When parents pile on, fragile kids can shut down. This mother chooses to focus on being supportive at home for both that child, her oldest, and a younger sibling. "They know," she says, "'If I didn't do my homework I'm not going to get yelled at by Mom; I'm going to get a bad grade and that's going to affect me.' Their actions are up to them."

If you're worried that your child is made overly anxious by the combination of parental and external pressure, you may need professional help to strike the right discipline balance—because no matter how off-balance things seem, lowering expectations to zero is almost never the right answer. Your message to your child—your future adult child—should always be "I know you can do this, and I will help you get to the point where you know it, too."

Rules for Parents

For me, it often helps to have a go-to when I'm feeling challenged by a moment that seems to need a disciplinary reaction from me. I need a reminder or a mantra of sorts that I can pop up when I'm at a loss. Here are a few of the things I say to myself when I need to respond not react, impose a consequence, or repeat myself again and again.

Don't engage. My daughters would be the first to tell you that they're an emotional pair. Even my sons can go in for the occasional rant. When there is a child stomping around my house, angry, frustrated, and letting it all out (often with a bonus "I hate you!" for good measure), I remind myself not to engage. *You don't have to go in there.* That's her mood, his problem, her time to vent. Sometimes there's even a good reason for it. That doesn't mean I have to join it.

Don't hold a grudge. This is really, really difficult for me. I can nurse a grievance for days, especially a real one, and who wouldn't be angered by a child who has a tantrum after winning a hockey tournament? Or who ignores the request to take the Starbucks cup out of the car door, with the result that when the door is slammed, it spills everywhere, causing the car to smell of vanilla steamer for the next three months? Those things make me feel justifiably angry. It's hard for me to remember that I have to be not just the grown-up, but the parent: the one who lets you make mistakes, loves you anyway, and doesn't keep rubbing it in.

Don't yell . . . back. Sometimes I yell at my children. I am a yeller. I grew up in a house of yellers. If I walk in on a situation that seems to me to require yelling, if I get a note from a teacher that demands my fast and furious response, I will find you, and I will yell at you. I'm working on it—I've learned that yelling doesn't make me happier, either. I haven't quite reached the no-yelling-at-all stage of personal Zen. But this I can do: If you yell at me, I almost never yell back. If I am angry, and I yell, that tells you how serious things are. It gets children moving. But if a child is yelling, and I yell back, then that child just dragged me into her drama. That never makes me happy.

Don't second-guess. Once the heat of the moment has passed, it can be tempting to ease up on a longer punishment (like two weeks without a phone). This is a very bad idea. If you're imposing a consequence, choose it carefully and stick with it. Holding firm the first few times means less begging later, and it's easier on you, too. *Decide what you want to do, then do it.*

Don't push them away. This, too, is about not holding a grudge. If anything, once something has gone really wrong, you want to bring your child closer. This is hard. As much as we try not to take our children's failures personally, we're often angry and disappointed when they mess up. It's natural not to want to be close to them for a while (and sometimes necessary when we need to cool off).

But once we've put things back into perspective, it's important to reconnect. Grounding has a big advantage beyond being painful—it gets the child home and under your wing. (Although at times, you find you've effectively grounded yourself, too.) One parent found at the end of her son's junior year in high school that not only had he not done any of his math work for the entire semester, but that he was planning to try to smuggle marijuana back from a long-planned summer trip with a friend's family. She canceled the trip, made him a place next to her desk, and had him work through the whole semester's math, all summer long, right under her eye. Once they got past the first part, it changed their relationship, and the son credits it with turning him into someone capable of going to college.

It's okay to enjoy it. If you must punish your children, you might as well see the funny side of it, especially when they're young. When I grounded one of my children for the first time, I regretted the things she was missing almost as much as she did. Three years later, when I grounded her younger brother, I was so able to squash those feelings that I called up a close friend, the mother of his best friend, and asked her to please invite my child for a sleepover to which he would not be allowed to come. "I want him to feel it," I said. He did. And I did the same for her a few weeks later.

Get working, side by side. After the smoke has died down, and things are on their way back to normal (or the modified normal that is your punishment), get that child and get to work. Tackle something. Prepare the garden. Clean out a section of the basement. Make brownies. Mend some metaphorical fences. This is not a punishment, but a way to dig back in and ground yourselves in the kind of work that puts us on the same team. Uniting your efforts toward a common goal can restore the balance in your family, and remind you and your child that you're in this together. "Kids absolutely want to do the right thing," says Dr. Ginsburg, as we wrap up our conversation. "They look to us to show them and tell them what's safe and what's right." They want, and need, our guidance as well as our love and support, when things are going well and when things are going wrong. It's all "discipline" and it can—it really can—make you all happier.

eight

FOOD, FUN, AND FAMILY TIME

Cooking and eating are polarizing. Love to cook. Hate to cook. Love to eat or not so much, for reasons of diet, personal history, and taste. Left to your own devices, you can indulge your own quirks, whether it's eating the exact same basic meal every night or spending hours putting together a fresh version of Lobster Thermidor. But once children enter the picture, you have to feed them, too. It's likely that you have a vision of what those meals "should" look like. Once "should" enters the picture, "fun" often exits.

I fall into the "love to cook and eat" camp, but even for me, the constancy of the requirement that we nourish these four children of ours is overwhelming. It's such an incredible amount of work, acquiring the food, preparing the food, serving the food, cleaning up after the meal. At a certain point, children become able to help, but we're talking thousands of meals before that point. Really truly thousands. *Thousands.* I feel like I should throw in the dishtowel on this chapter right now, because how can that be fun?

But of all the topics I'm covering in my quest to help all of us enjoy our family lives more, this is the one I feel most attached to—the one where I can honestly say, Okay, I got this. I don't always love the process. I don't always love the result. But cooking, eating, and sharing meals together are truly one of the ways I find joy in my family, and I want you to share that experience—in a way that works for you. Because this really matters. Like mornings, mealtime is family time. When it comes to getting everyone together all in one place with the same thing in mind, dinnertime is typically what we get.

In dual-income families, most parents and school-age children spend more weekday hours outside the home than in it. Researchers who observed interactions in middle-class families found relatively few hours when all family members were likely to be home simultaneously. Not surprisingly, those were concentrated in the early mornings and the late afternoon and evening. When we are all home together, we're most likely to congregate in the kitchen, and of all the things we do as a family, researchers find that we spend the most time eating together.

In other words, if family meals aren't happy, then your overall batting average for family happiness probably isn't as high as you'd like. This is an area that's ripe for change.

I'm among those who think eating together is important—a human ritual that we shouldn't sacrifice to outside pressures. Research has linked eating meals together (particularly dinner) to a host of benefits for children: stronger vocabularies, higher grades, a decreased likelihood of drug and alcohol use, and greater feelings of connection to family. In my own research, we found connections between eating meals together and parent satisfaction as well. Eating more meals as a family and considering everyone's desires when choosing those meals were among the factors that went along with a greater sense of satisfaction with life.

But even putting research aside, there is obvious enormous value for us as individual parents and children in the act of eating together, and every meal does not have to reflect some imaginary ideal. You and your partner may work different shifts, so that the whole family eats together only a few times a week. You might be dealing with food allergies, or living in your parents' house and eating at their table, or have children who split their time between two households. Those things matter less than we think. Our children are absorbing powerful memories about who we are, how we eat, how we sit, how we talk to one another, about the food, our lives, the people and things around us—but not all at any one single meal. Eating together is cumulative; the rituals evolve gradually. When your children eat in other houses, they'll compare those rituals and expectations. When their friends come to your house, you'll see little clues to how they expect a meal to go in how they act and respond to your meal. Family meals reflect family values. They show us not who we want to be, but who we are.

So, to sum up, family meals are great! Yay eating together!

It's still a lot of work.

What Goes Wrong

Ask people to name the one thing they like least about parenting, and meals rarely come up. Let them choose their top three, though, and there it is: "snacks and meals," "my toddler throwing food back at me," and "What, you want dinner *again*? We just had dinner last night."

The trouble with family meals is twofold. First off, we worry about what our kids are eating—whether it's good for them, good for the planet, sustainable for everyone, generating a lot of waste, helping them form a healthy lifetime relationship with food—you know the drill. We look around and we worry that what we're doing isn't good enough, and the fact that there's a billion-dollar industry dedicated to persuading your children (and you) to eat more of exactly the foods most of us would rather limit is just one of the things that can make meals a source of worry rather than a daily pleasure.

Second, we worry about the mechanics: buying the food, paying for it, storing it, preparing it, cleaning up after it, and all the rest. Women, in particular, feel pressure to prepare meals that meet external standards like "healthy" and "homemade" within an often-limited budget of both money and time, and can be disappointed when those meals aren't met with enthusiasm by children and partners.

That burden becomes even heavier for parents who don't feel competent in the kitchen. Americans spend more at restaurants than we do on groceries, and while it's hard to get a good number on how many of us feel like we don't know how to cook (survey answers range from 7 percent to 28 percent), it's hard to feel good about what we eat if we feel as though we have no ability to make it ourselves.

Then there's the built-in irony: the easier it is to get the food on the table, the less satisfied we tend to be with whether it meets our standards of how we want to feed our families. Convenience can be cheap, or it can be healthy, but it is almost never both. That means our two problems with food—what our families are eating, and how hard it is to get it on the table—are often in conflict. Improving both isn't easy, but it can be done.

How can you do what's best for you to get happier when it comes to food and family? By focusing on our bigger goals: happily enjoying healthy meals together, sharing good times around food, and taking pleasure in the experience and the company. How we achieve those things can differ among families and even within our own family depending on circumstances. I wouldn't cook different things for different people at the same meal; you might not let your child eat "chicken-french-fries" twice a day every day for a week on vacation (I have). But we can both be happier about making the choices that work for our family, even if those choices are different. For most Western parents, *there is nothing wrong* with our lives around food. If you can afford enough to eat, a table to eat it around, and a roof to eat under, finding the rest of what makes you and your family happy is just gravy.

If food is a medical issue at your house—if, for example, someone in the family struggles with an eating disorder—please remember that no one expects you to feel "happy" about that. Some of these strategies may help to bring more joy to something that's difficult, but still a big part of your daily family routine, while some just might not fit where you are now. In any area where we're on a rocky uphill path and it seems as if everyone else is rolling gently down a grassy slope, it's important to go easy on our expectations. Try to picture what your meals would look like if things were going well around your table, with your limits, rather than looking to some imaginary ideal. Build goals around that reality. It's almost always possible to get a little happier. But to do that, we need to look at where we are, make a choice to make things better, and then consider the mechanics: how our family plans and prepares meals, and how we eat them.

The Right Attitude for Change

The first step toward happier family meals is to really want happier family meals. If you see the whole thing as just a chore, you're writing off something wonderful and consigning what constitutes the bulk of time your family will spend together into the "have to" bin. The dinner hours are when we nourish our families in every sense of the word. "For me—like most people—it's sometimes the only time all day I have a meaningful conversation with my kids," says Jenny Rosenstrach, a popular food blogger and the author of *Dinner: A Love Story*. "We always say that the table is a safe place and I think it really has become that." Dinner in the Rosenstrach family is a priority, and as a result, they know that most nights, they'll have that time together.

But maybe all that pressure just makes you feel more anxious. For some of us, it isn't that we need to invest more in dinner or those evening hours. Instead, we might need to care *less* about achieving some personal standard of perfection at every meal. *You don't have to get it right every time.* No one single dinner makes a family. It's the accumulation of all that time together, in the kitchen, at the table, eating whatever it is you're eating. That time should be a source of peace and solace, and even joy, no matter what's on the plate or the conversational menu. "I don't mean to suggest that every night in our house we are having emotional epiphanies over the meatloaf," says Rosenstrach. It's just dinner, but with a family of individuals all going in different directions, she loves having an established time when they all expect to be together. Grilled cheese while quarreling over who gets the last sandwich half is still family time. It's so easy to let the perfect get in the way of the good when, really, it's enough that you're all there at all.

If either what your children eat or how you're getting it on the table is a significant source of unhappiness or stress in your life, you probably already know why. Maybe you dread the nightly mania of arriving home and diving straight into the witching hour and dinner prep, or battling the triple threat of dinner, homework, and bedtime. You might have your own issues around food and cooking, or resentments about the way the workload is distributed.

What would make your meals happier? Fewer panicked nights with no idea what to cook or last-minute runs through the drive-through? A faster system for getting food on the table when everyone gets home at the end of the day? Sharing the load more among family members, or cutting down on the complaints when everyone sits down to eat? Take some time to consider what would make the most difference for you, and then choose new strategies to support that change.

Planning and Preparing

Every day, for every meal, someone has to figure out what you're eating, who's making it, and where it's going to come from. For a lot of us, that means planning. At a minimum, it means planning not to plan. If you're like most families, breakfasts and lunches are more casual meals. Making those easier is mostly a matter of having simple things in the house that you feel good about offering or having your kids reach for. (If you're a family that cooks up a big breakfast or lunch on a regular basis, I imagine that's already something that makes you happy.) I'll talk more about those choices in the shopping section.

For most of us, dinner is different. This is the meal we expect to be cooked, to be balanced, to be eaten sitting around a table. It's the big leagues. Here's a little note from your future self—the one who, a few minutes or a few hours from now, will be watching the hands of the clock tick inexorably toward the evening meal:

Dear Past Me,

Help! It's dinnertime again (did we not just do this yesterday?)
and everyone keeps asking what's for dinner, and I have no idea.
I've been making decisions and behaving like a fully functional
adult all day and I am toast—couldn't you pick up the slack on this
one? Make a plan, buy a bunch of things that could be dinner, and
put a list of them somewhere for me, sign up for a meal service, not
have ordered takeout last night and the night before so I could order
it now because it was a long day? Anything? I know you probably
don't feel like thinking about this. But trust me, I feel like thinking
about it even less. I just want someone to tell me what to do, and
I'll do it.

Hopefully,
Dinnertime Me

I am a fanatical weekday meal planner, particularly during hockey season, when, with all four kids playing, afternoons and evenings become a cantata of pick-ups and drop-offs and precision timing. Every Sunday, I map out the week—who will be home for a sit-down dinner which nights? Which nights require a dinner that can be eaten in shifts? When will I be home to cook, when can I do some meal prep during the day, and when do we need a meal that can be ready within five minutes of my walking in the door or pulled together by a child? When will I just not want to cook? (Friday, every time.)

I make it easy on myself. Some days, the plan involves nothing but putting a prepared meal from the grocery store into the oven and slicing up some bread, or dropping frozen meatballs into the slow cooker with a jar of sauce and pressing start before I walk out the door at seven a.m. I plan takeout nights. I plan to make a box of macaroni and cheese.

Then I'm set. All I do at night is look at the list; I know the ingredients are there, I know whatever is planned will work for our timing, and the kids know what to expect for dinner, which they like. I get that little flash of worry during a work afternoon—*Shoot, what am I doing for dinner?*—and then I relax. Got it.

I don't always cook what I've planned. Things change. Someone is sick, and I move Thursday's soup to Tuesday. We decide to get takeout because something ran late. That's all fine. I rarely plan more than two weekly meals that "have" to be cooked or the ingredients will go bad, and I'm very willing to just stick stuff back in the freezer. It doesn't really matter if we follow the plan. What matters is that I have the plan.

Some people, though, really hate feeling as if they're boxed in by those planned meals. If that's you, happy non-planning parents recommend having ingredients for at least three go-to meals on hand and putting a list of meal ideas where you can find it easily, to avoid drawing a blank at the end of a long day. "I hated planning meals for a long time," says Inga Carter, of Portsmouth, New Hampshire, "because I would plan a week's worth of meals and then, invariably, by Thursday I wouldn't want what I had planned or life would get in the way, and then the rest of the week would go to hell, meal-wise. Then it occurred to me that I didn't have to assign days to meals. I could just plan a week's worth of meals, maybe with an idea of this meal on that day, but leave it open and make whichever one I felt like. It's been a couple years of that now and it's still working great."

Planning isn't necessarily about cooking. You can plan to have pasta with a jar of sauce and a bagged salad or to serve the eggplant parmesan from the prepared food section. In a family with two adults or older children, planning could mean as little as deciding who's on deck—who's going to shop, who's going to cook, and when. Lisa Woodruff, a mother of two in Cincinnati and the host of the *Organize 365* podcast is (in spite of being a professional organizer) not someone who likes to plan meals. Instead, she and her husband plan days. If it's his day, it's his problem (and she doesn't second-guess his choices). Preparing Monday's dinner might matter less if you know your partner is shopping Tuesday and that your teen is making dinner Wednesday.

You do you. Find the level of planning that makes you happier, and don't worry about what anyone else is doing. Consider that future self, the one staring into the fridge hoping the elves have dropped off a casserole. What will you wish you'd done, once you're standing in those shoes? That's all you need to do to make a happiness deposit, guaranteed to deliver a later payoff.

Shopping

I either don't like to grocery shop or, if I'm hungry, I like it too much. When my children were younger, my husband shopped on the weekends with my list. When they all entered full-time school, but we still needed after-school care, I decided to have our babysitter do the shopping. She gets more hours, which she needs, and I save money on all the impulse buys the kids or I would put in the cart if we were at the store. I only get the groceries I thought I needed at the moment when I made the list—the things I need to make the meals I planned, along with choices made by sensible me, who doesn't want to be tempted by a pantry full of potato chips and who knows that if there are no snacks in the house other than apples and peanut butter, people will eat apples and peanut butter. Except late at night, when I am rummaging desperately through the house looking for a salty snack to ease my stress, I love sensible me.

Because it makes me unhappy when I feel that my children are eating more convenience foods than real ones, I put things on the list that can be pulled out to eat almost as easily as a bag of chips: pre-shredded or sliced cheese, deli meat, bagels, tortillas, cherry tomatoes, cucumbers, fruits, frozen fruits that make easy smoothies, cheese tortellini, smoked salmon. I ask the kids to make lists of what they want. Anything that doesn't come in a box or a bag, I say. If those things are what we have, those are the things that get eaten.

When I do the shopping, I make a game of leaving with only the things on my list. I remind myself, when I see the displays on the ends of the aisles, that those are designed to tempt me, to convince me that it would be very handy to have a case of canned tuna in the house or a gallon-sized bottle of soy sauce. It wouldn't. The cans in the cabinet rarely get used, and the giant size of anything doesn't fit in my kitchen. I have already decided what we need, and that choice belongs to me, not to the marketing department at Frito-Lay.

That's not to say there's no junk food in the house—there is, and that's fine. We have plenty of treats and indulgences. But I'm happier when I decide what we need and buy it, and no more. There's more room in my cabinets and less food getting thrown away when it's past its sell-by date, or when some child conveniently chose to overlook the half-eaten bag of chips and opened a fresh one. The grocery store will be there. Even if there is a snowstorm or a hurricane, it will re-open, sooner than you think, fully stocked with more flavors of Oreos and Goldfish crackers than anyone could reasonably need.

Getting Food on the Table

I like to eat, which means I like to look forward to my dinner. It does not, however, necessarily mean I always want to cook that dinner. During one of the weeks when I was writing this chapter, I cooked exactly one thing—roasted brussels sprouts. We ate meals from the freezer, something prepared, or takeout every day. Sometimes I'm happier if I don't cook, and that's fine. Planning a week of easy nights might make you much happier than planning a lot of meals you won't really have the time or inclination to cook.

Some stages in life really lend themselves to keeping things simple in the kitchen. Even Jenny Rosenstrach, who declares herself to be maybe even a touch pathological about family dinner (she's kept a diary of everything she, and later her family, ate for dinner for more than nineteen years), says that sometimes you just need to "lower the bar." "When I was working full-time and my kids were very young, I didn't want dinnertime to be a fight. I just wanted it to be pleasant and to sit down together for as long as possible to lay the groundwork for the ritual," she says. "If you want to sustain the practice of regular family dinners, you can't expect every night to be osso buco."

What we really want is to feel good about what we're eating, and to be able to get those meals together, especially at the end of a long day, without a lot of angst, madness, and misery. I feel like I cook a lot, and most of our meals are things I've prepared, one way or another, but I do relatively little actual standing over a stove at 5:30 p.m. I've got three strategies for making the path from fridge to table (or from someone else's fridge to table) easier at the end of the day.

OUTSOURCE

In the past, pre-made meals usually meant a choice between cheap and unhealthy in most ways or pretty much what you might make at home, only at twice the price or more. But that's changing. Particularly if you live in or near a large urban area, your options might include chefs who come to your home and prepare a week's worth of meals, then leave them behind with cooking instructions, or who deliver prepared meals for your fridge or freezer. You might know a friend or neighbor or even a teenager who has started a small business doing something similar. Sharon Van Epps, a mother of three teenagers in Seattle, says the family gets a homemade pasta dinner delivery once a week from their old nanny. "Pasta cooks in three minutes, all I have to do is heat up the sauce. She varies it weekly and sends a little info about the Italian origins of that particular dish."

Kelli Avila, a mother of two toddlers in Boston, saw the need and started a similar business. Her Shoofly Pie Baking Company delivers small and large savory pies twice a week in just a few Boston neighborhoods. Lillie Marshall, a customer and the mother of two, says she and her husband rely on meals from Kelli and from a similar company four to five nights a week. "It's saved us," she says, "given that we have two kids under three and a half and both work more than full-time and hate to cook." Both Van Epps and Marshall say the time savings is worth the added expense to them—they're happier.

You can also outsource the planning and shopping part of meals to one of the many ingredient-delivery services. Some allow you to take delivery for ingredients for just a meal or two of your choice when you want them, while others require a regular subscription (but take the deciding when or what out of your hands). Some send whole ingredients, others chop for you. In this case, you need to time to cook, but not to prep. I've found that these services tend to favor meals that require someone to spend thirty to forty-five minutes in the kitchen cooking right before dinner, whereas I still favor meals that I can get ready ahead of time, allowing for me to be somewhere else, or doing something else, until right before we eat. But I have friends who swear by them, often using the easy instructions and the promise of having all the ingredients to persuade a partner or a child to do the cooking.

DON'T COOK, "ASSEMBLE"

This is the pasta-with-a-jar-of-sauce meal, or the make-your-own-taco using precooked chicken warmed in the slow cooker, canned beans (I put those next to the meat in the slow cooker), pre-shredded cheese, and toppings picked up at the salad bar. You might spend a little more on pre-chopped or even pre-cooked ingredients (or you might do it yourself on the weekend), but again, it may be worth the expense. "Almost anything you've prepared at home using mostly fresh or minimally processed ingredients will probably be healthier than the takeouts you didn't get," says Maya Adam, a mother of three and a lecturer on food and nutrition at Stanford who developed a massive open online course called "Child Nutrition and Cooking." "There are no inherently unhealthy foods. The question is always: what would I have been eating instead of this food? Homemade grilled cheese sandwiches may be less healthy than a quinoa and Persian cucumber salad with toasted pistachio nuts and shallot vinaigrette, but if the alternative is a fast-food hamburger and fries, go for the grilled cheese." Prepared foods like sauces and salad dressings can speed dinner assembly. Adam suggests looking for those with fewer ingredients, although she notes that those are often the more expensive products. If buying a few mass-produced prepared ingredients helps you prepare some of the meal at home, she says, it's still worth it.

COOK WHEN YOU HAVE TIME, NOT WHEN YOU DON'T

Here's Ellen Spirer Socol, a working mother in Westchester County, New York, describing her Saturday: "Between 7:30 and 10:30 this morning I made tomato sauce, béchamel sauce (for both lasagna and mac 'n' cheese), lasagna, mac 'n' cheese, and a batch of cookie dough. Sure, it would be nice to just sit and read a book or organize my office, but anything that gets another weeknight dinner done ahead of time is more important." Batch-cooking on the weekends and cooking double of everything, she says, so you can freeze another meal is "key." She spent three hours and got two meals for the fridge and four for the freezer (she froze some sauce separate from the lasagna), plus cookies, at a moment when she wasn't in a rush.

A friend and I do this for each other a couple of times a year—we each cook double of two or three freezable meals, then swap. We plan ahead, so that both families will like the food and we won't end up with multiple meatloaves. Sometimes we make a day of it—we do the cooking together in one of our kitchens, and we both go home with four or six no-cooking nights in hand. It's been a great way to expand both of our family palates—she favors Mexican food (enchiladas) and I cook a lot of Italian (meatballs)—as well as spend time together.

At the Table

As I said at the beginning of the chapter, food is one area where I give myself the happier parent gold star. I love food and cooking, and I'm passionate about the entire question of how we feed our families and how national policies as well as personal choices play into what shows up on our plates.

But there's what we buy and cook, and then there's the meal. For some families, it isn't planning, shopping, or cooking that's making us less than happy, but what happens once we sit down to eat. A few years into our family life, as my children and my friends' children began to express their opinions about food and eating (and after one memorable meal when a guest shook her head at what we'd prepared and asked if she could find her kid some cereal), I decided to set down our family rules about what happens at our table—and begin to work on how our kids should behave as they grew up and became guests themselves.

Our kids were three, four, five, and eight. The rules weren't new, but they'd been largely unspoken until then. Here they are:

1. **One family, one meal.** We cook one meal for the whole family every night, which includes at least one thing anyone will eat. There are no options, and there is no after-dinner snacking.
2. **You don't have to eat it, but you do have to look at it.** No one has to eat or taste anything, ever—but you do have to let it be on your plate.
3. **No insulting the food.** At our table, you can say "No, thank you," "I didn't care for that," and "That's not my favorite."

Unless you're asked for more details, that's it. No attitude, no faces, no "yuck," not ever.

4. **No pressure.** They eat what they eat. We don't worry about it and rarely comment. *If you see something, don't always say something.* The most anyone might say (and it's usually a sibling) is "That's good. You should try it."

5. **Food isn't a reward for eating.** If there's dessert, and you didn't really eat dinner, that's fine. Here's your ice cream.

Seven years later, very little has changed about our "rules." I've since found variations on the ones to do with eating and pressure everywhere, from the teachings of Ellyn Satter, nutritionist and author of *How to Get Your Kid to Eat (But Not Too Much)*, to Karen Le Billon's book *French Kids Eat Everything*, so they're not unique to our family by any means. I relaxed the rule about after-dinner eating when my children got older, especially since a child might eat dinner before a sports practice and need to eat again after, or there just might not have been enough dinner for a teen on a particularly hungry day. By then, I knew no one was skipping a less-favorite meal in the hope of filling up on something else afterward, because that just wasn't how they ate. I knew our way had worked for us when I expressed sympathy for my son as I served him meatloaf—not his favorite. "That's okay," he said. "I don't have to love it to eat it."

I love our rules, and they work. I've got research on my side: children who eat the same meals as adult members of the family eat healthier diets. Observing parents consuming nutritious foods like fruits and vegetables increases the likelihood that a child will also consume those foods. When a meal is shared, children and adults stay at the table longer, beginning and ending their meal together rather than wandering in and out—providing more opportunity for conversation. In cultures where a shared family meal means adults and children sitting together and eating the same foods, like in France and Italy, children develop a more positive attitude toward food and learn to prefer quality over quantity.

The middle two rules (it goes on your plate, but there's no pressure) create room for kids to grow and change around food. They can taste it without a big drama. They don't need to become cemented in their position that they like or dislike something, because if they leave it on the plate, no one will comment. Research shows that kids need to be exposed to a food multiple times before they try it or like it, but it's tough to make that shift if all of those times have involved shrieking, making faces, and being forced to taste in order to get dessert or leave the table. *People, including children—especially children—change* . . . if we let them.

Our rule about not insulting the food or the cook may be my favorite. The cook can be very sensitive; it's a lot of trouble to plan and make a dinner every night when she's tired after a long day, and she's not afraid to say so. And maybe throw things. I have, to be honest, served up some pretty dreadful mistakes in my time as family chef, and the only one to say "yuck" was me. That makes me very happy, or at least, it eliminates something that made me very unhappy. If I had it to do again I might make a rule that they thank the cook every night. Profusely. For making the meal, and for helping them learn how to eat it.

My way isn't the only way to be happy about food and family. I'll defend my "no insulting the food" rule to the death (if you take one thing and only one from this chapter, I'd make it that), but there are other approaches to things like trying new foods and feeling good about what your family is eating. Le Billon (*French Kids Eat Every-*

thing is one of my favorite books about children, families, and food culture) swears by the French rule "You don't have to like it, but you do have to taste it," also known as the "no thank you" bite. She also practices "Dessert only if you eat dinner," but not as a bribe. It's what she considers a natural consequence. Meals are eaten in a certain sequence; if at any point you break the order, the meal is over. That's a very different message than offering junk food as a reward for eating something healthy.

Rosenstrach is a passionate cook—but even more, she's a passionate defender of the importance of everyone sitting peacefully around the dinner table together. She's found that she's happier if she does a little "short-order cooking" once in a while: "If you serve something and your kid doesn't like it, make him or her a peanut butter sandwich and don't beat yourself up over it," she said.

The strategies that make you happier about food and family might not be the strategies that work for your brother, your best friend, or your boss. That's fine. As much as the latest food trend might push the idea that there's only one way to eat right, that's simply wrong. There's more than one way to enjoy cooking and eating, and you don't have to find the way for everyone. You just have to find yours.

Cooking for Kids Who Won't Eat

There's a long list of things that can make our time eating together less pleasant, but children who don't appreciate the food you've cooked are among the most challenging. "Selective" eaters (also known as picky) make it hard to create and enjoy a family meal, as do—for different reasons—family members with self-imposed eating restrictions on ingredients like meat or carbs. (This is different from the challenges of an allergic family member, which I'll talk about in the next section.)

When we are overly solicitous of a child's first responses to new foods, especially a very young child, we can inadvertently harden a mild resistance to trying new things into an ardent refusal to accept any but the easiest of flavors. With younger kids, it's often possible to head off picky eating with simple strategies, like allowing a child to feel hunger, offering a healthy variety of foods at meals, and allowing her to make her choices. But what of the older child who has already become a decisive eater—or rather, a decisive refuser of many foods? How can you enjoy sitting down together when every meal is a battle over "just try one bite" or a minefield of guilt for you, the parent of a child who eats nothing but pasta with olive oil and parmesan, ever?

It starts with releasing both the battle and the minefield. Two statements of fact: no child ever decided she liked something after an hour-long argument over "just one bite." And children in families with enough to eat rarely suffer physically from malnutrition. (We'll talk obesity and weight concerns in the next section, and if you have concerns that your child is developing an eating disorder, which can begin as early as kindergarten, find a doctor who will listen and help.)

For most of us, the road to a happier table starts with a conversation—away from the table—with your picky child. Does she want to change? I was a picky eater, and it was a constant source of embarrassment for me. A teenaged athlete might really want to find some healthier choices she's willing or able to eat; a younger child might be willing to have some fun doing "taste tests" and experimenting in the kitchen. If that's the case, you can strategize together. Pick one meal a week to include a new food or recipe, or for her to help cook. It was easier for me, as a child, to get my head around the idea that I might like something new than to readjust my conception of something I'd already decided I did not like.

For a child with no interest in changing (right now) or if your relationship around her eating is just too fraught to even suggest it, Sally Sampson, founder of *ChopChop*, a nonprofit kids' cooking magazine, and coauthor (with Natalie Digate Muth) of *The Picky Eater Project*, suggests shifting the focus away from the picky child and what she eats entirely. Make meals that accommodate her or can be customized and then do nothing more. Do require that the picky child join you at the table if she's out of that habit, but "don't focus on the food or what your child is or isn't eating—not a peep," she says. "Instead, ask them about their day, tell them about yours. Treat your child with the same courtesy you would an adult: don't make them eat anything they don't want and don't make a scene about their choices. How one child is eating should not be the topic of conversation when you're eating. If you need to have a conversation about it, have it anywhere else than your kitchen or dining room table."

Other parents do tend to expect us to nudge and push our kids to eat more or differently. Susan D'Entremont, a mother of two in Albany, says her pediatrician told her not to worry about her son's "tan diet." The more attention we pay to it, the worse the problem might get, he told her. "But even if we don't pay attention to it, others do. The most common comment is 'We would never allow that in our household.' I'm not sure what that means. You would pin your kid to the floor and force food down his throat?"

Her relaxed approach is gradually paying off. Now that her son is a teen, she says, "he will actually try a bite of something he hasn't before, so maybe someday . . ." For most kids, that day does come.

"My daughter, who ate white food for years, is now thirty-five and eats everything," said a friend. "It gets better." My mother could say the same.

It does. And even if it doesn't, you can feel better about your child's eating and eating with your child if you can embrace the idea that you choose what's available to eat, and she chooses what to eat, and really live it. What goes into her mouth isn't the only important part of a meal together. In fact, it's arguably the least. You're talking, you're laughing, you're together, you're modeling a good relationship with food and family. You can get iron from supplements and vitamin D from sunshine. You can't get a happy family meal together anywhere else.

Keeping It Simple When Things Get Complicated

If it's tough to be happy in the kitchen with a picky eater, it's even more difficult when the challenges are health related. If one of your children has food allergies, is putting on weight in a way that worries your pediatrician, or if you or your partner have your own food challenges, it can be hard to feel good about gathering the whole family around the same meal.

In some cases, like life-threatening food allergies and weight issues, keeping a child healthy means adjusting the way the entire family eats. In many food-allergic families, nearly everything is cooked at home to prevent contamination. It's a real commitment, but one that many parents of food-allergic kids say means the whole family eats less processed food, snacks less, and is more likely to come together around the table than if the temptations of prepared foods and frozen single-serving meals were more available—a silver lining.

If you're beginning to worry that your child is heavier than he should be—or if he's noticing—pause before you panic (and consult your pediatrician). It's important to remember that preteens often go through a stocky stage. They "grow outward before they grow up-ward," as Maya Adam puts it. But it can worry some children, and in some cases, it can be a sign of a problem. Either way, it's not a bad moment to take stock of family eating habits and see if some changes are necessary. That's what Adam did when one of her children started getting a little self-conscious about weight.

"Without making any conscious decisions to change our diet, I found myself doing things a little differently. I held back a little on the oil or butter in the pan. I cut back on the meat in our weekly meals and added a few more vegetables to everyone's plates. I made an extra effort to turn out some pretty-darn-good-tasting veggie dishes and I served them first (pretending the other food wasn't ready yet), to try and catch their hunger and make it work in my favor."

She didn't put an end to snack food, but made more things like cookies herself, from more healthful recipes. On nights when takeout was tempting, she pushed herself to make a different choice.

"As I made these subtle changes (which, by the way, the children hardly noticed) I realized something that has since become the key to my philosophy on food preparation: when the hand that prepares the food has a vested interest in the long-term health of the people con-suming that food, the food will almost always end up being higher quality, healthier, and, as you get better at it, probably more deli-cious."

When you're trying to make subtle shifts for a child's health, you need to change your meals overall. But when the challenges allow for more flexibility (a vegan family member; an adult who wants to cut back on carbs or meat without changing children's diets), many parents swear by the deconstructed meal—a technique that works in families with picky eaters as well.

Jenny Rosenstrach calls this "Venn diagram eating"—enough crossover that everyone is eating the same meal, but enough room to allow the mushroom-haters to have a pasta that's fungi-free. "You take a normally composed dish, like Cobb salad, and deconstruct it into separate parts. So one kid is having chicken, avocado, and tomatoes for dinner, and one is having hard-boiled eggs, bacon, and lettuce, but it's still the same dinner."

One of Melissa Ford's twelve-year-old twins has food allergies and "food and eating are just really stressful for him" (which is common in food-allergic children). "The other twin is a real foodie and loves to try new foods." The Washington, DC, mom makes a meal with sauce on the side and leaves some portions unseasoned. They make restaurants a "try new things" adventure for one child while letting the other stay within his comfort zone.

If you, as a parent, are the one with some challenges around food—you might yourself be a picky eater, or in recovery from an eating disorder or following a careful diet of your choice—then you need to give yourself the same grace and respect I've encouraged you to give your children, and ask of yourself the same flexibility. Put the foods you don't like on your plate, let your own choices go by without comment or excuse, and know that your children are watching you.

When Nicki Gilbert's then eight-year-old daughter asked, "Mom, when do grown-ups stop eating breakfast?" the California mother of four realized that she needed to make some changes. As a recovering anorexic, she kept very tight control over her eating. "I needed to learn that I could take care of myself with food instead of by denying myself," she says. Instead of keeping foods in the house that she had to resist, she made healthier purchases. "I focused on wanting to fill all of our bodies with good and healthy food," she says. "I try and encourage all of them to listen to their body, to ask themselves, 'Are you really hungry?' I don't think that I knew that."

Although she still follows a narrow diet herself, she makes meals that allow the whole family to sit down together. "I used to hate being in the kitchen because mealtimes were such a minefield for me, but now I have this different approach," she says. "I think I'm good at making meals that we all enjoy so there's always something for everyone, even me.

"The best thing about our meals is being together."

Pass On Your Family Food Values— and Your Respect for Others

The choices we make around eating tend to be very personal. We often make them a part of our identity: "I'm a healthy eater/an omnivore/an ice-cream lover/gluten-free." Typically, they involve both embracing one way of eating and rejecting, or at least setting aside, another—you can't eat everything. There are a lot of politics around those choices. Whether it's eating in a way that reflects your ethnic heritage, adopting a particular style (local, organic, fresh), or refusing to follow a fad or trend, how you eat can be seen by others as a judgment no matter how you intend it.

It *is* a judgment. You've made the choice you think is best for you and your family. If you didn't think yours was the right choice, you'd make a different one. The tough part, then, is the part where your choice interacts and overlaps with others: when it's your turn to provide preschool snack; when you have a child's friend over for lunch; when your family and another go out together to share a meal.

Those situations can amplify our choices—and so can our kids, who talk to one another about the food they're eating at a very young age. This can get confusing. Why does Lana say Oreos are delicious while Jonas says they're poison? You may not be walking around denouncing other people's food choices, but it's natural for children to compare themselves and their lunches, to look for similarities and differences, and to feel a need to defend even when no one was attacking. They may identify more closely with your family food choices than you ever meant for them to. When Lisa Saunders's daughter was young, the family "used to disparage McDonald's pretty regularly at home. Then one day a mom very kindly offered to take a bunch of kids there after an event, and my daughter announced, 'Oh no, my parents won't let me eat there. They think it's garbage!'" If you ever walk home, as Julie Zimmerman has, with a group of third graders after a school party and overhear one of them "badmouthing the birthday cupcakes in class that day because they were store bought," know that you are hearing her parents' words in her mouth—and that your children are repeating you in that same know-it-all tone.

Try to give your children the words they need to eat their way (which is to say, your way) without hurting or being hurt by others, and prepare them for differences. Some of our very closest family friends eat vegan, which means I've been talking with my children about why we eat eggs, dairy, and animals since they were very young. At the same time, I know that on the other side, our friends were doing much the same—offering the reasoning for their choices, while trying to teach their children not to force that reasoning on others.

We really don't all have to eat the same way to be happy, or to be healthy or moral or responsible. We don't even have to eat the same way all the time. We just have to be content with the way we're eating and sharing our meals now, and leave room for other ways to find happiness around food later on.

Make the Choices That Make You Happy

Just because you're cooking for your family when you cook doesn't mean you're not also cooking for yourself. Why not make your favorite meal regardless of whether you expect anyone else in the family to really like it? One of the prime reasons I enjoy most of our meals is that I choose most of our meals, and that means I almost always put my own tastes first, or at least on par with everyone else. That's consistent with my research, both the surveyed and the anecdotal—parents who make choices around meals (and vacations) while taking everyone's preferences into account are happier overall than those who cook with primarily the kids' tastes in mind. You probably make some meals that are designed to please your kids. Make some that are special for you, too.

If you're generally okay with things around cooking and eating, but you're just not getting much pleasure out of it, try something to shake things up in a way that fits in with your life right now. If you don't cook with your children much, invite them to get involved in a meal or even take over once in a while. If, on the other hand, you have little helpers always nearby, give yourself a break and cook solo. Indulge in a recipe/ingredient delivery service, serve breakfast for dinner, declare pizza Fridays. Find a way to find your joy.

These meals are your time together. They'll almost certainly reflect the entirety of your life: some will be good, some pretty awful.

Sometimes the conversation will be lovely and deep, sometimes goofy, sometimes angry, sometimes little but grunts. Some meals will be delicious, some serviceable, some laughably bad. You'll settle into your ways and your places, and the way you are together at the table will reflect the way you are together out in the world. So if it isn't what you want, if it isn't generally happy, it's right to want to change it. But you have time. You don't need a ten-point plan to make family dinners happier by next Tuesday. You have years to get this right.

Family dinners are about dinner, but first and foremost they're about family. So here's my final piece of advice for happier family meals: *sit down and eat.* Don't wait on the table. Stay in your chair, enjoy yourself, have a glass of wine if that's what you do. It's not a family meal if you're not really there, too.

nine

FREE TIME, VACATIONS, HOLIDAYS, BIRTHDAYS, AND OTHER ON-DEMAND "FUN"

W e have never taken a family vacation during which I have not, at some moment, vowed never to take another. One of my favorite comments about traveling with kids came from Kristen Howerton (who blogs at *Rage Against the Minivan*) on Facebook as she and her four kids, all under ten at the time, embarked on a trip to Machu Picchu. It went something like this: "Here we go! Off to take the kids to whine at one of the Seven Wonders of the World."

Vacations with children—and birthdays, holidays, and school breaks, along with that rare beast, "free time"—are supposed to be fun. But we know too well that while the fun is anything but guaranteed, one thing is certain: there will be a lot of work involved. For vacations, there will be the planning, the packing, the management of small children in unfamiliar and unchildproofed spaces, and the debates with older children about whether to put down the phone, turn off the video, or even set aside the book to look out the window. There will be times—usually weeks, if you're in the United States—when your children are on vacation and you are not, and those will be both complicated and expensive. Birthdays and holidays will include family pressures and children jacked up on sugar, late bedtimes, and high expectations, at their worst when you expect them to be at their best. Is everybody happy yet?

What Goes Wrong

That word, "expectations," is at the root of what makes special occasions with children so likely to be special in all the wrong ways. It seems to us, as parents, that there is a lot riding on these red-letter days. Many of our own memories of childhood center around the times when the camera came out and the grown-ups took off work and the cousins visited. We know these are the times our children will remember, too, and we want them to be good memories.

Vacations are under similar pressure. Vacations are worth the hassle: they're good for adult health and productivity, and have benefits for children and families. Children who travel can be more adaptable, curious, and aware of the world around them, and families told researchers they felt closer and more connected while on vacation. (The latter finding is from a Disney-funded survey, so it should be taken with some salt; they probably didn't ask if families also felt more stressed at the sight of each additional mouse-eared price tag.) Vacations are supposed to be relaxing, rejuvenating, a time to reconnect.

But we Americans pack our relaxation into a really small space. About a quarter of us have no paid time off at all, and the rest of us get an average of thirteen days a year for vacation and a bonus eight paid holidays. That's not a lot of hours for all of our family togetherness needs, and many of us either don't take all we're offered or spend significant chunks of that time shielding our laptop from the spray and sunshine at the water park.

Once the vacation begins, we get weighed down by that whole "supposed to" problem. There's this sense that this is our moment—that "quality time" for which we have traded in so much of our "quantity time." Few of us spend many afternoons or weekend days hanging out with our children, especially once they're elementary aged or older. Our leisure today tends to be both organized and age segregated, and even parents who are with their children during those hours, or parents who are at home most of the time, spend much of that time driving children to child-centered activities, practices, and lessons rather than on frivolous family fun. So when vacation time arrives, there we are, with our all-caps plan to relax, rejuvenate, and reconnect, burning precious resources in the form of vacation days and money and risking our very livelihoods with our absence from our desks in order to spend this time with these, our beloved offspring, *who do not seem to appreciate it.*

From here, "what goes wrong" on a family vacation is age and circumstance dependent, but there are so many possibilities. Children get sick on planes and then pass their germs through every member of the family on holiday. Rental cars lose their air-conditioning or their windows get stuck open. Work crises greet us in the hotel lobby, teenagers are bored and show it, the campsite or water park you'd counted on is closed for repairs. Even the memories gathered on the vacation might not be the ones you were counting on. Jessica Sanders, a Utah mother of three who writes *The Happiest Blog on Earth*, says that she and her husband saved for a year to take their children on a trip to Disneyland. "We spent two days at the resort, a few days at the beach, and time exploring Los Angeles museums and sights. We did so many incredible things most kids don't ever get to experience," she says. When they got home, her father-in-law asked their four-year-old what she liked best about the trip. "She said, 'Grandpa! We got to go to McDonald's three times!'"

How Can We Put the Fun Back in Family Time?

I included birthdays, holidays, vacations, and general free and leisure time in the same chapter because they have two big things in common: first, we feel a lot of pressure to get them "right," and second, the only way to really feel happy under mandatory-fun conditions is to get to work on changing that mind-set. There are, of course, plenty of ways to make all of those things better and easier, and I'll offer as many as I can in the final section of the chapter. But before any of the tricks and tips for family vacations and toddler birthdays can help, we have to pull the valve on the pressure. Yes, vacations, holidays, birthdays, and leisure are "supposed" to leave us with beloved family memories. That's because they do, pretty much regardless. Even (possibly especially) when things are very much not going according to plan.

CHANGE YOUR NARRATIVE

One of the secrets of "quality time" in the form of vacations and special occasions is that, although it feels rare, you actually get a solid quantity of it. Enough to create traditions, enough that it will quickly feel as though you have "always" done this or that. Between a child's birth and his eighteenth birthday, you get 940 Saturdays, as pediatrician Harley Rotbart counted up in his book *No Regrets Parenting*. You get eighteen Christmases, eighteen summers, and some set number of family vacations, which stretch out before you when your children are babies and catch up to you quickly after all. That may sound like me reminding you that your time is limited, but those are decently large numbers. They're finite, yes, and we humans don't like that much, but there's lots of room in there for error, if you want to call it that. Plenty of time for missed connections and rainy beach vacations. More importantly, plenty of time for doing nothing much.

When it comes to letting up on some of the pressure we feel around vacations and holidays, one of the first things to do is to embrace the idea of truly unscheduled time. As in, no plans. You wake up in the morning with a completely open slate, and then you do something you want to do, and then you do something someone else wants to do, and you fit in some meals and any necessary personal hygiene in there, and before you know it, you're ready to go to bed. No playdates, no lessons, not even a dinner reservation. Just a day or more doing whatever comes up.

The problem is, many of us, especially Americans, tend to be afraid to do nothing. It's not our way. A survey by Hilton International found that more than half of travelers with children say they pack so much into their vacation that they need "a vacation from their vacation" when they return. "There's this general sense right now that our children's time, and the times when we're with them, should be spent productively," says Lisa Damour, who writes a column on adolescence for the *New York Times* and is the author of *Untangled*. "That's the baseline. We're working toward this faraway goal that our kids come out okay, and we don't know what that looks like, exactly, but we know that watching YouTube videos with them does not feel connected to that goal but driving them to ballet class does."

Instead, says Damour, we need to rely on our gut feeling that all of the time we spend with our children, whether it's watching mindless television, reading aloud, or just being in the same space together, occasionally leaning over to share a headline on our phones, adds up to something. "I have this fantasy that someone will do an actual research study that shows that just hanging out with your kids doing nothing leads to them coming out okay. I think we'd all feel so much better."

If, when you're planning a vacation or for the time you can share with your kids over their school breaks, you make "just hanging out doing nothing" one of your goals, you've set a lovely low bar that you're bound to clear. You can make similar shifts in all your special occasion intentions: we will have eight fifth graders here, and they will celebrate my son's birthday. Will they hit a piñata with a stick? Maybe. Or maybe the piñata will prove recalcitrant, and eventually, his older brother will take it up the stairs and throw it down at them. That's still a birthday celebration (and arguably more memorable than the classic piñata version). After a long year of school and all of the activities that go along with it, Naomi Hattaway, the founder of an international social network based in Virginia, took a break this summer with two of her children (eleven and fourteen; she also has a twenty-two-year-old) and "didn't sign up for one activity. Not one." Instead, they traveled and, even when home, "slept until ungodly hours and stayed up past midnight nearly every night. We ate a lot of ice cream, logged more dog walk miles than we have ever collectively in our past, and explored our neighborhood coffee shops like never before."

Scheduling unscheduled time can really change the way we interact with our kids. So many of our arguments with children, especially when they're young, come from transitions. Every parent has wondered how it can possibly be so hard to get them to pack themselves up to go to the swimming pool with friends when they love the pool and their friends, and wanted nothing more than to go an hour ago when you made the arrangements.

I don't have an answer for that, but I think it centers around the words "have to." We have to go. We have to be on time. We have to get in the car now. Suddenly, what was supposed to be fun has become part of the constant give-and-take that is parenting. As Julie Falatko, a children's book author from Maine who spends vacations camping out with her husband and three children in their RV, puts it: sometimes travel just feels like "a new and different venue for my husband and me to discipline the children."

More genuinely free time, whether it's at home or away, might help to reduce that sense of always being the disciplinarian on duty. If you don't need to be anywhere, there's no need to drag the kids to the car. It also gives you all an opportunity to make decisions together and not in a "here, you pick one thing to do on our vacation" kind of way. Instead, with a wide-open schedule, everyone gets to throw things out there. "We ditched the meal planning and decided at the last minute what to eat and where," says Hattaway. "We took advantage of five-dollar movies at the theater on Tuesdays." Less "have to" meant more time to play and a more relaxed attitude for everyone.

This business of being together, in your own house, in a vacation house, or at a family member's home, without having some set plan is something that takes practice, especially if your screen-time rules don't offer an easy out for the "bored" child, or if you're the parent of siblings who are likely to use the time to engage in some rivalry. Do it enough, though, and particularly when your children reach an age where they can entertain themselves and even feed themselves or take themselves outside for a while, you'll begin to crave it. The "do nothing day" will become one vacation ideal. Many families (us included) build it into vacation plans, choosing hotels or vacation rentals that allow for unstructured time and sudden changes of plan.

Joseph Hinson, who built my website, is a father of three in Virginia. He and his wife designed their summer vacation around the idea of unscheduled time. They drove a pop-up camper around the East Coast for a month, scheduling little beyond camping spots. "We saw bears, walked under waterfalls, went tubing, biking, and connected with our world in a way that was incredible," he says. "It's hard to get back to the normalcy of life after that experience." Now they're resisting scheduled weekends and afternoons, and trying to bring some of that feeling of freedom and family connection back into their ordinary life. They spend time with friends, but they also reserve "family fun days" every week. "So far they've ranged from seeing beautiful sites within an hour of our house on weekends to doing breakfast for dinner in front of our projector outside. We want to feel like we're in control of our life, instead of it just happening to us."

Unstructured time can also mean that you've made plans, but you're happy to change them. Ruth Rau, a mother and toymaker in Winchester, Virginia, says that after years of vacationing with her two boys, she has learned to take a more laid-back approach. "We spend more time in fewer places," she says. "We don't try to cram everything in, and we don't make many plans we can't change." On their way to the zoo while staying with family friends one summer, she says, they saw a sign for a model train show. "All of the kids wanted to see the trains. So we ditched the zoo and spent a lovely leisurely morning walking around a shaded model train exhibit, talking to locals, then found the most wonderful little coffee shop and had a picnic on the lawn." A year later, she says, her kids (now four and five) still talk about the day with the trains. "And I still remember the feeling that exploring life with my kids is pretty sweet."

As you ease into a comfort with doing less, consider the real goal of your time, whether it's a vacation, summer break, or a holiday. "Seeing the Grand Canyon" or "celebrating Thanksgiving" is only part of it. "What we've come to understand is that vacations with kids are all about getting out of the house," said Falatko. "You try to do something memorable, and we're all together, so they have to figure out how to play together even more than they usually do." In my research on siblings, one thing that came up again and again is that all the bickering matters less in families where siblings also share memories of good times. Family vacations and holidays are often where those memories are formed. *Soak up the good.* "What it's about for me," said Falatko, "is the enforced togetherness, which makes us all remember what we like about each other in the first place."

Once you've adjusted your expectations when it comes to vacations and special occasions, there are still practical things you can do to increase your happiness when the pressure feels like it's on. These big events might represent future memories and past traditions, but they're also, on a simpler level, experiences to be built with your family, your to-do list, and your wallet. Most of us get better at vacations, family holidays, and birthdays with practice, and other people's advice can help.

Planes, Trains, and Automobiles: Families on the Move

When a vacation or a family holiday involves packing up and heading out, it's the rare parent whose excitement isn't tinged, or entirely overwhelmed, with a sense of stress. There's so much to remember, so much to plan, so much to pack. How can we get it all together and keep it that way over the course of four flights, a rental car, and two different hotels in two states?

EXPECT MORE FROM YOUR KIDS

When my children were three, five, and seven, my husband, my mother, and I took them to China on a trip to adopt their youngest sister. As if that trip alone weren't challenge enough, three days after our arrival in Beijing, the Chinese government quarantined us as part of their efforts to combat the spread of the H1N1 flu virus (you might remember it as swine flu). They hospitalized my husband and moved my mother, the three children, and me to a quarantine facility—a former luxury hotel, moldy and full of holes in the walls after being shut down for years, now staffed by government employees, only one of whom spoke English. Daily temperatures hovered in the nineties. The hotel was un-air-conditioned and the entertainment options limited to a single badminton net and a long-unused fountain full of koi fish, some belly-up. Chinese food was served buffet-style three times daily and did not include the typical kid's menu options (although we were once served hot dogs, wrapped in Chinese buns, for breakfast).

This was obviously not your ideal vacation scenario, but in looking back, the thing I see most clearly is that everything I panicked about regularly before traveling with my kids really isn't a big deal. The absence of snacks wasn't a crisis, nor was the unfamiliar food (and watching your children eat what's in front of them for a week because there isn't anything else will forever change your approach to feeding them). Extremely limited TV and video games weren't, either (this experience predated tablets by a year or so). They were hot and bored, but who hasn't been hot and bored? It was a surreal week (and in many ways a frightening one), but it wasn't a catastrophe in the ways I would have expected it to be if you'd asked me to prepare for it. It was, once we were really convinced they weren't going to remove the children and that they were going to let us go eventually, not that bad.

Most of us won't spend our less-than-perfect vacations in government quarantine, but even when fear isn't a factor, children can put up with a lot more than we think they can. They don't really have to be entertained every minute; they don't have to love every meal; they can spend some time—hours, or even days—doing something they don't enjoy for the sake of someone they love, or possibly because the people in the hazmat suits have already taken Daddy and might come back for Mommy, too. Nothing is going to make a six-hour delay on the tarmac with a two-year-old easy, but you can expect more than we usually do from older children in the way of tolerating both the less-than-ideal and the outright disastrous. Talk ahead of time about how you'll handle tough situations (or difficult extended family members, if that's a common problem). Come up with coping tools and plans, pack snacks, and try to agree not to make things worse.

GET HELP FROM YOUR KIDS

One of the reasons vacations don't contribute to our happiness as parents is that they're so much work. If only someone else would do just one thing, we think, this would be easier. Planning, packing for, and masterminding a vacation can feel like a job, not a joy. If you're traveling with a partner or a spouse, your workload is lessened, but still, it is work.

Our children can take some of this on. You can give a very young child a list: five pairs of underwear, three shirts, and three pairs of shorts, even if you're planning to edit his selections. You can ask them to choose a book and put crayons in a baggie to bring along. Children that young may not be much help, but they're learning to expect to help later. A six-year-old with a general list of what she needs should be able to get out her clothes for a trip, subject to your approval. A nine-year-old with the same list should be able to pack his side of the suitcase, although you'll probably still need to check to be sure he didn't choose his favorite holey sweats as "pants." At twelve, a child should be thinking through how many days you'll be there and what you'll do and making his own list.

If your destination allows for it (for example, a trip to a family member's house), don't check their work. Let them forget a swimsuit and borrow from a cousin, or forget underwear and end up at a chain store with the whole family impatiently waiting to head to the beach. Don't be too hard on them about it. Packing is a valuable life skill.

Bruce Feiler, author of *The Secrets of Happy Families*, recommends getting children involved in the planning piece as well. Have them choose somewhere to go or do, he suggests, and map out the details and even, as they get older, make any calls or arrangements. Younger kids could be put in charge of how to get to the airplane gate or searching for something specific, like nearby mini-golf. Show them where to start (here is the big map of the airport; those are what the signs we follow look like) or help them with search terms, and then step aside.

Getting your children involved in the work as well as the play that goes into family travel makes the whole thing more of a team effort, and it can also help a child who is anxious around travel feel some control over it. As their "help" becomes real help, their participation becomes a piece of the joy of the family trip, both because it adds to the feeling that you're all in this together and because you really didn't have to pack for five.

TAKE TURNS AT EVERYTHING,
INCLUDING GRUMPINESS

It's a good idea to take everyone's interests into account as much as you can when planning a trip—to "take turns" doing something that's more important to one family member than to others. I like bookstores. My youngest daughter likes candy stores. There's room in our trip for both, and it's fair to ask that I don't whine and demand to know if we're done yet while she's watching someone pull taffy.

Activities shouldn't be the only place where happy vacationing families make trade-offs. "Let's face it," says Claudia Luiz, a New York psychoanalyst and author with two daughters of her own, "it is not realistically possible for all family members to feel happy or even behave calmly and maturely throughout the whole vacation." She includes parents in that one, and here's her suggestion: take turns being unhappy, and by unhappy she means grumpy, angry, sad, frustrated, annoyed, and everything else.

How does that work? Picture a daughter begging for pigtails, and a mother engaged in a frustrated search for the hairbrush with just three minutes to go before the family is supposed to meet her own parents in the lobby for breakfast. *I won't spend my whole vacation looking for things!* She's banging things around in the bathroom, and everybody else has a choice: join in (*It's not my fault! Geez, don't make such a big deal of it!*) or let her take her turn while saying nothing, or maybe helping look for the brush.

You don't have to go in there applies to the moods and tempers that periodically take over us on vacation and during holidays, too. When one child is having a meltdown over a dropped Popsicle, her siblings can choose to let her accusations (*You pushed me!*) go, and her parents can decide not to enter into a shouting match over her desire for a replacement. Vacations and holidays can be stressful, even if we do manage not to pack them with expectations. Parents are worried about keeping the trains running; children are out of their element (especially children who really thrive on a schedule).

"The hardest part is that tensions and frustrations are so contagious," says Luiz. Parents have a hard time seeing a child unhappy when vacations are supposed to be fun. "If everyone is tired, it's not uncommon for everyone to become simultaneously disgruntled." If that happens, and you've planned for taking turns, it's possible—with a big effort and the putting on of the big-kid pants—to declare that you're going to let others have a turn at being grumpy right now. If you can stay calm and cheerful while allowing a child or your partner to feel something else, your emotions might catch on with a child or two as well.

One thing to remember, said Luiz, is that this kind of taking turns isn't necessarily going to be fair play. Some family members will inevitably require more "turns" at grumpiness than others. This has been true for years with our children. My younger daughter does not enjoy traveling, and it does not matter if it's a theme park or an art museum—there are certain predictable things that are going to go wrong every time. For too long, we fought her, then, for years, we worked around her; now, at eleven, she knows her own foibles and can often be headed off from an angry episode with a reminder that we know this is hard work for her, and we'll try to make it easier. Her siblings have learned that they don't want to get on her train, although they do get frustrated with her effect on their fun, which is reasonable. It may be new, but we still bring our old selves along. Wherever you go, there you are.

MAKE DEPOSITS BEFORE YOU
MAKE WITHDRAWALS

This brilliant advice comes from Jason Kotecki, a writer, artist, and speaker from Madison, Wisconsin. "Kim [my wife] and I are willing to do some things we aren't thrilled about (like heading to the hotel pool when we really just want to crash on the bed) so that we can ask our kids to do things that might not be thrilling to them (like waiting patiently for a table at a restaurant). You can't just keep asking things of your kids and expect it to go well," he says.

Especially with younger kids, the "before" aspect is key. It's hard for them to wait for anything, let alone to check out that pool. Your itinerary probably already required them to accept the unfamiliar, to sit still, to nap in strange places, and to use all their patience. Planning activities that meet their needs first sets you up for a more successful longer trip. "By the same token, parents shouldn't spend their whole time catering to the whims of the kids," says Kotecki. The withdrawals, too, are part of the deal.

ADULTS GET TO HAVE FUN, TOO

A survey by Hilton International found that well over half of parents who travel with kids make their children's happiness the first priority on vacation. That's a mistake. The adults on a vacation deserve to see and do the things they hope to, and if that means children queuing for the *Mona Lisa*, then queue they should. Our research found that the happiest parents took both parent and child interests into account when planning a vacation; a trip to London does not need to be all Harry Potter, and not every family vacation should be taken at Disneyland.

FIND YOUR FIVE THINGS

How often do you find your vacation plans dictated by the "Top Ten Things to See" section of the guidebook—or, even more likely, "Top Ten Destinations for Kids"? They're a great place to start, but most top tens aren't going to cover your personal top priorities. I grew up traveling with my father, who was and is a serious train buff, and our trips always included the local rail or transport museum (as well as a lot of scenic train rides). We have friends who seek out Roman ruins, fossil-hunting sites, or natural hot springs. My husband likes to bike on every possible trip. On the kid front, we really do seek out candy stores—the kind that make local specialties, or maybe just local fudge—and we always encourage our kids to spend some time with the guidebook and pick something they're excited about. Sometimes they pick something really special; sometimes it's some absolutely ordinary thing you could do anywhere (*Oh, look, yet another fake outdoor climbing wall*). That's okay.

Take some time to think about what you really like to do on vacations. I like to choose my own top five:

1. Eat.
2. Visit grocery stores and farmers' markets, or take a cooking class.
3. Go to "time travel"–style exhibits of working houses and farms from the past.
4. Walk the streets/hike the trails.
5. Find a local bookstore for local memoirs.

Notably missing from that list? Art museums. Going to the tops of tall buildings to look out at the view, a common human drive that has clearly skipped me, although I know my children enjoy it. Shopping. Theater. Casinos. Bars. That's not to say I won't enjoy doing those things, particularly with someone else who's really excited to go. But if I'm putting them on an agenda from some misguided sense that I "have" to go to the top of the Empire State Building in order to have *seen* New York City, then I have misunderstood the word "vacation." *You do you.*

When you plan ways to fulfill your own vacations wants, it's easier to appreciate what the family members you travel with really enjoy as well, and vice versa.

SPEND WISELY

Oh, the perils of "getting your money's worth." For many of us, a shorter vacation with a few more perks may be a happier trip than one that maximizes money and minutes. "Getting a suite is worth it!" says Ashley Crossman Hakrama, a mother of two and Web designer from Jacksonville, Florida. "Having a second room to put the little ones to sleep and then still hang out is what makes it a vacation. I have spent nights in the bathroom Netflix-ing with my husband because the kids are asleep and we don't want to wake them. I would much rather leave a day earlier and have a better room." Keisha Blair, a mother of three from Canada, told me the exact same thing, adding, "No sex on a vacation is no good!"

Think hard about what has value to you. A subway in the morning may be affirmatively entertaining for your family and part of the fun, while the same trip in the other direction at nap time is well worth the splurge on a cab. Our family has tended to resist traveling far unless we have a lot of time, reasoning that we need to spend at least a week somewhere to make a long flight "worth it." But last year, we grabbed the opportunity to spend a long weekend in England with friends. It seemed foolish. Who buys overseas air tickets and spends twelve hours in the air (total) for just three and half days? But it turned out to be one of our most successful family trips. Our travel lovers adored the idea that we would just pick up and go like that, our travel stress victim could reassure herself that she'd be back home in just a few days, and because it was a short trip, we only tried to do a couple of things. In terms of pleasure gained for money spent, it turned out to be an absolute bargain.

DO NOTHING, BUT DO IT OUTSIDE

Many of us make nature and outdoor activities a part of our vacation plans, but too often we focus on doing one thing (a boat ride, a camel ride) or seeing another (a geyser, a canyon). We don't plan time to simply be present outside, lingering on a beach into the evening, spending four hours poking along a trail we could walk in less than half that time, sitting on a park bench for long enough that our kids can do whatever it is they're planning to do with all the pinecones and rocks they've been gathering.

Being outside and close to the natural world does make us happier. There's significant research into the subject: staring at a eucalyptus tree for ten minutes makes you more generous, proximity to the ocean correlates with happiness, and a few days spent in nature are associated with improvements in creativity, an increased attention span, and lower hyperactivity and aggression. You can get plenty of benefits by dipping your toe into the woods, but it's worthwhile to do so much more. Most visitors to Yellowstone National Park never leave the pavement (and some never leave their cars). A short hike can get you away from the crowds, and a willingness to stay a while gives you plenty of time to soak up the green while your children explore.

DECIDE ABOUT THE SCREENS, AND THEN LET IT GO

We take an annual vacation to the same beach hotel every year. While we're there, we do much the same things in much the same places that we have since our oldest son was three, but with increasingly different children—and increasingly different technology.

Every year, I make the same mistake. Instead of deciding what we'll do about television and our ever-growing family supply of portable technology, my husband and I try to play every day by ear, which means that too often, we're reading by the pool and they're tech-ing by the pool, and we're nagging.

It would be far better to pick a plan and stick to it. *Decide what to do, then do it.* Jason Kotecki saves kid tech time for trips, so that videos and video games "are special for road trips and long airplane rides. I also load up their devices with brand-new apps for them to explore. Some are educational, some are just for fun." Other parents allow tech during travel, but seek out Wi-Fi-free destinations or limit phone use on arrival, fearing that kids will replace family time with the same gaming and texting they do at home. "We've taken the kids to Disney and felt like they'd rather have stayed home with their iPads," one mother complained. It can feel hard to strike the right balance of tech use and family time, and easier to respond by banning it altogether.

Nancy K. Baym, the author of *Personal Connections in the Digital Age* and a principal researcher at Microsoft, says parents should resist the urge to regulate without discussion just because we don't like the idea of a teen "glued to her phone." Her suggestion for finding a happy medium for all? Talk to your child about what she wants from vacation, and how her gadget is or isn't a good part of that. Sharing photos on social media? You might very well be doing the same, and now is a good time for a discussion about how it feels when our friends post vacation pictures and how much is too much. Texting with friends? Maybe she could prep them for the idea that she'll be checking in nightly but not available all day.

Teenagers, says Dr. Baym, are often as interested in finding some time to disconnect as we are, "but we can't assume they want the same experience that we do." Instead, we should wait to impose limits until we have asked whether they're interested in limiting themselves. As I've said before, though, you take the same child on vacation that you have at home. If tech use is a problem or an ongoing battle when you're not on vacation, that's not likely to change with the scenery. Try to find a reasonable compromise before you leave rather than snatching the device away and starting a battle. Tell your teen you'd like to take a vacation from your regular argument and come up with something new together, like tech-free hours for all (including adults) combined with tech-full hours in which you won't comment on usage. (And, parents of younger children, take heart. This isn't an inevitable future. Plenty of teenagers—a majority, even—use tech reasonably and responsibly, on vacation and off.)

DON'T PUSH THE AGE BARRIER

Your children will get older, and when they do, they'll appreciate those trips you long to take with them that much more. They'll be able to enjoy the "kids club," the ropes course, the hike, the boat trip. You will, too, because you won't be focused on entertaining them or keeping them from falling into the Grand Canyon. The same goes for children's classes and camps. The age rules are there for a reason, and children too young to meet them usually don't enjoy the experience, no matter how precocious. Let kids be little before you expect them to be big.

When my oldest son was two, we took him to Disney World. He was too young for the rides and screamed at the site of every costumed character or firework. His favorite thing was an unimpressive playground that could have been anywhere. My biggest memory of the trip is of pacing the hotel grounds, trying to get him to nap so we could return to the park in the evening, cursing and crying while he cheerfully kicked his feet, wide awake. He remembers nothing.

This is not a good way to spend your time or money. Do something you want to do that your child fits into, or spend the money on a babysitter and get away, even if it's just to a local hotel that offers baby- and toddler-free sleep. Whenever possible, save the family destinations for when you have a family that's ready to enjoy them.

PLAN LIKE A PRO

Nobody knows your family like you do. You know the baby will blow her diaper, so "pack blowout bags," says Jason Kotecki: individual gallon-sized bags with paper towels, a diaper, wipes, a towel saturated with stain remover, and a fresh set of clothes. I know one of my children will wander off no matter what I do, so when she was younger, I wrote our contact information on her arm or clothing, and even now, I give her very specific instructions for what I want her to do when she finds herself unable to spot us. Pack snacks for the blood sugar crash, headphones for the child who needs some space away from the crowd, Band-Aids for the kid who will run ahead and then skin her knee. Make a list of three possible emergency mid-excursion ice cream/coffee shops or find a park that's close enough to the museum for one parent to duck out with a child who can't take the hushed crowds. There's a difference between allowing for spontaneous fun and wishful thinking. Being prepared in the same way you would at home can allow you to weather a minor catastrophe and keep going.

Holiday Travels and Travails

You may want to host the perfect get-together or manage to bring well-mannered, clean, and appropriately clad children to the festivities. But there are a lot of moving parts when it comes to holidays with extended family, and many of them are outside of your control—starting with the members of your extended family themselves.

Much of the narrative-changing advice for vacations applies here. Holidays do pile up. You get enough of them to make up for the seeming disasters (which, again, often make great memories). But to your attempts to expect less and enjoy more you can add another mantra when it comes to the family holiday: you are not in this alone.

That applies in both a practical way and a more emotional one. You can and should ask for help if you're having trouble with the more material aspects of a family holiday, like cooking for a crowd, decorating like your grandmother did, or just managing three children under five at a large outdoor gathering. That may mean more hands; it might mean someone else picks up the bill for the groceries or the wine.

But if the story you're telling yourself about a family holiday is that things are going all wrong, and it's all your fault, then that is where "you are not in this alone" really applies. When what's happening is that you're not living up to someone else's expectations (or your children aren't), then that other person—your parent, your in-law, or even your child—might not be meeting you halfway.

My husband was raised Jewish, and his aunt and uncle keep kosher, which means (among other things) that they don't eat meat and dairy at the same meal. When I host Thanksgiving, I used to feel a lot of pressure to get that exactly right. I worried mightily about serving nothing that they wouldn't eat and keeping dishes separate. I researched whether every ingredient needed to meet some additional standard that I wasn't familiar with.

Before many years passed, I realized that I was trying too hard. Our aunt and uncle wanted to enjoy the annual family get-together, and they wanted everyone else to enjoy it, too, which meant they didn't care if the kids buttered their rolls, and they didn't want me to lose sleep over the gravy. It's not that I don't still want to give them a wonderful kosher meal. I do. But I also know, now, that they would never want to make me feel terrible if I made a mistake. They're the perfect guests in that they want things to be a success as much as I do.

It may be that not everyone at your family gatherings is working toward that goal, and if that's the case, the only way to learn to enjoy yourself anyway is to find a way to build that into your own expectations. I know plenty of people who work at that for a lifetime, but knowing that the entire burden of a happy holiday doesn't rest with you should contribute to your ability to keep yourself in balance over the trouble spots and not beat yourself up afterward.

Do Birthdays Better

It's hard for your children to be happy when you're not happy.

This is true when it comes to vacations and travel, yes, but it came up in particular while I was getting things ready for my younger daughter's birthday. As we made cupcakes to take into her classroom, I asked my then-ten-year-old what's important about the treats you take in.

"It should just be something you like, but that other people like, too," she said. "And you don't want it to be too hard, because it's like, your birthday, and if it's too complicated it might taste too interesting, or just take too long and then in the morning you're all stressed, and your mom is yelling, and you just want it to be your special day. It should just be something you can share with your friends on your special day. Plus, I like things out of a box because it's easy."

Making birthdays and holidays fun and joyful for you—even if it means you "do less" for your children—makes those special occasions happier for your entire family. Everything doesn't have to be perfect for things to be wonderful, and sharing the work that goes into creating a great day makes it more fun for everyone, especially kids, who are very, very tolerant of imperfectly frosted cupcakes and haphazardly displayed decorations, especially if they created them themselves.

It can be hard for parents to feel that same joy in an imperfect celebration. Birthdays invite both you and your children to draw comparisons, and we tend to build a mental story around what we think those we love expect from us (like homemade cakes) that may or may not be true. Add on the weight of the memories and nostalgia that surround those red-letter days and you can easily find yourself dreading birthdays instead of looking forward to them.

Birthdays are a very social thing. The fact that every other child in the class has produced cupcakes for a birthday means that if you fail to provide cupcakes, your child isn't just disappointed, but singled out. If every other child in the same class has had a birthday party that included every classmate, you may feel obligated to do the same. We get caught up in the cycle of striving for perfection, as painstakingly described in the very scholarly *Gender and Consumption: Domestic Cultures and the Commercialisation of Everyday Life*, edited by Emma Casey and Lydia Martens:

> Birthday parties are rarely organised as singular expressions of parental/child relations but rather as part of a broader gendered sociality in which networks of gifts and children are circulated in rounds of reciprocity. The increasingly aestheticised and elaborated nature of children's parties and their intertwining of material culture, social relations and commerce is a form of consumption that is not merely an extension of women's domestic work, but is rather a testament to the ways in which mothering and consumption have become a mutually constitutive phenomenon.

If "rounds of reciprocity" doesn't make you want to make a cake out of a box mix and throw the kids on the lawn to play in the snow or the sprinkler, I don't know what will. You will be happier about celebrating your child's birthday if, instead of looking to the "network of gifts and children circulating" in your community, you consider, first, your own limits and values, and second, what your child wants— and know, too, that this is not necessarily easy. For many families, birthdays aren't just a single day but multiple celebrations for schoolmates, family, and friends. That's not new, and it's also not just in the realm of the privileged. One mother of a third grader living in a homeless shelter in New York City told me that they'd had three parties—one with family, one with friends, and one with the shelter community. Parents want to make our children feel special on what's seen as a big day, and if parties or gifts are the norm where you are, it will be hard to buck that trend (but it won't necessarily impact your child in the ways that worry you).

Ask your child what's important to her. A two-year-old might tell you that all she wants is to have the big kids next door over, and even if that's a slick thirteen-year-old girl and a hulking sixteen-year-old boy, you might be surprised how happily they'll come over and play hide-and-seek for an hour. Keep your own strengths, values, and budget in mind. If you're lucky, your child's dream birthday party will be something simple, but if she asks for something that doesn't work for you—for a petting zoo you can't afford, or a trip to the trampoline park that's two hours away that you can't imagine making—it's okay to say no. Your child will remember the party you have, not the party you don't have.

You also don't have to adhere to the "every child in the class" custom—even if your school recommends it. If big, homegrown parties are your thing, indulge your urge to barbecue (unless your child wants nothing to do with crowds). If, on the other hand, the idea of hosting twenty three-year-olds (and, presumably, one parent or caregiver each) fills you with dread, do not do that thing, even if your child has been to multiple parties along those lines already. Do you know who will pause, come the end of the school year, and say to herself, "Hmmm . . . we hosted little Fenella for Arethusa's birthday, but Fenella's mother did not do the same" and strike you off some master social list somewhere?

Exactly no one whose opinion you value and, almost certainly, actually no one at all. Instead, consider that maybe the big party hosts just like throwing big parties, while many of your fellow preschool parents will thank you for setting a simpler standard, like three friends for a build-your-own ice cream sundae party. Make it a surprise or host it over a break from school if you're concerned that the kids will bring it up, but know, too, that at some point, children do discover that not every child is invited to every party.

That will also work out just fine—although I have absolutely worried over the child who has come home to report birthday after birthday without an invitation. Try not to encourage your child in a belief in this reciprocity system, and when it's his turn, invite the friends he wants without much consideration of who else invited who when. (I say "much" because few of us, and few kids, would want to leave out the friend whose small party you went to last week.) If you're worried that children won't attend because your child is struggling socially or has special needs, talk to the parents of the invitees in advance of the party and decide what works best instead of leaving it to chance.

Savor the Calm and the Crazy

All of these moments, from vacations to holidays to birthdays, offer opportunities to *soak up the good*. There will be moments of chaos. There will be times when you're caught between two generations, when your mother just doesn't understand your daughter and your father thinks your son is an irresponsible goon, but that's what you've got. There will luau parties held inside during a flash thunderstorm and Thanksgivings when your vegan uncle is trying to convert your meat-loving brother-in-law while your teenager texts from inside a locked bathroom. *There is nothing wrong* in those moments, even as everything seems to go wrong around you. And there will be, if you're lucky, moments of peace while stirring the gravy, moments of exhausted bliss in the wreckage of the piñata, and moments of just settling in on some random park bench somewhere along your journey and watching all the members of your family do what they do. Those are your memories, and you get to have that cake, and eat it, too.

THE END OF THE BOOK,
NOT THE JOURNEY

A not-so-surprising thing happened while I wrote this book: I got happier. Not just a little happier, either. I've just been reading *The Year of Living Danishly*, in which the writer asks all kinds of Danish people to rate their happiness on a scale of one to ten and is repeatedly surprised by the consistency (nines and tens, every one). With my feet still firmly on American soil, I'd say I went from a six or seven to a nine, or maybe even a ten, even without Denmark's characteristic elevation of cozy happiness to a national art form. I can imagine a few things that could *happen* that would make me feel happier, but I can't think of anything more I could *do*. There are still things I could do better, more consistently, so maybe a nine. But a nine is good. A nine is great. At nine, I spend far less time feeling grumpy, frustrated, and annoyed, and far more at sort of a pleasant equilibrium. I notice when things are going well. I let a lot of small things go.

Of course, that was the goal, but that doesn't mean I wasn't a little surprised. I thought I was pretty happy to begin with. I knew we had some problem spots, but I didn't expect the changes I was making to have such power.

There were other things happening that probably helped push my happiness along. My children got older, and while bigger kids do have bigger problems, they also generate far fewer sippy cups and are more pleasant on long car rides. I took a leave from my day job to work on the book, and while my schedule has always been flexible, that space made it easier to accept the natural spikes in a family schedule, like the periods when everyone needs a checkup and a dentist visit and a trip to the eye doctor, the viruses that keep kids home from school one at a time for days and then weeks on end, and the increased demand for parent participation in school and activities that always appears around the holidays or when school draws to a close.

I don't discount those things, but the changes I made to my own life, and to the stories I told myself about what was happening and the ways I approached it, really made a difference. A few stand out as downright life changing.

What do I do differently? For starters, I let the good times be the good times. I revel in the ordinary. I remember that this is the life and the family we chose and that here we are, having what we wanted. In the introduction, I quoted Michel de Montaigne: "My life has been full of misfortunes, most of which never happened." I don't dwell on those imaginary catastrophes anymore, or project my worries out into a distant future where my children, aged forty and beyond, are still fighting over who gets the seat next to the door on the passenger side of the car. (Ask me why that's more desirable. Go ahead, ask me. *I have no idea.*) I keep things in perspective when it comes to worries about the larger world. Just a few generations ago, my life would have been so much more difficult on a daily level. Consider all we've gained—combustion engines, antibiotics, electricity, doctors who wash their hands before childbirth. We are still a society and a world with challenges and inequalities, but we can appreciate all we have without disregarding what we can still achieve. I want to be happy, and the wanting turns out to go a long way.

Alongside those big thoughts are small daily actions. The phrase *If you see something, don't always say something* has been a magic bullet for me when it comes to both daily discipline and the mundane brotherly and sisterly bickering that forms the soundtrack to so much of our family life. Like the young teacher I described in the homework chapter, who thought she was expected to assign something every night, some part of me still felt that my role in successfully raising these children to adulthood was to correct them every time they did wrong. In a completely positive and constructive way, of course. If they screwed up, in ways big or small, I needed to immediately teach them what was right.

This was exhausting, ineffective, and largely impossible. Even assuming I saw every transgression, attempting to respond to them all left me certain that any quality my words held was getting buried in the sheer quantity. It is sometimes useful to stop your children and say, "Wait a minute, how do you think that makes your brother feel?" Do it every time they squabble, though, and you become a nattering cliché, perkily oozing the same pleas to "use your words" and "talk about what you're really feeling" while your children carry on exactly as before.

Faced with a choice between letting them become background noise or becoming background noise myself, I realized that I had to let more things go. Their bickering often signified nothing beyond a generalized disgruntlement that they were taking out on one another, or a route to a decision among competing interests regarding things like what to watch on television or who sat in which seat in the car. Theirs was a loud, acrimonious road, to be sure, but they could take it, or, if their battle was bringing me down, I could tell them to stop it. All of them, that is. I did not need to single out the one who was being unreasonable or the one who was being bossy. I did not need to care. For me, with these kids, at these ages, the right thing to do 90 percent of the time was just tune it out.

My daughters came home from school recently squabbling, as they often do. One called the other a "wimp," the other retaliated with a barrage of intentional annoying behavior that culminated in her walking around her sister in circles, singing a tuneless song while her sister tried to read. Once, I would have interfered, stopped first the name-calling, then the intentional annoyance (which was annoying me, too). I didn't. I picked up my laptop and walked away without comment, without even much of a second thought. There were no real explosions—there wasn't much arguing, even. Both name-caller and singer got bored, and less than half an hour later they were baking a cake. The transition from school back to family provokes something like this almost every day. It's a pattern, not a problem. If I don't get involved, it ebbs away naturally. If I do, the drama can stretch well into the evening.

I tried to stop seeing every disciplinary infraction, too. This is trickier. It takes vast quantities of repetition to persuade children to hang up coats, to go to bed on time, or to consider the feelings of others when entering elevators or holding a conversation in a public place. Certain things recur nearly constantly. Don't run. Don't run. Don't run. *Don't run.* If I don't say anything, they often don't *see* anything.

Still, sometimes I just let them run. I don't scold the kid who ran into the person exiting the elevator. I let them have the crazy loud argument in the grocery store. Not everything is worth calling out.

I've found that each one of my kids goes through periods of being more difficult, which means it's often just one of the four constantly getting the admonitions while the others are standing around looking innocent and polishing their halos. That mantle passes from kid to kid, but while it might all even out, I don't like the feeling of picking on this one or that one all day long. The constant corrections can really take a toll on our relationship at what is often a challenging time already. That's when I want to choose my battles, and if that means I don't look like the greatest parent of all time as my child hangs off the front of the grocery cart, that's okay. I'm a happier one.

I said in the introduction that happier parents move from greater involvement with younger children toward cultivating independence as kids get older. My children are, for the most part, at or entering that "older" part of the spectrum, and that changes my job description. Nearly always, I need to teach them how to do something and then leave them to do it, even if that means homework doesn't get done, laundry turns pink, or insufficient practice leads to not making the cut at some activity or another.

Sometimes it's hard to let go of that tight control, especially when not all of my parenting peers are on the same page (although many are). Because it's more natural for Americans to worry that we're not doing enough than that we're doing too much in nearly everything we do, when I realize I've stepped back in areas where others have stepped up, I question myself. (Those happy Danish, incidentally, are much more likely to chide one another for everything from overwork to overdressing to, yes, overparenting. They've got a solid societal expectation that everyone should do less.)

I'm raising future adults, not perfect children, and that looks different. Embracing that narrative has made me happier about those seeming failures. It takes time to learn to be good at being a grown-up.

Personally, I'm still working on it. My kids have lots of space to improve, and we're all much better off if I'm not trying to micromanage their every move.

I've also increased my happiness dramatically with a very mundane change: I sleep more. I've been writing about healthy sleep for children and teenagers for years, but in writing the chapter on mornings, I finally sold myself on the idea of healthy sleep for me. I set aside my belief in myself as a genetically programmed night owl, took my own advice, and counted backward from the time on the alarm to the time I'd need to go to bed to get eight hours of sleep. Then I did it. First for one week, and then another, and then another.

I felt the difference immediately. Although it still isn't easy for me to get up at 6:20, and I never became someone who sings in the mornings, I gained more in patience and resilience and the ability to respond instead of react from that one simple change than from anything else I tried. I even, grudgingly, accepted the research that says that we're better off sticking to essentially the same sleep routine on the weekends. I go to bed at close to the same time every night, although I allow myself some morning slack. Sometimes I get nine or ten hours of sleep. Sometimes I *need* nine or ten hours of sleep.

The person I am when I have had enough sleep is more pleasant for everyone to be around, including me, as well as more productive. That version of me is also more able to tolerate sibling battles and discipline challenges, and respond in the moment in the way I will wish I had responded later. She doesn't worry as much about what other people think, she's generally more optimistic, and she doesn't have nearly as many voices in her head constantly berating her for failures and things left undone. I like her much better.

I try to be happy, I let more things go, I get more sleep—together, all of those things, along with other changes I've made as I wrote have meant a big shift in my overall state of mind. The phrase "If momma ain't happy, ain't nobody happy" definitely applies in our house. I'm capable of a black cloud of gloom and fury that is almost immediately contagious (a friend who does the same once called that his superpower). Just as that cloud spreads, nearly everything else I'm feeling spreads, too. Even small shifts in my mood move my children. If I am rushed, they are rushed; if I am anxious, they are anxious. And if I am happy, everyone is happier.

And my being happier makes a big difference to the happiness of my entire family. One of my greatest challenges as a parent has been that my well of patience isn't very deep, and while children excel at picking up on our emotions and mirroring them back to us, they don't moderate their own behavior based on where we are on our personal emotional roller coasters. So often, when your day has been long, when it has just been one thing after another, when any external observer would agree that you've given enough, they demand more. They're sick, they can't sleep, their best friend just texted them something awful, they just can't figure out a way to end this essay for English class. They need you now, and it isn't optional. There's no clocking out at the end of the day.

The less happy I am, the faster my well runs dry. When that happens, my reaction to a crisis tends to make me even more unhappy. Grudgingly, angrily, grumpily, sometimes nastily, I do only whatever is physically necessary. I go through the motions, holding without hugging and longing for my own bed.

When I'm happier, I'm far more able to drag the bottom of that well. I take the deep breath and open up, fully, to the problem and the child behind it, no matter how late, no matter how hard. I tell the child who has vomited grape juice onto the rug for the third time that it is okay and I mean it. I hold the child whose phone is pinging with anger and exclusion and I give her a safe and loving place to be even if she takes it all out on me.

I'm not perfect (far from it), but I'm so much more able to keep parenting as my best self than I once was. And as I found my way toward the generosity of spirit that feeds that ability, I found something that surprised me. Scraping the bottom of that well makes me happier, too. When I find it in me to give one more thing to one more child, I give something to myself, too. A moment that had me on the edge, about to snap or scream or yell or cry, becomes a moment to *soak in the good*. Happiness is cumulative. The more things that feel right, the more things that feel right.

I'm happier every time I pull that off, and I know I pull it off more often. Last night, at dinner, one of my children pulled a "conversation card" from the middle of the table (from a box of such cards meant to encourage family dinner conversations, which normally sits unused) and handed it to me. "You read it," he said.

"What are your best and worst qualities?"

They shared theirs in characteristic ways. ("Sometimes I like to be annoying on purpose," declared my youngest son, with a dimpled grin.) When it was my turn, I started with the bad, as one does. "I lose my temper really easily," I said. "I don't have much patience."

"But you do!" said one. "You have lots of patience. You're always doing things slowly and waiting for us."

"And you mostly don't yell," said another. "Plus you make the best Rice Krispies treats because you're patient. Most people burn the butter or the marshmallows." An excellent use of patience.

Scraping the bottom of my well turns out to deepen it. Just like taking time to *soak up the good* makes us more able to see the good around us, the more often you locate that loving patience within yourself, the easier it gets to find. At the same time, so many of the things I learned from parents who had found happier ways to deal with things I found challenging meant I wasn't dipping into my well as often, either. So maybe it's deeper, or maybe there's just more left in there. However it works, happiness is self-perpetuating. The happier I am as a parent, the easier it becomes to feel happy.

I still live in my house with my four amazing, glorious, delightful, stubborn, challenging, bickering children and my equally wonderful, but mostly not all the other things, husband. But it feels as if we have more room for one another somehow. I keep coming back to what Denise Pope said in the homework chapter, or Sally Sampson said in the food chapter, which amounted to much the same thing: when we're not putting all our energy into getting our kids to eat or study or do anything else exactly the way we want them to, we can put it into a much more positive place. We can talk about other things, like birds and maple sap production and town politics. We can enjoy each other. We can be happy together.

That makes all the rest of it, from the mornings to the meals to the inevitable bursts of the hard kind of discipline, better.

I said in the introduction that I didn't want to spend these years in a haze of resigned exhaustion, longing to be or do something else. For the most part, I don't. That doesn't mean I'm not sometimes exhausted, or that our weeks aren't still peppered with those days when we zip madly from one place to another picking up, dropping off, and then figuring out who we've forgotten where.

That's okay. I choose those days, just as I choose the slower ones where everyone basks in all the time in the world to do all things, and the other slower ones where they spend their time challenging one another to find new and inventive ways to announce that they're bored.

This is what I wanted. I wish it would go on forever. It won't.

But it is, right now, good.

ACKNOWLEDGMENTS

So many people had a hand in this book somehow that I almost hesitate to start thanking you. I'm bound to leave someone out. I'm going to intentionally leave someone out, just so I know who I've forgotten. You know who you are.

But for now, let's start at the beginning—thanks to Lisa Belkin, who set everything in motion, to Megan Liberman and Rick Berke, who took a chance on me at the *New York Times*, and even before them to Hanna Rosin and Emily Bazelon, who did the same at *Slate*. Megan, the day I got your first phone call goes down in my personal archives as one of the best days of my career, and I missed your supportive editorial push every day after you left.

As for the book itself, the first thanks go to Laurie Abkemeier, who took me on as a client long before I had that big ol' *New York Times* sticker of approval on my forehead, and then to Lucia Watson, who saw what the book could be and let me run with it. To the team at Avery, who are as I write this making me feel like a valued and treasured part of the coming year's catalog (see me using cool publishing words there?), thank you, thank you. Anne Kosmoski, Alyssa Kasoff, and Farin Schlussel, you've done all the work so far; Lindsay Gordon and Megan Newman, you've so clearly got everyone's backs. And thank you Suzy Swartz, who took good care of me and all my emails and who is going to go on to great things.

Dawn Reiss, you helped me write this book; without you, the research portions would look something like this: TK, TK, I know I read something about this somewhere. Matthew Weinshenker, thank you for helping me turn a bunch of questions into a bunch of data and for reining in my enthusiastic embrace of those results.

To the hundred and more experts and fellow parents I interviewed directly for this book one way or another, thank you. God knows I would have absolutely no ideas on happier mornings, among other things, if it weren't for you all. The world would be a better place if nobody ever had to get up earlier than they wanted to in order to go somewhere they weren't awake enough to go to yet, but since we can't have that, the world is a better place with you all in it. My Facebook community—you, too, are at the core of this. I hope you spotted each and every discussion we had over the course of many years of trying to figure this whole parent thing out. *Motherlode* readers and commenters, you're in here, too. I miss you all.

Sarah and Jess, you are my writing group and my rocks. Stickers and chunks will get us everywhere.

Mom, Dad, Rob, Sam, Lily, Rory, Wyatt—I already said it at the beginning. Ain't no book about happier parents without a happy family behind it. At least some of the time.

NOTES

INTRODUCTION: THIS COULD BE FUN

3 **We give up our own hobbies and pleasures:** Jeanne E. Arnold, Anthony P. Graesch, Enzo Ragazzini, and Elinor Ochs, *Life at Home in the Twenty-First Century: 32 Families Open Their Doors* (Los Angeles: The Cotsen Institute of Archaeology Press, 2012), 70.

3 **headlines like "How Having Children Robs Parents":** Georgia Grimmond, "How Having Children Robs Parents of Their Happiness," *Post Magazine*, September 16, 2015, http://www.scmp.com/magazines/post-magazine/article /1858685/how-having-children-robs-parents-their-happiness.

3 **"cocktail of guilt and anxiety":** Judith Warner, *Perfect Madness: Motherhood in the Age of Anxiety* (New York: Riverhead, 2006), 4.

4 **one study linking happiness to nudism:** Keon West, "Naked and Unashamed: Investigations and Applications of the Effects of Naturist Activities on Body Image, Self-Esteem, and Life Satisfaction," *Journal of Happiness Studies*, January 21, 2017.

5 **we can build stronger partnerships:** Kaisa Malinen, Ulla Kinnunen, Asko Tolvanen, Anna Rönkä, Hilde Wierda-Boer, and Jan Gerris, "Happy Spouses, Happy Parents? Family Relationships Among Finnish and Dutch Dual Earners," *Journal of Marriage and Family* 72, no. 2 (April 2010): 293–306.

5 **and friendships:** Suniya S. Luthar and Lucia Ciciolla, "Who Mothers Mommy? Factors That Contribute to Mothers' Well-Being," *Developmental Psychology* 51, no. 12 (December 2015): 1812–1823.

5 **share leisure activities with our families:** Ramon B. Zabriskie and Bryan P. McCormick, "Parent and Child Perspectives of Family Leisure Involvement and Satisfaction with Family Life," *Journal of Leisure Research* 35, no. 2 (2003): 163–189.

5 **doing things that are pleasant for all parties:** Kelly Musick, Ann Meier, and Sarah Flood, "How Parents Fare: Mothers' and Fathers' Subjective Well-Being in Time with Children," *American Sociological Review* 81, no. 5 (September 2016): 1069–1095.

5 **things in our lives that correlate with happiness:** Tomas Jungert, Renée Landry, Mireille Joussemet, Geneviéve Mageau, Isabelle Gingras, and Richard Koestner, "Autonomous and Controlled Motivation for Parenting: Associations with Parent and Child Outcomes," *Journal of Child and Family Studies* 24, no. 7 (July 2015): 1932–1942.

10 **relationships with their parents are happier, too:** Mark D. Holder and Ben Coleman, "The Contribution of Social Relationships to Children's Happiness," *Journal of Happiness Studies* 10, no. 3 (June 2009): 329–349.

1. MORNINGS ARE THE WORST

24 **Researchers have worked with preschoolers:** Amy R. Wolfson, Elizabeth Harkins, Michaela Johnson, and Christine Marco, "Effects of the Young Adolescent Sleep Smart Program on Sleep Hygiene Practices, Sleep Health Efficacy, and Behavioral Well-Being," *Sleep Health: Journal of the National Sleep Foundation* 1, no. 3 (September 2015): 197–204; Annie Murphy Paul, "We Tell Kids to 'Go to Sleep!' We Need to Teach Them Why," *Motherlode, New York Times*, July 10, 2014, https://parenting.blogs.nytimes.com/2014/07/10/we-tell-kids-to-go-to-sleep-we-need-to-teach-them-why.

26 **survey of one thousand new parents:** Lisa Belkin, "Parents Losing Sleep," *Motherlode, New York Times*, July 23, 2010, https://parenting.blogs.nytimes.com/2010/07/23/parents-losing-sleep.

2. CHORES

43 **they require their own children to do them:** Jennifer Breheny Wallace, "Why Children Need Chores," *Wall Street Journal*, March 13, 2015.

44 **our children's sense of being part of a larger whole:** Elinor Ochs and Carolina Izquierdo, "Responsibility in Childhood: Three Developmental Trajectories," *Ethos* 37, no. 4 (December 2009): 391–413.

45 **with a sense of being adrift:** Andrew J. Fuligni and Sara Pedersen, "Family Obligation and the Transition to Young Adulthood," *Developmental Psychology* 38, no. 5 (September 2002): 856–868; Gay C. Armsden and Mark T. Greenberg, "The Inventory of Parent and Peer Attachment: Individual Differences and

Their Relationship to Psychological Well-Being in Adolescence," *Journal of Youth and Adolescence* 16, no. 5 (October 1987): 427–454.

46 **whether it's a five-year-old in Peru's Amazon:** Shirley S. Wang, "A Field Guide to the Middle-Class U.S. Family," *Wall Street Journal*, March 13, 2012.

51 **deeply invested in raising caring, ethical children:** Carl Desportes Bowman, James Davison Hunter, Jeffrey S. Dill, and Megan Juelfs-Swanson, "Culture of American Families Executive Report," Institute for Advanced Studies in Culture, 2012, http://iasc-culture.org/survey_archives/IASC_CAF _ExecReport.pdf; Making Caring Common Project, "The Children We Mean to Raise," Harvard Graduate School of Education, 2014, http://mcc.gse.harvard.edu/files/gse-mcc/files/mcc-research-report.pdf?m =1448057487.

51 **moral qualities as more important than achievement:** Marie-Anne Suizzo, "Parents' Goals and Values for Children: Dimensions of Independence and Interdependence Across Four U.S. Ethnic Groups," *Journal of Cross-Cultural Psychology* 38, no. 4 (July 2007): 506–530.

51 **thirty-three schools in various regions:** Making Caring Common Project, "The Children We Mean to Raise."

52 **predictor for young adults' success:** Marty Rossmann, "Involving Children in Household Tasks: Is It Worth the Effort?," University of Minnesota, 2002, https://ghk.h-cdn.co/assets/cm/15/12/55071e0298a05_-_Involving -children-in-household-tasks-U-of-M.pdf.

55 **building skills in children:** Julie Lythcott-Haims, *How to Raise an Adult: Break Free of the Overparenting Trap and Prepare Your Kid for Success* (New York: St. Martin's Press, 2015), 166.

63 **endorses paying for excellent work:** Ron Lieber, "Don't Just Pay for Chores. Pay for Performance," *Motherlode, New York Times*, August 28, 2014, https:// parenting.blogs.nytimes.com/2014/08/28/dont-just-pay-for-chores-pay-for -performance.

3. SIBLINGS

75 **Parent-reported and observational studies:** Hildy Ross, Michael Ross, Nancy Stein, and Tom Trabasso, "How Siblings Resolve Their Conflicts: The Importance of First Offers, Planning, and Limited Opposition," *Child Development* 77, no. 6 (November/December 2006): 1730–1745.

76 **the same researcher found:** Laurie Kramer, Sonia Noorman, and Renee Brockman, "Representations of Sibling Relationships in Young Children's Literature," *Early Childhood Research Quarterly* 14, no. 4 (December 1999): 555–574.

76 **two-thirds of children still share a room:** Danielle Braff, "Why Parents Are Choosing to Have Kids Share Rooms Even When There's Space," *Chicago Tribune*, May 20, 2016.

77 **spend about 33 percent of their time:** Ji-Yeon Kim, Susan M. McHale, D. Wayne Osgood, and Ann C. Crouter, "Longitudinal Course and Family Correlates of Sibling Relationships from Childhood Through Adolescence," *Child Development* 77, no. 6 (November/December 2006): 1746–1761.

78 **manage their own emotional response:** University of Illinois College of Agricultural, Consumer and Environmental Sciences, "As Siblings Learn How to Resolve Conflict, Parents Pick Up a Few Tips of Their Own," June 25, 2015, http://news.aces.illinois.edu/news/u-i-study-siblings-learn-how-resolve -conflict-parents-pick-few-tips-their-own.

79 **when parents don't intervene:** Laurie Kramer, Lisa A. Perozynski, and Tsai-Yen Chung, "Parental Responses to Sibling Conflict: The Effects of Development and Parent Gender," *Child Development* 70, no. 6 (November/December 1999): 1401–1414.

84 **constantly wind up on the losing side:** Richard B. Felson, "Aggression and Violence Between Siblings," *Social Psychology Quarterly* 46, no. 4 (December 1983): 271–285.

84 **tacitly endorse that result:** Michal Perlman and Hildy S. Ross, "The Benefits of Parent Intervention in Children's Disputes: An Examination of Concurrent Changes in Children's Fighting Styles," *Child Development* 64, no. 4 (August 1997): 690–700.

104 **"outnumber negative ones by about five to one":** Christine Carter, "Siblings: How to Help Them Be Friends Forever," *Greater Good Magazine*, January 20, 2010.

4. SPORTS AND ACTIVITIES

108 **engage in organized sports:** Committee on Sports Medicine and Fitness, "Intensive Training and Sports Specialization in Young Athletes," *Pediatrics* 106, no. 1 (July 2000): 154–157; C. Ryan Dunn, Travis E. Dorsch, Michael Q. King, and Kevin J. Rothlisberger, "The Impact of Family Financial Investment on Perceived Parent Pressure and Child Enjoyment and Commitment in Organized Youth Sport," *Family Relations* 65, no. 2 (April 2016): 287–299.

108 **unsupervised "free" playtime has decreased:** Garey Ramey and Valerie A. Ramey, "The Rug Rat Race," National Bureau of Economic Research, Working Paper no. 15284, August 2009; Sandra L. Hofferth and John F. Sandberg, "How American Children Spend Their Time," *Journal of Marriage and Family* 63, no. 2 (May 2001): 295–308.

109 **time parents spend chauffeuring children:** Garey Ramey and Valerie A. Ramey, "The Rug Rat Race."

109 **compared to 12.4 in 1975:** Laura Vanderkam, *168 Hours: You Have More Time Than You Think* (New York: Portfolio, 2010).

109 **fewer risky behaviors:** Alia Wong, "The Activity Gap," *The Atlantic*, January 30, 2015.

110 **traveling for the sake of sport:** Karla Jo Helms, "The Sports Facilities Advisory Deems Youth Sports and Sports-Related Travel 'Recession Resistant'—Youth Sporting Events Create $7 Billion in Economic Impact," Cision PR Web, November 20, 2017.

112 **We get involved ourselves:** Nicholas L. Holt, Katherine A. Tamminen, Danielle E. Black, James L. Mandigo, and Kenneth R. Fox, "Youth Sport Parenting Styles and Practices," *Journal of Sport and Exercise Psychology* 31, no. 1 (2009): 37–59; Michael Jellineck and Stephen Durant, "Parents and Sports: Too Much of a Good Thing?," *Contemporary Pediatrics* 21, no. 9 (September 2004): 17–20; Stephen S. Leff and Rick H. Hoyle, "Young Athletes' Perceptions of Parental Support and Pressure," *Journal of Youth and Adolescence* 24, no. 2 (April 1995): 187–203; Gary L. Stein, Thomas D. Raedeke, and Susan D. Glenn, "Children's Perceptions of Parent Sport Involvement: It's Not How Much, But to What Degree That's Important," *Journal of Sports Behavior* 22, no. 4 (December 1999): 591–601.

121 **a small but significant association:** E. Glenn Schellenberg, "Long-Term Positive Associations Between Music Lessons and IQ," *Journal of Educational Psychology* 98, no. 2 (May 2006): 457–468.

126 **90 percent of kids tell surveys:** "Youth Sports Statistics," Statistic Brain, March 16, 2017, https://www.statisticbrain.com/youth-sports-statistics.

126 **pleasure for their kids by behaving:** Jens Omli and Diane M. Wiese-Bjornstal, "Kids Speak: Preferred Parental Behavior at Youth Sports Events," *Research Quarterly for Exercise and Sport* 82, no. 4 (December 2011): 702–711.

135 **If you're willing to give up:** Madeline Levine, *Teach Your Children Well: Why Values and Coping Skills Matter More Than Grades, Trophies, or "Fat Envelopes"* (New York: Harper Perennial, 2006), 20.

5. HOMEWORK

139 **percentage had increased to just over 50 percent:** Claudia Goldin, "America's Graduation from High School: The Evolution and Spread of Secondary Schooling in the Twentieth Century," *Journal of Economic History* 58, no. 2 (June 1998): 345–374.

140 **In high school, electives:** Steven Katona, "High School Students Choosing High-Level Courses Over Electives," WUFT News, February 24, 2015, https://www.wuft.org/news/2015/02/24/high-school-students-choosing-high-level-courses-over-electives.

140 **nationwide increase in homework load:** Tom Loveless, "Homework in America," The Brookings Institution, March 18, 2014, https://www.brookings .edu/research/homework-in-america.

142 **One small study:** KJ Dell'Antonia, "When Homework Stresses Parents as Well as Students," *Motherlode, New York Times*, September 10, 2015, https:// parenting.blogs.nytimes.com/2015/09/10/when-homework-stresses-parents-as -well-as-students.

149 **"Take an interest," said Julie Lythcott-Haims:** KJ Dell'Antonia, "'Impossible' Homework Assignment? Let Your Child Do It," *Well Family, New York Times*, March 22, 2016, https://well.blogs.nytimes.com/2016/03/22 /fourth-grade-book-report-let-your-fourth-grader-do-it.

156 **I thought it was impossible:** KJ Dell'Antonia, "'Impossible' Homework Assignment? Let Your Child Do It," *Well Family, New York Times*, March 22, 2016, https://well.blogs.nytimes.com/2016/03/22/fourth-grade-book -report-let-your-fourth-grader-do-it.

6. SCREENS ARE FUN, LIMITING THEM IS NOT

167 **more than 7.5 hours a day:** "The Common Sense Census: Plugged-In Parents of Tweens and Teens 2016," Common Sense Media, December 6, 2016, https://www.commonsensemedia.org/research/the-common-sense-census -plugged-in-parents-of-tweens-and-teens-2016.

168 **about six hours a day:** "Zero to Eight: Children's Media Use in America 2013," Common Sense Media, October 28, 2013, https://www.commonsensemedia .org/research/zero-to-eight-childrens-media-use-in-america-2013.

168 **about 2.5 hours a day:** "Zero to Eight: Children's Media Use in America 2013," Common Sense Media, October 28, 2013, https://www.commonsensemedia .org/research/zero-to-eight-childrens-media-use-in-america-2013.

173 **asked one thousand kids:** Catherine Steiner-Adair, *The Big Disconnect: Protecting Childhood and Family Relationships in the Digital Age* (New York: HarperCollins, 2013).

175 **64 percent of teenagers:** Charlotte Eyre, "Young People Prefer Print to e-Books," *The Bookseller*, September 30, 2015.

176 **Somewhat dubious statistics:** Martha de Lacey, "Baby's First Facebook Update! Photos of Newborns Now Appear on Social Media Sites Within ONE HOUR of Their Birth," *Daily Mail*, August 27, 2013.

176 **249 parent-child pairs:** KJ Dell'Antonia, "Don't Post About Me on Social Media, Children Say," *Well Family, New York Times*, March 8, 2016, https:// well.blogs.nytimes.com/2016/03/08/dont-post-about-me-on-social-media -children-say.

179 **Even the American Academy of Pediatrics:** American Academy of Pediatrics, "Media and Young Minds," *Pediatrics* 138, no. 5 (November 2016).

179 **teaching them something they did not know:** "Study Finds Infants Can Learn to Communicate from Videos," Emory Health Sciences, January 22, 2015, http://news.emory.edu/stories/2015/01/upress_infants_learn_from_videos/index.html.

185 **certain amount of time can ease transitions:** Alexis Hiniker, Hyewon Suh, Sabina Cao, and Julie A. Kientz, "Screen Time Tantrums: How Families Manage Screen Media Experiences for Toddlers and Preschoolers," Proceedings of the 2016 CHI Conference on Human Factors in Computing Systems (San Jose, California, May 7–12, 2016): 648–660.

186 **relieve anxiety for many children:** KJ Dell'Antonia, "Four Moments When Video Games Are Good for Kids (and How to Make Them Even Better)," *Motherlode, New York Times,* December 10, 2015, https://parenting.blogs .nytimes.com/2015/12/10/four-moments-when-video-games-are-good-for -kids-and-how-to-make-them-even-better; Robert George, "Video Games Prove Helpful as Pain Relievers in Children and Adults," *Medical News Today,* May 9, 2010; Melissa Osgood, "The Key to Reducing Pain in Surgery May Already Be in Your Hand," Cornell University, Media Relations Office, April 29, 2015, http://mediarelations.cornell.edu/2015/04/29/they-key-to-reducing -pain-in-surgery-may-already-be-in-your-hand/.

199 **Relatively few parents:** "Zero to Eight: Children's Media Use in America 2013," Common Sense Media, October 28, 2013, https://www.commonsensemedia .org/research/zero-to-eight-childrens-media-use-in-america-2013.

7. DISCIPLINE

206 **punishing a child and reducing bad behavior:** Jim Edwards, "Baseball & Discipline in the 1950s," *Everyday Christian Family,* November 28, 2013, http://everydaychristianfamily.com/baseball-discipline-in-the-1950s.

217 **effective discipline includes three things:** Committee on Psychosocial Aspects of Child and Family Health, "Guidance for Effective Discipline," *Pediatrics* 101, no. 4 (April 1998).

223 **82 percent of high school:** Lene Arnett Jensen, Jeffrey Jensen Arnett, S. Shirley Feldman, and Elizabeth Cauffman, "The Right to Do Wrong: Lying to Parents Among Adolescents and Emerging Adults," *Journal of Youth and Adolescence* 33, no. 2 (April 2004): 101–112; Lisa Heffernan, "What I've Learned: When Teens Lie," *On Parenting, Washington Post,* February 24, 2015, https://www.washington post.com/news/parenting/wp/2015/02/24/what-ive-learned-when-teens-lie.

8. FOOD, FUN, AND FAMILY TIME

232 **interactions in middle-class families:** Elinor Ochs and Tamar Kremer-Sadlik, editors, *Fast-Forward Family: Home, Work, and Relationships in Middle-Class America* (Berkeley: University of California Press, 2013), 32.

234 **and can be disappointed:** Sarah Bowen, Sinikka Elliott, and Joslyn Brenton, "The Joy of Cooking?," *SAGE Journals* 13, no. 3 (August 2014): 20–25.

234 **spend more at restaurants than we do on groceries:** Michelle Jamrisko, "Americans' Spending on Dining Out Just Overtook Grocery Sales for the First Time Ever," *Bloomberg Markets*, April 14, 2015.

247 **adult members of the family eat healthier:** Valeria Skafida, "The Family Meal Panacea: Exploring How Different Aspects of Family Meal Occurrence, Meal Habits and Meal Enjoyment Relate to Young Children's Diets," *Sociology of Health and Illness* 35, no. 6 (July 2013): 906–923.

247 **increases the likelihood:** Jennifer Orlet Fisher, Diane C. Mitchell, Helen Smiciklas-Wright, and Leann Lipps Birch, "Parental Influences on Young Girls' Fruit and Vegetable, Micronutrient, and Fat Intakes," *Journal of the American Dietetic Association* 102, no. 1 (January 2002): 58–64.

247 **children and adults stay at the table longer:** Elinor Ochs and Margaret Beck, "Serving Convenience Foods for Dinner Doesn't Save Time," *The Atlantic*, March 11, 2013.

248 **more positive attitude toward food:** Paul Rozin, "Human Food Intake and Choice: Biological, Psychological and Cultural Perspectives," in Harvey Anderson, John Blundell, and Matty Chiva (eds.), *Food Selection: From Genes to Culture* (Paris: Danone Institute, 2002): 7–24, http://ernaehrungsdenkwerkstatt .de/fileadmin/user_upload/EDWText/TextElemente/Ernaehrungspsychologie /Rozin_Ernaehrungsverhalten_Danone_Publikation.pdf.

248 **quality over quantity:** Paul Rozin, Abigail K. Remick, and Claude Fischler, "Broad Themes of Difference Between French and Americans in Attitudes to Food and Other Life Domains: Personal Versus Communal Values, Quantity Versus Quality, and Comforts Versus Joys," *Frontiers in Psychology* 2 (July 2011): 177.

9. FREE TIME, VACATIONS, HOLIDAYS, BIRTHDAYS, AND OTHER ON-DEMAND "FUN"

260 **bonus eight paid holidays:** Rebecca Ray, Milla Sanes, and John Schmitt, "No-Vacation Nation Revisited," Center for Economic and Policy Research, May 2013, http://cepr.net/documents/publications/no-vacation-update -2013-05.pdf.

260 **either don't take all we're offered:** Harvard University T. H. Chan School of Public Health, "The Workplace and Health," edited by NPR/Robert Wood Johnson Foundation/Harvard School of Public Health, July 11, 2016, https:// www.rwjf.org/en/library/research/2016/07/the-workplace-and-health.html.

283 **cycle of striving for perfection:** Emma Casey and Lydia Martens, *Gender and Consumption: Domestic Cultures and the Commercialisation of Everyday Life* (London and New York: Routledge, 2007).

BIBLIOGRAPHY

Alcorn, Katrina. *Maxed Out: American Moms on the Brink*. Berkeley: Seal Press, 2013.

Anand, Paul. *Happiness Explained: What Human Flourishing Is and What We Can Do to Promote It*. Oxford: Oxford University Press, 2016.

Bronson, Po, and Ashley Merryman. *NurtureShock: New Thinking About Children*. New York: Twelve, 2009.

———. *Top Dog: The Science of Winning and Losing*. New York: Twelve, 2013.

Brown, Brené. *The Gifts of Imperfection: Let Go of Who You Think You're Supposed to Be and Embrace Who You Are*. Center City, MN: Hazelden, 2010.

———. *Daring Greatly: How the Courage to Be Vulnerable Transforms the Way We Live, Love, Parent, and Lead*. New York: Avery, 2015.

Bruni, Frank. *Where You Go Is Not Who You'll Be: An Antidote to the College Admissions Mania*. New York: Grand Central Publishing, 2016.

Callahan, Alice. *The Science of Mom: A Research-Based Guide to Your Baby's First Year*. Baltimore: Johns Hopkins University Press, 2015.

Caroline, Rivka, with Amy Sweeting. *From Frazzled to Focused: The Ultimate Guide for Moms (and Dads) Who Want to Reclaim Their Time, Their Sanity and Their Lives*. Austin: River Grove Books, 2013.

Carter, Christine. *Raising Happiness: 10 Simple Steps for More Joyful Kids and Happier Parents*. New York: Ballantine Books, 2011.

———. *The Sweet Spot: How to Accomplish More by Doing Less*. New York: Ballantine Books, 2017.

Caviness, Ylonda Gault. *Child, Please: How Mama's Old-School Lessons Helped Me Check Myself Before I Wrecked Myself.* New York: TarcherPerigee, 2015.

Coontz, Stephanie. *The Way We Never Were: American Families and the Nostalgia Trap.* New York: Basic Books, 2016.

Damour, Lisa. *Untangled: Guiding Teenage Girls Through the Seven Transitions into Adulthood.* New York: Ballantine Books, 2017.

David, Susan. *Emotional Agility: Get Unstuck, Embrace Change, and Thrive in Work and Life.* New York: Avery, 2017.

Douglas, Ann. *Parenting Through the Storm: Find Help, Hope, and Strength When Your Child Has Psychological Problems.* New York: Guilford Press, 2017.

Duckworth, Angela. *Grit: The Power of Passion and Perseverance.* New York: Scribner, 2016.

Duhigg, Charles. *Smarter Faster Better: The Secrets of Being Productive.* New York: Random House, 2017.

Dweck, Carol S. *Mindset: The New Psychology of Success.* New York: Ballantine Books, 2008.

Faber, Adele, and Elaine Mazlish. *Siblings Without Rivalry: How to Help Your Children Live Together So You Can Live Too.* New York: W. W. Norton, 2012.

———. *How to Talk So Teens Will Listen and Listen So Teens Will Talk.* New York: HarperCollins, 2006.

Faber, Joanna, and Julie King. *How to Talk So Little Kids Will Listen: A Survival Guide to Life with Children Ages 2–7.* New York: Scribner, 2017.

Fass, Paula S. *The End of American Childhood: A History of Parenting from Life on the Frontier to the Managed Child.* Princeton: Princeton University Press, 2016.

Feiler, Bruce. *The Secrets of Happy Families: Improve Your Mornings, Rethink Family Dinner, Fight Smarter, Go Out and Play, and Much More.* New York: William Morrow, 2013.

Ferguson, Andrew. *Crazy U: One Dad's Crash Course in Getting His Kid into College.* New York: Simon & Schuster, 2012.

Gawdat, Mo. *Solve for Happy: Engineer Your Path to Joy.* New York: North Star Way, 2018.

Ginsburg, Kenneth R. *Raising Kids to Thrive: Balancing Love with Expectations and Protection with Trust.* Elk Grove Village, IL: American Academy of Pediatrics, 2015.

Guernsey, Lisa. *Into the Minds of Babes: How Screen Time Affects Children from Birth to Age Five.* New York: Basic Books, 2007.

Haelle, Tara, and Emily Willingham. *The Informed Parent: A Science-Based Resource for Your Child's First Four Years.* New York: TarcherPerigee, 2016.

Hanson, Rick. *Hardwiring Happiness: The New Brain Science of Contentment, Calm, and Confidence.* New York: Harmony Books, 2013.

Harris, Michael. *The End of Absence: Reclaiming What We've Lost in a World of Constant Connection.* New York: Current, 2015.

Heitner, Devorah. *Screenwise: Helping Kids Thrive (and Survive) in Their Digital World*. New York: Bibliomotion, 2016.

Homayoun, Ana. *Social Media Wellness: Helping Tweens and Teens Thrive in an Unbalanced Digital World*. Thousand Oaks, CA: Corwin, 2018.

Hyman, Mark. *The Most Expensive Game in Town: The Rising Cost of Youth Sports and the Toll on Today's Families*. Boston: Beacon Press, 2013.

Jensen, Frances E., with Amy Ellis Nutt. *The Teenage Brain: A Neuroscientist's Survival Guide to Raising Adolescents and Young Adults*. New York: HarperCollins, 2016.

Kindlon, Dan. *Too Much of a Good Thing: Raising Children of Character in an Indulgent Age*. New York: Hyperion, 2001.

Koh, Christine, and Asha Dornfest. *Minimalist Parenting: Enjoy Modern Family Life More by Doing Less*. New York: Bibliomotion, 2013.

Lahey, Jessica. *The Gift of Failure: How the Best Parents Learn to Let Go So Their Children Can Succeed*. New York: HarperCollins, 2015.

Lamb, Sabrina. *Do I Look Like an ATM?: A Parent's Guide to Raising Financially Responsible African American Children*. Chicago: Chicago Review Press, 2013.

Lancy, David F. *The Anthropology of Childhood: Cherubs, Chattel, Changelings*. Cambridge: Cambridge University Press, 2016.

Le Billon, Karen. *French Kids Eat Everything: How Our Family Moved to France, Cured Picky Eating, Banned Snacking, and Discovered 10 Simple Rules for Raising Happy, Healthy Eaters*. New York: HarperCollins, 2012.

Levine, Madeline. *Teach Your Children Well: Parenting for Authentic Success*. New York: HarperCollins, 2013.

Levs, Josh. *All In: How Our Work-First Culture Fails Dads, Families, and Businesses—And How We Can Fix It Together*. New York: HarperCollins, 2015.

Lieber, Ron. *The Opposite of Spoiled: Raising Kids Who Are Grounded, Generous, and Smart About Money*. New York: HarperCollins, 2016.

Likins, Peter. *A New American Family: A Love Story*. Tucson: University of Arizona Press, 2012.

Louv, Richard. *Last Child in the Woods: Saving Our Children from Nature-Deficit Disorder*. Chapel Hill: Algonquin Books, 2008.

Lythcott-Haims, Julie. *How to Raise an Adult: Break Free of the Overparenting Trap and Prepare Your Kid for Success*. New York: Henry Holt, 2015.

Markham, Laura. *Peaceful Parent, Happy Siblings: How to Stop the Fighting and Raise Friends for Life*. New York: TarcherPerigee, 2015.

Mead, Margaret. *And Keep Your Powder Dry: An Anthropologist Looks at America*. New York: Berghahn Books, 2000.

Mullainathan, Sendhil, and Eldar Shafir. *Scarcity: Why Having Too Little Means So Much*. New York: Henry Holt, 2014.

Naumburg, Carla. *Parenting in the Present Moment: How to Stay Focused on What Really Matters*. Berkeley: Parallax Press, 2014.

Ocampo, Roxanne. *Flight of the Quetzal Mama: How to Raise Latino Superstars and Get Them into the Best Colleges*. United States: CreateSpace Independent Publishing Platform, 2016.

Ochs, Elinor, and Tamar Kremer-Sadlik. *Fast-Forward Family: Home, Work, and Relationships in Middle-Class America*. Berkeley: University of California Press, 2013.

Orenstein, Peggy. *Cinderella Ate My Daughter: Dispatches from the Front Lines of the New Girlie-Girl Culture*. New York: HarperCollins, 2012.

Payne, Kim John. *The Soul of Discipline: The Simplicity Parenting Approach to Warm, Firm, and Calm Guidance—From Toddlers to Teens*. New York: Ballantine Books, 2015.

Pope, Denise, Maureen Brown, and Sarah Miles. *Overloaded and Underprepared: Strategies for Stronger Schools and Healthy, Successful Kids*. San Francisco: Jossey-Bass, 2015.

Pugh, Allison J. *Longing and Belonging: Parents, Children, and Consumer Culture*. Berkeley: University of California Press, 2012.

Race, Kristen. *Mindful Parenting: Simple and Powerful Solutions for Raising Creative, Engaged, Happy Kids in Today's Hectic World*. New York: St. Martin's Griffin, 2014.

Raghunathan, Raj. *If You're So Smart, Why Aren't You Happy?* New York: Portfolio, 2016.

Rubin, Gretchen. *Happier at Home: Kiss More, Jump More, Abandon Self-Control, and My Other Experiments in Everyday Life*. New York: Three Rivers Press, 2013.

———. *Better Than Before: What I Learned About Making and Breaking Habits—To Sleep More, Quit Sugar, Procrastinate Less, and Generally Build a Happier Life*. New York: Crown, 2016.

Sandler, Lauren. *One and Only: The Freedom of Having an Only Child, and the Joy of Being One*. New York: Simon & Schuster, 2014.

Schulte, Brigid. *Overwhelmed: How to Work, Love and Play When No One Has the Time*. London: Bloomsbury, 2015.

Selingo, Jeffrey J. *There Is Life After College: What Parents and Students Should Know About Navigating School to Prepare for the Jobs of Tomorrow*. New York: William Morrow, 2017.

Senior, Jennifer. *All Joy and No Fun: The Paradox of Modern Parenthood*. New York: Ecco, 2015.

Shumaker, Heather. *It's OK to Go Up the Slide: Renegade Rules for Raising Confident and Creative Kids*. New York: TarcherPerigee, 2016.

Siegel, Daniel J., and Mary Hartzell. *Parenting from the Inside Out: How a Deeper Self-Understanding Can Help You Raise Children Who Thrive*. New York: TarcherPerigee, 2014.

Smith, Emily Esfahani. *The Power of Meaning: Crafting a Life That Matters*. New York: Crown, 2017.

Vanderkam, Laura. *168 Hours: You Have More Time Than You Think.* New York: Portfolio, 2010.

———. *I Know How She Does It: How Successful Women Make the Most of Their Time.* New York: Portfolio, 2017.

Willingham, Daniel T. *Raising Kids Who Read: What Parents and Teachers Can Do.* San Francisco: Jossey-Bass, 2015.

Wolf, Anthony E. *"Mom, Jason's Breathing on Me!" The Solution to Sibling Bickering.* New York: Ballantine Books, 2003.